Draw Ne

Draw Near to God

John Paul II

*Translated from Italian
by Carlos Alonso Vargas*

Lamp Press

Marshall Morgan and Scott
Lamp Press
34–42 Cleveland Street, London, W1P 5FB. U.K.

British Library Cataloguing in Publication Data
John Paul II. *Pope*
  Draw near to God.
  1. Catholics. Christian life – Devotional works
  I. Title
  242

  ISBN 0–551–01905–0

Text set in Bembo by Input Typesetting Ltd, London
Printed in Great Britain by Cox & Wyman Ltd, Reading

Contents

Abbreviations

AA	Apostolicam Actuositatem
AAS	Acta Apostolicae Sedis
Adv. Hae.	Adversus Haereses (Against Heretics)
AG	Ad Gentes
CT	Catechesi Tradendae
DH	Dignitatis Humanae
Div. inMis.	Dives in Misericordia
DS	Denzinger-Schanmetzer
DV	Dei Verbum
EN	Evangelii Nuntiandi
FC	Familiaris Consortio
FF	Fonti Francescane (Franciscan Sources)
GetS	Gaudium et Spes
HV	Humanae Vitae
Ins.PVI	Insegnamenti di Paolo VI (Teachings of Paul VI)
LG	Lumen Gentium
LE	Laborem Exercens
MC	Marialis Cultus
NA	Nostra Aetate
PO	Presbyterorum Ordinis
PT	Pacem in Terris
RH	Redemptor Hominis
RSV	Revised Standard Version of Scripture
SC	Sacrosanctum Concilium
SD	Salvifici Doloris
S Th.	Summa Theologiae
UR	Unitatis Redintegratio

Introduction: How to Use this Book

This collection of daily meditations by Pope John Paul II is arranged according to the Church's Year. First come readings for the great fasts and festivals: Advent, Christmas, Epiphany, Lent, Easter, Pentecost; then follow six readings for other feasts or solemnities throughout the year; finally come daily readings for use during the periods known as 'ordinary time', the days between Epiphany and Lent, and between Trinity Sunday and Advent.

Index to Seasons and Festivals of the Church's Year

Fixed Dates for which Special Readings are Provided

PRINCIPAL CELEBRATIONS OF THE LITURGICAL YEAR

Year	Sunday Cycle	Weekday Cycle	Ash Wednesday	Easter	Ascension	Pentecost	Corpus Christi	Weeks in Ordinary Time				First Sunday of Advent	Year
								Before Lent		After Pentecost			
								Until	Week	From	Week		
1990	A	II	28 Feb.	15 Apr.	24 May	3 June	14 June	27 Feb.	8	4 June	9	2 Dec.	1990
1991	B	I	13 Feb.	31 Mar.	9 May	19 May	30 May	12 Feb.	5	20 May	7	1 Dec.	1991
1992	C	II	4 Mar.	19 Apr.	28 May	7 June	18 June	3 Mar.	8	8 June	10	29 Nov.	1992
1993	A	I	24 Feb.	11 Apr.	20 May	30 May	10 June	23 Feb.	7	31 May	9	28 Nov.	1993
1994	B	II	16 Feb.	3 Apr.	12 May	22 May	2 June	15 Feb.	6	23 May	8	28 Nov.	1994
1995	C	I	1 Mar.	16 Apr.	25 May	4 June	15 June	28 Feb.	8	5 June	9	3 Dec.	1995
1996	A	II	21 Feb.	7 Apr.	16 May	26 May	6 June	20 Feb.	7	27 May	8	1 Dec.	1996
1997	B	I	12 Feb.	30 Mar.	8 May	18 May	29 May	11 Feb.	5	19 May	7	30 Nov.	1997
1998	C	II	25 Feb.	12 Apr.	21 May	31 May	11 June	24 Feb.	7	1 June	9	29 Nov.	1998
1999	A	I	17 Feb.	4 Apr.	13 May	23 May	3 June	16 Feb.	6	24 May	8	28 Nov.	1999

In our society,
with its many problems,
we see more and more every day
a deep need for certainty,
a fervent desire
for a pure and committed love,
a yearning for truth,
and for soberness and integrity.
This is a time of history
which is full of spiritual
and cultural conflict.
We see
in all of its great significance
the meaning of Christ's words:
'He who loses his life
for my sake will find it' (Matt. 10:39 RSV).
That holiness,
which all of us should strive for,
can be compared
to a distant summit,
which requires
a hard and tiring ascent every day.
But do not be discouraged;
resume your daily journey with joy and a generous spirit;
restore your spiritual strength
through prayer and reception of the Eucharist.
Set your eyes continually on the summit.
Be confident that you will reach it
with the help of the Lord!

John Paul II

Advent

The First Sunday of Advent
Men Will See the Son of Man

Men will see the Son of Man coming on a cloud with great power and glory (Luke 21.27).

Advent guides our thoughts towards *the beginning*, because the mystery of creation points to the very first coming of God. And the beginning points to the end: Christ's Second Coming.

The Gospels speak of the signs of the end. The things of this world will undergo destruction and pass away. In fact, the passing away of created things constantly reminds us that this world will end. The first Sunday of Advent leads us to think about this important mystery of the *beginning* and the *end* of creation.

The mystery of the fleeting nature of things and the mystery of death itself is evident in everything around us. No one doubts that the things of this world undergo destruction, and the visible world passes away. No one doubts that man in this world dies. Human life is fleeting. Through the passing away of the world and through the death of man, God – the one that does not pass away – is revealed. He is not subject to time. He is eternal. He is the one 'who is and who was and who is to come' (Rev. 1.8).

Advent is, above all, a reminder that God is eternal. He has no beginning and no end.

In Anticipation of the Lord's Coming upon the Earth

With this understanding of God's eternal nature and omnipotence and the beginning and the end of all things, the church invites us to prepare ourselves again for the coming of God.

This is he who is totally other above all of creation. He is the infinite divine Spirit. Yet he embraces simultaneously all those things that are created and all those things that breathe. 'In him we live and move and have our being' (Acts 17.28).

Thus, he is not only outside the created world enthroned in his unsearchable Godhead. He is *in* our world. Creation itself is pervaded by his presence. And that presence always tells of his coming. It announces to us that he comes. God, as the Creator and the Lord of all, comes eternally to this world which he has called into being out of nothing.

He also sustains everything he has created. He is divine providence itself. The world has in him – in God – its true destiny. All those things that have being because of God's power and omnipotence continue to exist through him.

Every created thing 'declares the glory of God' and bears witness to his presence and to his coming. God's advent is manifest in the very existence of the world, in its origins and in its development.

We should always live in anticipation of the Lord's coming upon the earth, as Christ says in the Gospel of St Luke (Luke 21.25–8, 34–6).

Your Deliverance is Near at Hand

In Jesus's sermon from Luke where the Lord refers to the end of the world, he warns us of catastrophes, signs of coming destruction, and all those things that will provoke 'the anguish of the nations'. Christ addresses the people of his day and of our day, because his words are for all peoples of every age. He exclaims, 'Stand erect and hold your heads high, for your deliverance is near at hand' (Luke 21.28). This ringing call is the challenge of Advent. The Lord sums up all that the word advent means to us.

Thus, God is not only enthroned above his creation. It is not only that all created things bear witness to him as the omnipotent Creator. It is not only that the changing world around us causes us to think about his changeless, eternal nature. No, he also enters into the history of our world. He becomes one with us in our human condition.

Men will see him as 'the Son of Man' (Luke 21.27). Advent means precisely that coming. It means above all else that God took on human flesh. It means the mystery of the incarnation. 'In those days, in that time, I will raise up for David a just shoot,' says the prophet Jeremiah (Jer. 33.15).

Redemption properly understood means the presence of the just one in the midst of sinners. Advent, then, is closely linked to the mystery of sin, which entered human history from the very beginning. God comes to work salvation in our midst. 'He shall do what is right and just in the land' (Jer. 33.15).

The Coming of the Redeemer

We know of Jesus' birth on that glorious night in Bethlehem. We know of his life and his death on the cross. With the word of his saving gospel and, ultimately, through his death and resurrection, he has proclaimed 'what is right and just' on the earth. Let us 'stand erect and hold our heads high'. For in this coming of the just one, in his paschal mystery, our salvation is assured.

Advent means the coming of the Redeemer, the Son of Man, born on that night in Bethlehem. From that glorious moment, he shows us himself in the whole of human history from beginning to end.

He shows us that mankind's history upon the earth is not merely a passage towards death. It has meaning and leads to the completion of all things. In that sense, Advent points to another coming of the Son of Man, this time as the Judge at the end of the world. He has come to plant the seeds of the gospel through his incarnation and his passion. He will come a second time to judge the nations and to reap the fruit of the harvest. He will come to lay bare the secrets of every conscience and every heart at the end of time.

In this way, man's history upon the earth is not only a passage towards death. It is above all a preparation for the truth of judgment. It is a preparation for the fullness of life in God.

Learning the Ways of God

The readings of the liturgy encourage all of us in the church to grasp the truth of Advent: God's coming. It shows us what man's response should be to this coming which is at once both near and distant. Man should lift up his soul, just as the responsorial psalm invites us to do: 'To you I lift up my soul, O LORD' (Ps. 25.1).

What does it mean to lift up one's soul? Above all, it means to learn the ways of God. 'Guide me in your truth and teach me' (Ps. 25.5), the psalmist cries out. He knows that God 'shows sinners the way; he guides the humble to justice' (Ps. 25.8–9).

Along this way, God makes known 'his covenant' (Ps. 25.14). Through this covenant, the intentions of God towards man are made clear to everyone. To make these intentions possible for man, he gives us his *grace*: 'All the paths of the LORD are kindness [grace] and constancy' (Ps. 25.10).

That is how the responsorial psalm reveals to us the

basic call of Advent which the church finds in the words of her Lord and which are addressed to everyone: 'So be on the watch. Pray constantly for the strength . . . to stand secure before the Son of Man' (Luke 21.36).

December 8th
The solemnity of the Immaculate Conception
The Mystery of the Beginning

The liturgy of the Immaculate Conception leads us to consider 'the mystery of the beginning'. The first reading, in fact, is taken from the book of Genesis. Here we see the beginning of salvation history in the sin of the first man and woman. The first fore-shadowing of the Redeemer is recorded for future generations: the Protoevangelium.

Yahweh God speaks to the evil one who is hiding under the form of the serpent: 'I will put enmity between you and the woman, and between your off-spring and hers; he will strike at your head, while you strike at his heel' (Gen. 3.15).

The Immaculate Conception is presented as a con-trast to this scene of the fall. This contrast is with the original sin of our first parents. The Immaculate Conception means freedom from the inheritance of that sin, Mary's deliverance from the effects of the disobedience of the first Adam.

Deliverance comes at the price of the obedience of the second Adam: Christ. It is precisely by virtue of this price, in consideration of his redeeming death, that the spiritual death of sin does not ever touch the mother of the Redeemer.

He Proclaims Peace

I will hear what God proclaims. The Lord proclaims peace
to his people, to his faithful ones, and to those who put
their hope in him. 'Near indeed is his salvation to those
who fear him, glory dwelling in our land' (Ps. 85.10).

These are the words of the psalm we pray. And behold,
they are fulfilled as the Virgin of Nazareth hears the message of God by way of his messenger: 'You shall conceive
and bear a son and give him the name Jesus . . . The Holy
Spirit will come upon you and the power of the Most
High will overshadow you; hence, the holy offspring to
be born will be called Son of God' (Luke 1.31–5).

The Virgin of Nazareth responds to what God tells
her. She listens attentively. She doesn't merely receive the
Word made flesh. She obeys the Word and answers: 'I am
the servant of the Lord. Let it be done to me as you say'
(Luke 1.38). This is how Advent is fulfilled – the first
advent of mankind.

Advent means nearness of salvation; it means God's
glory on earth. Advent is an encounter with God himself.
The psalm speaks about that: 'Kindness and truth shall
meet; justice and peace shall kiss' (Ps. 85.11).

Behold! The Word is made flesh in the womb of the
Virgin. Justice comes down from God. It comes as grace
and peace: the grace and peace of reconciliation with God
in the eternal Son.

What does this justice offered to man in Christ require
as a response? What must man carry in his heart? He must
carry faithfulness, because 'truth shall spring out of the
earth, and justice shall look down from heaven' (Ps.
85.12).

That is precisely what happens in the heart of the
Immaculate Virgin. That is why right there in her heart
the first advent of mankind is fulfilled. She becomes the
model of the church through her faith-filled response. And
the annunciation becomes the definitive advent.

The Time of Mary

Advent is in a special way the time of Mary. She bears the long-awaited Messiah who is the hope of the ages. In a certain sense, it is in her that we find the summit and the full meaning of Advent. The solemnity of the Immaculate Conception, which the liturgy celebrates during the season of Advent, witnesses to that in a most eloquent way.

Even though on September 8th each year the church venerates Mary's birth with a special feast, Advent introduces us even more deeply into the sacred mystery of her birth. Before coming to the world, she was conceived in the womb of her mother. Yet at that very moment, she was born of God himself, who accomplished the mystery of the Immaculate Conception: She was born 'full of grace'.

That is why we repeat, with the apostle to the gentiles: 'Praised be the God and Father of our Lord Jesus Christ, who has bestowed on us in Christ every spiritual blessing' (Eph. 1.3). And Mary was blessed in a very special way, in a unique and unrepeatable way. In Christ, God chose her before the creation of the world to be holy and immaculate in his eyes (Eph. 1.4). Yes, the eternal Father chose Mary in Christ. He chose her for Christ. He made her holy, even most holy. And the first fruits of this divine election and calling was the Immaculate Conception.

Light of the First Advent

O immaculate one!
Mother of God and of men!
You are the light of the first Advent!
You are the morning star which precedes the coming
    of the Messiah.
Now that the church and mankind are drawing near
    to the end

of the second millennium after Christ's coming –
be for us the light of this new Advent,
be its morning star
so that darkness will not overcome us!
Near the end of the second millennium, threatening
 clouds are gathering on the horizon of mankind
 and darkness is falling
over human souls.
Intervene, O Mary, and speak
with your convincing voice of a mother.
Speak to the hearts of all those who decide the fate of
 nations.
Speak so that through true understanding
they may find the way towards honourable and just
 solutions
in settling the conflicts that divide them.
Persuade those who bear arms throughout the world
to welcome the call to peace,
a call which rises towards them from the martyred and
 defenceless populations of the earth.
Revive, O Mary, in the hearts of all
the sense of human solidarity
towards those who, unable to meet their essential
 needs, are dying of hunger;
towards those who, fugitive from their own countries,
 are looking for a refuge for themselves and for their
 own;
towards those who, having been unemployed for a
 long time, feel that their future is dangerously
 threatened.
Protect, O Mary, the childlike innocence
of today's children, who will be the men and women
 of the coming millennium.
We ask this through Christ our Lord. Amen!

Mary: The Beginning of the Newborn Church

In the fullness of her mystery and her mission, Mary is the church's pre-eminent member. She also helps usher in its beginning. She is so closely linked to the church in salvation history that she appears as almost an incarnation and a living image of the church herself, the bride of Christ. From the very first moment of her life, she has all the richness of grace that Christ gives to his church.

In this light the eighth chapter of *Lumen Gentium* comes to mind. Interpreting St Luke's insight, this work of the Second Vatican Council tells us: 'After a long period of waiting the times are fulfilled in her, the exalted Daughter of Zion, and the new plan of salvation is established.' At this crucial point in history, Mary is at the meeting place of the Old and New Covenants. She represents the end of the messianic church of Israel and the beginning of the newborn church of Christ. She is the last and perfect expression of the children of God born of Abraham under the Old Covenant and the first and highest expression of the new children of God born of Christ. With Mary, we see the promises, the foreshadowing, and the prophecies of the Old Testament church fulfilled. With her, we also see the New Testament church begin, without stain or wrinkle, in the fullness of the grace of the Holy Spirit.

Model of the Church

'The Holy Spirit will come upon you and the power of the Most High will overshadow you' (Luke 1.35). The church regards Mary, the Mother of God, as her own prototype or model. This truth has been expressed by the Council in the last chapter of the constitution on the church: *Lumen Gentium*. Today, once again, we become aware of this truth.

'The Holy Spirit will come upon you and the power of

the Most High will overshadow you.' Doesn't the Mother of God – in the light of these words of the Gospel – appear to be the model and figure of the church?

Yet the church was born through the coming of the Holy Spirit on the day of Pentecost! The Holy Spirit descended upon the apostles who were gathered in the upper room together with Mary. The church was born when 'the power of the Most High' filled the apostles with the Holy Spirit to protect them from their own weaknesses and from falling away as they faced persecution for the sake of the gospel.

On the solemnity of the Immaculate Conception, the liturgy leads us to return to the beginning of the history of creation and of salvation. In fact, it takes us back even before the dawn of creation.

Hail, Full of Grace

In the Gospel according to Luke, Mary listens to these words: 'Rejoice, O highly favoured daughter!' (Luke 1.28). Or, as we usually say, 'Hail, full of grace!' This greeting comes to her, as our reading from the letter to the Ephesians indicates, from the mind of God himself. It is the expression of eternal love, the expression of her election 'in the heavens in Christ'. 'God chose us in him before the world began, to be holy and blameless in his sight' (Eph. 1.4).

The Virgin of Nazareth hears this salutation: 'Hail, full of grace'. It tells of her particular election in Christ.

In him, the God and Father of our Lord Jesus Christ has chosen you, O daughter of Israel, to be holy and blameless. He chose you before the world began. He has chosen you to be immaculate and holy from the very first moment your human parents conceived you. He has chosen you out of love for his Son. For in the mystery of the incarnation, the Son of God has found the mother of divine election in all her fullness: the mother of divine grace. That is why the messenger salutes you as one 'full of grace'.

Mary's Anticipation Is the Hope of the Nations

The anticipation of the Virgin, who is 'blest among women' (Luke 1.42), sums up all of the hope that the people of God had placed in the promises made to the patriarchs. And, through the people of Israel, the hope of all mankind is gathered in this great expectation.

Let us also seek to appropriate Mary's attitude of expectant faith, a faith which is so deeply rooted in the history of her people and the hopes of all mankind. Let us grasp its meaning as we walk down through the centuries. It is a path that is firmly established on the hope of a salvation that comes from God alone.

Mary is blessed because she has believed in the fulfilment of the Lord's words to her (Luke 1.45). She knows that God will not fall short of his own promises. She is 'happy' and at the same time 'blessed' by God. Those two states of being cannot be separated because the first one is the effect of the second.

The word of blessing, uttered by God, is always a source of life and therefore of happiness. Throughout Scripture, happiness comes through the giving and communicating of life, whether physical or spiritual. Whoever is 'blessed' by God with his life is also 'happy'.

Mary anticipates with great joy the gift of life. Yet it is a life by which she herself is both saved and made happy, since that life is the very Son of God himself.

The Immaculate

The Immaculate Conception does not merely mean that Mary has been given a special place above the rest of us.

It is not as if she has been taken out of the midst of all of us who inherit the sin of our first parents.

Quite the opposite is true. She is at the very heart of the spiritual warfare which rages against the prince of darkness and the father of lies, the one who opposes the woman and her offspring.

Through the book of Genesis, we can see the immaculate one in all the stark realism of her election. We can see her at the culminating point of that enmity: under the cross of Christ on Calvary. It is there that 'he will strike at your head while you strike at his heel'. At the price of his own life, Christ brings us victory over Satan, over sin, and over death.

Virgin and Mother

'Mary the Immaculate stands at the foot of the cross: She conceived, brought forth, and nourished Christ; presented him to the Father in the temple; shared her Son's sufferings as he died on the cross. Thus, in a wholly singular way she cooperated by her obedience, faith, hope, and burning charity in the work of the Saviour . . . For this reason she is a mother to us in the order of grace' (LG, 61). Such is the teaching of the Council.

And that is why the Mother of God is also intimately connected to the church. She is a figure or a likeness of the church, as St Ambrose has taught, in the order of faith, of love, and of perfect union with Christ. In fact, 'in the mystery of the church, which is also rightly called "mother and virgin", the Blessed Virgin Mary has walked ahead, presenting herself in an eminent and unique way, as virgin and as mother' (LG, 63).

The Virgin Is Herself a Wholly Blessed Gift

The angel said to Mary: 'You shall conceive and bear a son and give him the name Jesus' (Luke 1.31). The fulfil-

ment of these words is very near. All of the liturgy of
Advent is full of this expectation.

During the last days of this holy season, we hail him
who is to come with the wonderful Advent antiphons,
which sum up the mystery of the incarnation. To him
who is to be born of the Virgin and given the name Jesus,
the church proclaims:

O Wisdom, springing forth from the Most High,

O Adonai, ruler of Israel,

O Root of Jesse, who art lifted up like a banner for the
nations,

O Key of David, who openest and no one can close,
and who closest and no one can open,

O Dawn of the east, splendour of eternal light and sun
of justice,

O King of the gentiles and chief cornerstone,

O Emmanuel!

'The virgin shall be with child, and bear a son, and shall
name him Emmanuel' (Isa. 7.14). These are Isaiah's words
written centuries before Christ.

Mary, along with Joseph, is drawing near to Bethlehem.
The advent of the Saviour is reaching its zenith. And Mary
is herself a wholly blessed gift that fills our hearts with
expectation and hope.

The Lord Is Near

The Lord is near! Behold the words of the prophet
Zephaniah and be filled with joy: 'Be glad and exult with
all your heart, O daughter Jerusalem! . . . The King of
Israel, the LORD, is in your midst, you have no further
misfortune to fear . . . Fear not, O Zion, be not discouraged!' (Zeph. 3.14–16).

God's nearness, his presence in the midst of his people
Israel, is the source of our strength against all sorts of evil,
the prophet tells us. The presence of God is a saving help.
He is 'a mighty saviour' (Zeph. 3.17). This is the source

of the renewal of our spirits. For God's nearness, his presence among men, manifests his love – a love that overcomes all evil.

The New Testament bears witness to this truth. For instance, Paul in the letter to the Philippians tells us: 'Rejoice in the Lord always! I say it again. Rejoice! The Lord is near' (Phil. 4.4–5). Rejoice in his saving presence and have an unshakable confidence in God. The apostle then writes: 'Dismiss all anxiety from your minds. Present your needs to God in every form of prayer and in petitions full of gratitude' (Phil. 4.6).

The expression 'the Lord is near' is an invitation to intimacy with him, an intimacy which is realised in a direct way through prayer. It is during prayer that we open up ourselves to God and share with him our very lives.

God Calls Man

The Lord is near. Rejoice. Become kind and gracious, eager to forgive others.

The Lord is near. May he give his peace to you! The apostle writes: 'God's own peace, which is beyond all understanding, will stand guard over your hearts and minds, in Christ Jesus' (Phil. 4.7).

What a great blessing such peace really is! It is above all the peace of a good conscience. For God's nearness helps us to see the need to examine our conscience, to search our thoughts and actions before him.

The ministry of John the Baptist on the banks of the Jordan is an excellent example of this need. That is why the liturgy of Advent brings it to our attention more than once. John is the messenger who announces that the Messiah is close at hand. He offers penitents the 'baptism of repentance' in anticipation of him who 'will baptize in the Holy Spirit and in fire' (Luke 3.16).

It is through John's ministry along the Jordan that the

children of Israel have heard that God's coming is near. In this light, the first question posed by the crowd is: 'What ought we to do?' (Luke 3.10, 12). John the Baptist replies by calling the people to true righteousness. He even includes tax collectors and soldiers in the call. We see that as God draws near he calls for conversion, for renewal, and a change in conduct.

God, who is coming, is close at hand. He calls to each person through the inner voice of the conscience. If the voice of that conscience does not sound, then that person has not encountered God. He has not tasted God's closeness 'in Spirit and truth' (John 4.23). He has let God pass him by, or maybe such a person has even turned away from God.

He Has Become One of Us

Our Christian faith is characterised by God's nearness to us. When the Apostle Paul tells us, 'The Lord is near', this truth resounds constantly throughout our lives. God is near because he has revealed himself to man. He has spoken through the prophets and, in this final age, he has spoken through his Son (Heb. 1.1–2).

God is near because in the Son, in the eternal Word, he *has become man*. Born in Bethlehem of the Virgin Mary, Jesus of Nazareth 'has worked with a man's hands, has thought with a man's mind, has loved with a man's heart' – as we read in a document of the Council. 'He has really become one of us, like unto us in all except in sin' (GetS, 22). He even became poor, obedient unto death. He was condemned to death on the cross. It could be said that in his act of drawing near to men, he has overcome every limit.

Moreover, as God draws near he takes on the form of bread and wine in the Eucharist. He has become food for our souls. Once more, through this way of the Sacrament

of the Eucharist, he has overcome every limit that man
could ever imagine.

What Ought We to Do?

What is our response to God's nearness? We ask, just as
the children of Israel asked by the Jordan: 'What ought
we to do?' This God knows the inner mystery of man,
because he came in order to be the light of human consciences and of human hearts.

What is our response to his nearness? To his presence?
Are we full of deep adoration, dedication to the Lord, and
confidence in him? This is the kind of response the liturgy
of Advent invites us to make.

Or have we done otherwise? Have we acted in ways
that conflict with the spirit of Advent? Have we become
too familiar with God's closeness to us? Have we grown
accustomed to it in a casual way? Have we lost sight of
the deep inner truth that God holds out to us in Advent?
Have we become indifferent to it?

Or do we respond to God's nearness, to his divine
presence by saying, 'yes' to him? Or, quite simply, does
his presence disturb us?

The liturgy of Advent presses us to address such questions. They are essential. They relate not only to our
moral self and to our behaviour but are addressed to the
core of our being, to our Christian conscience.

The Lord is near! 'Rejoice,' writes the apostle. Our joy
will be true and deep when we understand and welcome
the full truth of John the Baptist's cry on the banks of the
Jordan. We can never forget that God who is infinitely
near is an infinitely holy God!

The Mystery of the Incarnation

Advent comes close to its fulfilment in human history.
We find expressions of this in the liturgy.

Behold, in the reading of the letter to the Hebrews, we hear the words of the Son of God: 'Sacrifice and offering you did not desire, but a body you have prepared for me . . . "I have come to do your will, O God" ' (Heb. 10.5, 7).

In these words, God's coming into our midst takes on the shape of the mystery of the incarnation. God has prepared this mystery from eternity, and now he is fulfilling it. The Father sends the Son. The Son welcomes the call. By the Holy Spirit he becomes man in the womb of the Virgin of Nazareth. 'The Word became flesh' (John 1.14). The Word is the eternally beloved and eternally loving Son. Love means unity of purpose and of will. The Father's will and the Son's will become perfectly united. The fruit of this union is personal love itself, the Holy Spirit. And then, the fruit of personal love is the incarnation: 'a body you have prepared for me.'

The Lord is near. He comes.

Obedience to Faith

At the visitation Elizabeth praises first of all Mary's faith: 'Blest is she who trusted that the Lord's words to her would be fulfilled' (Luke 1.45).

In fact, at the annunciation, Mary gives her assent and shows her obedience in faith. This assent, her *fiat*, is *the key moment*. The mystery of the incarnation is a divine mystery but at the same time a human mystery. In fact, he who takes on a body is the Son of God and the Word of God. Yet, simultaneously, the body he takes on is fully human: This is the wonderful economy of God's plan of salvation.

At that very moment when the Virgin of Nazareth utters her *fiat* 'Let it be done to me as you say', the Son is able to tell the Father: 'A body you have prepared for me.' Thus, God's advent is fulfilled also through human action and through the obedience of faith.

Mary's Heart of Faith

The Father has prepared a human body for the Son
through the working of the Holy Spirit who is love. The
mystery of the incarnation means a special outpouring of
this love: the Holy Spirit's descent on the Virgin of Nazareth, on Mary.

'The Holy Spirit will come upon you and the power of
the Most High will overshadow you; hence, the holy
offspring to be born will be called Son of God' (Luke
1.35).

The Holy Spirit, with his divine power, acts first of all
in Mary's heart. In this way, her faith becomes the source
of the mystery of the incarnation. 'I am the servant of the
Lord. Let it be done to me as you say' (Luke 1.38)!

The Children of God

The liturgy puts before our eyes not only the eternal
obedience of the Son: 'I have come to do your will, O
God.' It not only puts before our eyes the obedience of
her who was chosen from beforehand to be his earthly
mother. No, it also puts before our eyes *the place* in which
the mystery of the incarnation is to be fulfilled.

Yes, at the very heart of Micah's prophecy, we hear of
the town: Bethlehem. This is the very place where the
eternal Son is to be revealed for the first time in his human
body. The Son of God as the Son of Man – Mary's Son.
The prophet says: 'But you, Bethlehem Ephrathah, too
small to be among the clans of Judah, from you shall come
forth to me one who is to be ruler in Israel; Whose origin
is from of old, from ancient times' (Mic. 5.2).

Such origin 'from of old, from ancient times' is actually
from times without beginning! It is the eternity of the
only begotten Son of God. 'When she who is to give birth
has borne, the rest of his brethren shall return to the
children of Israel,' the prophet further announces (Mic.

5.3). This human birth of God's Son from the Virgin starts the new Israel, the new people of God. This is the people of God who are to be Christ's 'brethren', who through grace will become *sons in the Son of God*. They will be 'empowered to become children of God', as St John says in the prologue to his Gospel (John 1.12).

The place where all of this is to be fulfilled, a place which will be remembered for all time in salvation history, is the small town of Bethlehem Ephrathah.

Every Day Should Be an Advent

In Advent, we are urged by grace to have the inner attitude of faith and expectancy of all those who have waited on the Lord, all those who have believed and loved Jesus. This approach to Advent enables our faith to become vibrant as we constantly meditate and feed upon his word. For the Christian this continues to be the first and fundamental point of reference for his spiritual life, a life that must be nourished by prayers of adoration and praise to God. Of these, the *Benedictus* of Zechariah, the *Nunc dimittis* of Simeon, and especially the *Magnificat* of the Blessed Virgin are matchless models.

This inner attitude of faith in Advent is reinforced by our reception of the sacraments, above all those of Reconciliation and the Eucharist, which cleanse us and enrich us with Christ's grace. They make us *new men* in tune with Jesus' exhortation: 'Reform your lives!' (Matt. 3.2; Luke 5.32).

From this perspective, every day can and should be an advent for us as Christians. Because the more we cleanse our souls, the more we make room for God's love in our hearts. Then Christ will be able to come inside and be born in us every day.

The Eternal Way to God

Advent gives us great joy because we are 'going up to the house of the Lord' (Ps. 121.1). We can see the end of this great pilgrimage, which is what earthly life is supposed to be. We are called to dwell in 'the house of the Lord'. That is our real home.

Advent is the anticipation of the day of the Lord, of the hour of truth. It is the anticipation of that day when 'He shall judge between the nations, and impose terms on many peoples' (Isa. 2.4). God's fullness of truth will be the foundation of the definitive and universal peace of Christ, which is the object of hope for all men of good will.

In this way, Advent helps us realise anew man's eternal way to God. Every year it is a new beginning of this way. Man's life does not lead down an impassable road. No, it is a way that leads to our encounter with the Lord at the end of time!

In Advent, there is also a foretelling of those ways which will lead the shepherds and the wise men from the east towards the manger of the newborn Jesus at Bethlehem.

The Transformation of Man

The way of Advent leads towards the inner life of man, which is in many ways under the weight of sin. Our encounter with God does not take place merely from without but also deep inside of us. It involves such a transformation of our inner being that we are able to respond to the holiness of him whom we encounter. This inner transformation consists of *putting on the Lord Jesus Christ*. Thus the historical sense of Advent is penetrated by the spiritual sense.

In fact, Advent is not supposed to be only the memory of salvation history before the Saviour's birth, even though that has very high spiritual meaning when properly understood. Still beyond that and more deeply, Advent reminds us that all of man's history – the history of each one of us – is to be understood as a great advent. Our lives are meant to be lived in anticipation, instant by instant, of the coming of the Lord. Then, he will find us ready and watchful, and we will be able to receive him worthily.

Promise of Salvation

The Advent season brings spontaneously to our lips prayers for our salvation. In this way, we look back on the watchful wait for salvation through the whole of the Old Testament and continuing on into the New. 'In hope we were saved,' says St Paul (Rom. 8.24), and 'it is in the Spirit that we eagerly await the justification we hope for, and only faith can yield it' (Gal. 5.5). Even the final words of the Bible are a prayerful cry for the coming and the full manifestation of the Lord Jesus as the Saviour: 'Come, Lord Jesus!' (Rev. 22.20).

Salvation! It is man's great aspiration. The holy Scriptures witness to that on every page. They invite us to discover where true salvation for man is. They tell us who our deliverer and our redeemer really is.

The foundational experience of salvation which the people of God experienced in the Old Testament was the liberation from slavery in Egypt. The Bible calls it redemption, ransom, liberation, and salvation. That was the first form of redemption and salvation which the people of God experienced collectively in history. The memory of this salvation is the hallmark of Israel's faith.

The second great event of salvation in the Bible is the liberation of the exiles in Babylon. Both events – liberation from Egypt and from Babylon – are interwoven through the books of the prophets and connected one with the other. The liberation of the exiles in Babylon is a second redemption, or rather a continuation and a fulfilment of the first one. And its author is again God, the holy one of Israel, the deliverer and redeemer of his people. In the words of Jeremiah, 'The days are coming, says the LORD, when I will fulfill the promise I made to the house of Israel and Judah' (Jer. 33.14).

Christmas and Epiphany

25th December: Christmas Day

Behold, I Announce the Midnight of the Saviour's Birth

This Midnight extends from east to west. It follows all of the meridians encompassing the whole earth. In the east it has preceded us. In the west it is yet to come.

Behold, I announce the Midnight of the Saviour's birth in all places and at all moments as it passes through the globe. I announce the Midnight! I, the custodian of the great mystery. I, the Bishop of Rome, announce everywhere the Midnight of Christmas.

'Sing to the LORD a new song, his praise from the end of the earth' (Isa. 42.10). Sing, O earth! Sing, because you have been chosen by God, chosen from the whole universe! And the whole universe has been chosen together with you. Sing, O earth! 'Let the heavens be glad and the earth rejoice; let the sea and what fills it resound; let the plains be joyful and all that is in them! Then shall all the trees of the forest exult' (Ps. 96.11–12). Sing, O earth! Because you have been chosen before time to be the birthplace of God who takes on human flesh.

Let the whole earth be gathered around that unique Midnight! Let the power of all created things speak! Let it speak with the existence of all created worlds! Let it speak with the language of men!

Behold, a man speaks. His name is Luke the Evangelist. He says: 'The days of her [Mary's] confinement were completed. She gave birth to her firstborn son and wrapped him in swaddling clothes and laid him in a manger, because there was no room for them in the place where travelers lodged' (Luke 2.6–7). That is how the Son of God came into the world.

Mary was the wife of Joseph, a carpenter at Nazareth who belonged to David's house. The Christ Child was born in Bethlehem because Mary and Joseph had to travel there to register in the census decreed by Caesar Augustus. That is what man has said of the Saviour's birth.

Simultaneously with man, the angel of the Lord speaks. He speaks to the shepherds when, in the middle of Bethlehem's dark night, 'the glory of the Lord shone around them, and they were very much afraid' (Luke 2.9).

He says to them: 'You have nothing to fear! I come to proclaim good news to you – tidings of great joy to be shared by the whole people. This day in David's city a savior has been born to you, the Messiah and Lord. Let this be a sign to you: in a manger you will find an infant wrapped in swaddling clothes' (Luke 2.10–12).

Man and the angel of the Lord speak about the same reality and point to the same place: the Lord's birth at Bethlehem.

Let the Earth Exult

The angel speaks about something that man would not dare to say: In Bethlehem the Messiah, the anointed one, has been born. This is the anointed one who comes to visit mankind in the power of the Holy Spirit. He will judge the earth. He will judge the world with justice. He will 'sacrifice himself for us, to redeem us from all unrighteousness and to cleanse for himself a people of his own' (Titus 2.14). He will sacrifice himself for us: that is his judgement! 'Watchman, how much longer the night?' (Isa. 21.11).

Behold, I announce the Midnight. From the depths of Bethlehem's night, which is the night of all mankind, a gift has been given. 'The grace of God has appeared, offering salvation to all men' (Titus 2.11).

What is grace? Grace is divine pleasure. It is focused fully on this child who lies in the manger. For this child is the eternal Son, the Son of divine pleasure, the Son of eternal love.

Yet this child is Mary's Son. He is also the Son of Man, true man. The divine pleasure of the Father focuses on man: what grace! 'Peace on earth to those on whom his favour rests' (Luke 2.14), the angels tell the shepherds, the sons of men.

From Bethlehem this divine grace begins to shine forth on men of all times. It is the beginning of glory, of that glory which God possesses in the highest. To this glory man has been called in Jesus Christ. Yes, a marvellous grace has visited men on this glorious night.

Let the earth exult! You, O earth, which are man's dwelling. Receive once again the splendour of that night. Gather around that splendour. Proclaim to all created things the joy of redemption. Announce to the whole world the hope of the redemption of the world. 'Let the plains be joyful and all that is in them! Then shall all the trees of the forest exult before the LORD' (Ps. 96.12–13).

Behold, he comes. Behold, he is already among us: Emmanuel. All the power of the redemption of the world is in him.

Alleluia!

The Feast of Goodness

Children grasp easily the mystery of Christmas, even though that mystery is so deep not even an adult will ever fathom it completely. To understand Christmas, in some ways, we must remain children all the time. We must be like little children – as Jesus said – to enter the kingdom of heaven (Mark 10.15). And we must be like truly good children to understand Christmas.

For Christmas is above all the feast of goodness: It speaks to us of God's goodness and kindness in giving us Christ. In fact, Jesus has become a babe to teach us goodness.

This goodness consists of our love and obedience as God's children. It means loving the Father, the Son, and the Holy Spirit, loving all men, and obeying God's commandments.

Room for Charity

Our modern society changes so quickly. We hear so much about technological breakthroughs for the betterment of man, particularly in areas like medicine. Yet, increasingly, there seems to be less room for charity and kindness. In fact, there is tremendous spiritual poverty and misery in our day. We see it in the aimlessness and loneliness of many people today. It is a poverty of the soul.

The church urges us to renew our charity and kindness for others during this season of God's goodness and grace. We remember that in the incarnation of the Word 'the kindness and love of God our Savior appeared' (Titus 3.4).

Drawing Near to All Men

The mystery of Christmas sheds its light on the Christian's call to brotherly love. To this inexhaustible fountain of grace and love, we are invited to draw close with eyes of faith and with true wisdom. Wisdom shows us how we can live as brothers, drawing our inspiration and strength from the mystery of God made man. In fact, as we draw ever closer to Bethlehem, we see how small our God, who is great and infinite, has made himself. How similar he is to us in all things, yet he is God. See how he has identified with us and drawn near to us. As we draw closer to Bethlehem with the simplicity and wisdom of the shepherds and the wise men, Jesus will teach us to draw near to all men, starting with the humblest and the smallest, so we can help them all live for God.

The Night when the Light Appeared

The night of Bethlehem probably seemed similar to so many other nights which in their unchanged rhythm take turns blanketing our planet.

But it was a special night. For in a small corner of the earth, in the vicinity of Bethlehem to the south of Jerusalem, the darkness of night was transformed into light.

This light illumines the night with a tremendous and awe-inspiring mystery. In its splendour, it surrounds some shepherds who are in the vicinity 'keeping night watch by turns over their flocks', and it leaves them 'very much afraid'.

From out of the dazzling light comes an angelic voice: 'You have nothing to fear! I come to proclaim good news to you – tidings of great joy . . . This day in David's city a Saviour has been born to you' (Luke 2.10–11).

The promised child is born.

The dazzling light and the angelic voice indicate the place and the meaning of his birth. He has really been born. He has been born in a stable built for animals, because there was no room for him in any human home. He has been born during a census of the whole population of Israel, while Caesar Augustus rules over the Roman Empire and Quirinius is governor of Syria. The one who is born belongs to the house of David, so he is born at Bethlehem, which is 'the city of David'. He is born of the Virgin. Her name is Myriam, that is, Mary. She is the wife of Joseph from David's house and both of them have come from Nazareth to enrol in the census.

And from the midst of this great light that surrounds the shepherds, these simple folk are told: 'In a manger you will find an infant wrapped in swaddling clothes' (Luke 2.12).

God Became Flesh for Our Sake

God became flesh for our sake! The divine Word became
a man like us. Thus, we are assured both in human history
and in our own personal lives that he is always present
with his love, with his salvation, and with his providence.

We begin to see that Christmas demands faith, because
Christmas is a mystery. Our reason cannot succeed in
trying to understand how God could possibly have loved
us to such a degree. The shepherds are given a sign. They
will find him in a manger. There the infant Jesus has been
placed by the Blessed Mother: a sign of extreme poverty
and of God's supreme humility. Such a thing baffles the
intellect. It teaches us that to welcome the message of
Christ, the divine Redeemer, reason must be laid aside.
Only humility, which melts into trust and adoration, can
comprehend and welcome God's saving humility.

Then let us turn every day to meditate on that manger
scene. Let us ask Mary and St Joseph to pray that we
might be given the grace of adoring humility and of confident faith!

1st January
Solemnity of Mary the Mother of God
Holy Mary, Mother of God

We want to consecrate ourselves to you,
because you are the Mother of God and our mother,
because your Son Jesus has entrusted us to you,
because you have been willing to be the mother of the
    church.
We consecrate ourselves to you, all of us who have
    gathered together as your children.
I consecrate to you the entire church with her pastors
    and all the faithful:
the bishops, who in imitation of the Good Shepherd

watch over the people who have been entrusted to
them;

the priests, who have been anointed by the Spirit;

the religious brothers and sisters, who offer up their
life for the kingdom of Christ;

the seminarians, who have welcomed the Lord's call;

the Christian spouses in their life-long union of love
for each other and their families;

the lay people committed to apostolates;

the young people, who are longing for a new society;

the children, who deserve a more human and peaceful
world;

the sick, the poor, the prisoners, the persecuted, the
orphans, the despairing, and the dying.

Pray for Us Sinners!

Mother of the church,
we take refuge under your protection
and we entrust ourselves to your care.
We ask you to pray for the church,
that she may be faithful in the purity of faith,
in the sureness of hope,
in the fervour of love,
in apostolic and missionary zeal,
in the commitment to promote justice and peace
among the children of this blessed world.
We entreat you for the whole church that she may
always remain in a perfect communion of faith and
love, united to the See of Peter with close ties of
obedience and love.
We commend to you the seeds we plant for the
salvation of souls,
our faithfulness to preferential love for the poor and
the Christian formation of our youth,
more priestly and religious vocations,
for the generosity of those who consecrate themselves
to Christ's mission,
for the unity and holiness of all families.

Now and at the Hour of Our Death

Virgin of the Rosary, Our mother!
Pray for us now.
Grant to us the priceless gift of peace,
of forgiving all wrongs and harbouring no grudges,
for the reconciliation of all men as brothers.
May violence and warfare cease.
May dialogue grow and may men live in peace with
  each other.
May new ways of justice and prosperity open up.
We ask this of you whom we invoke as Queen of
  Peace
now and at the hour of our death!
We entrust to you all the victims of injustice and
  violence,
all those who have died in natural disasters,
all those who at the hour of their death turn to you as
  mother and patron,
so that with you we may glorify together
the Father, the Son, and the Holy Spirit.
Amen.

The Mystery of the Holy Family

The church experiences the joy of the nativity of her Lord
in *the mystery of the family, of the Holy Family*. It is a
deeply human truth. By the birth of a child, the marriage
relationship of man and woman, of husband and wife,
becomes more perfectly a family.

At the same time, the nativity of Jesus is a great mystery
of God which is unveiled before the eyes of men, a mystery that is hidden in the faith and in the hearts of Mary
and Joseph of Nazareth. At the beginning, the two of
them are the only witnesses to the birth of the child who
was born in Bethlehem as the Son of the Most High.

To the two of them, Mary and Joseph, God makes

known the mystery of the family which he forms with them and through them when Jesus is born.

As we, too, look with the eyes of faith we see that the Holy Family is a special expression of God's nearness to us. It also shows us the dignity of all human families in the eyes of the Creator. In fact, Christ has given us the Sacrament of Matrimony as a sign of that great dignity. The Apostle Paul even calls this sacrament 'a great fore-shadowing' of the relationship between Christ and the church (Eph. 5.32).

An Invitation to Inner Life

Three new figures appear on the horizon of Christmas: the wise men coming from the east. God's epiphany draws near. In the liturgy of the church, the feast of Epiphany means manifestation, because God reveals himself and shows forth his glory.

This understanding of the feast makes us think first of the star that appears overhead to guide the wise men. We also think of their long journey from the east following that distant star on the horizon.

But there is a deeper meaning to this understanding of the feast of Epiphany. The Holy Spirit invites us to consider the inner path these wise ones have trod. This is an inner path to God and the manifestation of his glory. It begins with the mysterious encounter of the human intellect and human heart with the light of God himself. In the words of St John, 'The real light which gives light to every man was coming into the world' (John 1.9).

These three wise men were undoubtedly following this light even before the star appeared to them. God was speaking to them in the wonder of all created things, saying, 'I am. I exist. I am the Creator and the Lord of the whole world.'

At a certain moment, beyond the veil, he drew them even closer to himself. He began to reveal to them the truth of his coming into the world. They were made aware of the divine design of salvation in some way they could not fully understand.

And the wise men responded with faith to that inner epiphany with God.

The Meaning of the Star

The wise men recognise the meaning of the star because of their faith. That faith commands them to start off on a long journey towards a distant land. They are headed towards Jerusalem, the capital of Israel, where the truth about the coming of the Messiah has been handed down from generation to generation. The prophets had foretold his coming, and the authors of holy books had written about the Messiah. God, who spoke to the hearts of the wise men by his inner epiphany, had spoken down through the centuries to the chosen people.

This long-awaited coming is fulfilled the night of God's birth in Bethlehem. That night is already the epiphany of God's coming, God who is born of the Virgin and who is placed in a simple manger.

This God hides his coming in the poverty and obscurity of a lowly birth in Bethlehem. Such is the epiphany of his divine humility. Only some shepherds come to adore the Christ Child.

Now the wise men come. God, who has hidden himself from the eyes of men living nearby, reveals himself to these men who come from far away. They come guided by the star of faith that reveals the Messiah. Thus, the words of Isaiah are fulfilled: 'Nations shall walk by your light, and kings by your shining radiance. Raise your eyes and look about; they gather and come to you' (Isa. 60.3–4).

The Family: A Community of Peace

The family is called by the word of the living God to be a community of peace and of friendship. Like the Holy Family, each family calls all individuals and nations to form such a community. Above all, to develop fully, the family needs a social life of peace and brotherhood that protects the rights of each member. Yet the family today is subject to great tension because of trends in modern society. The family finds itself facing fragmentation and the breakdown of authority. Parents find it difficult to pass on genuine Christian values to their children. The trend towards urbanisation causes overcrowded suburbs, housing problems, and a higher rate of unemployment or underemployment. And all of this has a negative effect on the family.

The church's firm opposition to moral evils that are attacking the family and married life is due to her deep conviction that these evils are contrary to God's plan for mankind. These evils violate the sacredness of marriage and the values of human life. The church has the responsibility to defend the rights of the family and the total welfare of mankind. That is the reason why she renews her commitment to proclaim the full truth about man.

6th January
The Feast of the Epiphany of the Lord
Grace Leading to Faith

'The mystery was made known to me by revelation' (Eph. 3.3 rsv). The church draws upon these words of the Apostle Paul in the letter to the Ephesians to understand the meaning of the Epiphany. In fact, this feast has been called the Epiphany since the early days of the church. We want to venerate the grace of God on this feast for it leads men to faith.

Yes, the mystery of Christ is made known to man through faith. This is the essence of the feast of the Epiphany. In a certain way, this faith is revealed to the inner man who has spiritual vision, just as one day Jesus reveals himself to Paul of Tarsus on his way to Damascus. Thus, Paul becomes a special witness because of his conversion to faith. As he himself states: 'I am sure you have heard of the ministry which God in his goodness gave me in your regard' (Eph. 3.2).

The apostle bears witness to the grace of the Epiphany. And the church goes back to his words because in that witness we find all those who have been called in Christ by faith. All who believe become 'sharers of the promise through the preaching of the gospel' (Eph. 3.6). Paul underscores for us the great call to preach the gospel to the gentiles now that we believe. This is the call to bring the light of God's revelation to the nations. This is the call of the feast of Epiphany.

A Mystery Revealed Through the Holy Spirit

The wise men of the east are the first gentiles to receive the revelation of faith in Christ. They are the first ones to draw near the mystery of the inheritance which God has offered to all men in Jesus Christ: the incarnation of his eternal Son.

They draw near that mystery which is revealed to the apostles, even before the gospel is made known as the way leading to faith. In them we find an example of pre-evangelisation. We see God preparing their souls for salvation. This is also a work of the Holy Spirit. It reveals the meaning of the star which the wise men follow on their journey towards Jerusalem. For the star symbolises that their salvation is still afar off.

During the time of the Epiphany, the liturgy of the church leads us on our own journey towards Jerusalem.

We turn our hearts towards the holy city which has become 'the city of the great king'. Even if the people of Jerusalem are unaware that the king of glory has been born in their midst, we still rejoice. For she is the city of the great king.

The Coming of the Wise Men

Yet the Jerusalem of the Epiphany is not only the Jerusalem of Herod at the time of the wise men. From God's perspective, it is also the Jerusalem of the prophets.

In the holy city are preserved the testimonies of those who have foretold the coming of the Messiah down through the centuries under the inspiration of the Holy Spirit. The prophet Micah speaks of the birth of the Messiah King in Bethlehem, for instance. Isaiah, the messianic prophet *par excellence*, gives a truly unique witness to the Epiphany: 'Rise up in splendour, [Jerusalem]! Your light has come, the glory of the LORD shines upon you. See, darkness covers the earth, and thick clouds cover the peoples; but upon you the LORD shines and over you his glory appears' (Isa. 60.1–2).

This prophecy of Isaiah expresses so well the reality of the Epiphany. The glory of the Christ inhabits the holy city of Jerusalem. He dispels the darkness and shines his light upon his people.

The prophet now foretells that all of the peoples living in darkness will stream to God's holy city; 'Nations shall walk by your light, and kings by your shining radiance. Raise your eyes and look about; they all gather and come to you; Your sons come from afar, and your daughters in the arms of their nurses' (Isa. 60.3–5). These amazing words of Isaiah find their first fulfilment in the coming of the wise men to Jerusalem.

We Have Seen the Star at Its Rising

'We observed his star at its rising and have come to pay him homage' (Matt. 2.2). This is what the wise men tell the inhabitants of Jerusalem upon their arrival in the holy city. They inquire about 'the newborn king of the Jews'. These are the very words that we recite at the feast of the Epiphany: the manifestation of Jesus as the Messiah, the Son of God, and the Saviour to the peoples who have lived in the darkness of paganism.

.The wise men, representatives of the pagan peoples, remind us of our own search for God. They perceive his presence in the wonders of creation. To find the truth which they had only glimpsed through nature and study, they undertake a journey full of unanswered questions and great risks. Their search ends in a discovery and in an act of deep humble adoration before the infant Jesus and his mother. They offer him their precious treasures and receive in return the priceless gift of Christian faith and joy.

May the wise men be our guides so that our daily walk will always have as its aim Jesus himself, the eternal Son of God and the Son of Mary.

Sunday after 6th January
The Baptism of the Lord
God's Servant Brings Saving Grace

The Word of God presents Jesus of Nazareth to us as the 'servant of God' foretold in the book of Isaiah. He is the chosen one and the delight of God. As God's servant, he will fulfil his mission with total commitment to the Lord's will and show exemplary humility before men. Thus, God establishes him 'as a covenant of the people', as 'a light for the nations', to give sight to the blind and freedom to prisoners.

This mysterious servant of God is Christ, who comes to bring salvation to mankind. He is revealed in the waters of Baptism. In the Gospel of St Luke, Jesus is baptised by John. The heavens are opened. The Spirit of God comes down on Christ as a dove. And a voice – the Father's – says: 'This is my beloved Son. My favour rests on him' (Matt. 3.17).

Now the prophecy is fulfilled. God's favour rests on his servant, the Father's favour for his eternal Son. For the Son has taken on human nature. In deep humility, he has asked John to baptise him with water. Yet John the Baptist is only a precursor of the Christ, and his Baptism in water is only a preparation for the Messiah's coming – a preparation for grace. Jesus, the humble servant of God, brings grace and baptises with the Holy Spirit and fire.

From this point until Ash Wednesday (see p. 38) the reader is invited to use readings from the Ordinary Time section (p. 140), except for the Feast of the Presentation (2nd February) which has a special reading (pp. 128–30).

Lent

Ash Wednesday
Rend Your Hearts, Not Your Garments

'Rend your hearts, not your garments' (Joel 2.13). The church announces the coming of Lent in the words of the prophet Joel. During the prophet Joel's time, the call to fast had to be combined with the warning – 'Rend your hearts, not your garments!'

Jesus, too, had to warn those of his day:

Be on guard against performing religious acts for people to see.

When you give alms, for example, do not blow a horn before you in synagogues and streets like hypocrites looking for applause.

When you are praying, do not behave like hypocrites who love to stand and pray in synagogues or on street corners in order to be noticed.

When you fast, you are not to look glum as the hypocrites do. They change the appearance of their faces so that others may see they are fasting (Matt. 6.1, 2, 5, 16).

In the past when the church announced Lent, it had to encourage people to be on their guard against mere show and against hypocrisy in fasting, prayer, and almsgiving.

Nowadays mere show is not the main danger.

The real danger is that the proclamation of Lent goes unheeded. For many today, Lent remains 'a herald's voice in the desert, crying' (Mark 1.3). They do not respond to the call.

Return to Me

'Return to me with your whole heart' (Joel 2.12). This is God's personal call to each member of the church. God speaks in the first person: 'Return to *me* with all your heart.' This is his message every Lent. That is why Lent is called a 'powerful season', because it is in this season more than any other that God himself speaks to us. He calls. He enters personally into man's life. He knocks at men's hearts.

God wants us for himself. His love for us is very intimate for he knows each of us in the depths of our being. He knows that man cannot be satisfied unless he returns and is converted to God alone. And that is why his love is 'jealous'. 'Then the Lord became jealous for his land', says the prophet (Joel 2.18). The holy jealousy of God's love is the climate of Lent from Ash Wednesday up until the Sacred Triduum – which are the three great feasts of Holy week: Holy Thursday, Good Friday, and the Easter Vigil.

Remember You Are Dust

How can we return to God and be converted to him alone? Conversion begins by turning inward and quieting yourself in God's presence. Then your heart and conscience can begin to awaken.

'Go to your room, close your door,' Jesus instructs us (Matt. 6.6).

Conversion to God cannot happen in the midst of distraction. Reflection and a clear focus on the Lord are necessary. Man must find his true and highest self and, at the same time, his deepest self.

Why deepest? Why true and highest? Because his understanding of man relates to his creation and the creation of the world. To all the creatures of the visible world around him, man stands out as lord and master. He is called to subdue all creatures under him and to have dominion over the earth. This is the first commandment he receives from the Creator.

Not only has God made man the crown of creation, God has also shaped man in the depths of his being. Because man is also spirit, he can achieve where the rest of creation falls short. Man's fundamental nature as both spirit and flesh does not allow him to find ultimate meaning in mere physical creation.

Man cannot satisfy his deepest self through the visible world. Not even by subduing creation and progressing in his ability to develop, to create, and to discover – can he find true happiness in his inmost self. 'What profit would a man show if he were to gain the whole world?' asks Jesus (Matt. 16.26). No, man cannot fulfil his deepest self in this way.

This is the first message of Lent, the message of Ash Wednesday. It is a deep and a powerful message: 'Remember you are dust, and to dust you shall return.'

How, then, can we truly find fulfilment?

The Seed of Immortality

How can man fulfil himself through the world when it sows the seeds of his destruction and is ruled by the law of death? The reality of death is the end of the man who seeks his life in the world around him.

Yes, there can be for us certain immediate and fleeting fulfilments in this short span of life. But they do not last. 'To dust you shall return,' God tells man.

Man must quiet himself and look into the depths of his being. He will find deep within himself in God the seeds of his own immortality. There, he will discover the futility of his efforts to find fulfilment in what does not last.

It is at that moment that he begins to understand why God calls, 'Return to me!' Yes, 'Return to me with your whole heart.'

The Season of God Who Speaks

For man there is no fulfilment without God. This is the meaning of conversion. This is the messianic message. God is love. Man has turned from God to seek fulfilment in what will not satisfy him. And God has called man back from sin through his Son.

In love God does not hesitate to sacrifice his own Son. He does not hesitate to treat as sin, out of love for us, him who had known no sin, 'so that in him we might become the very holiness of God' (2 Cor. 5.21).

The church speaks in the name of God. She calls us to an awareness of our sin and a knowledge of God's love. Her language is particularly radical. 'Radical' means 'going back to the roots'.

Such a radical call is essential at the beginning of Lent. We must cry out with the psalmist: 'In the greatness of your compassion wipe out my offense. For I acknowledge my offense, and my sin is before me always. Against you only have I sinned. . . . A clean heart create for me, O God' (Ps. 51.3, 5–6, 12).

Lent is the season in which God speaks intimately to us. It is the season for us to listen, to receive redemption, to be made new.

He Brought Us out of Egypt

'He brought us out of Egypt' (Deut. 26.8). Thus, we start our study of the great biblical themes of Lent. The first theme is the liberation of God's people from slavery in Egypt. That theme is at the heart of the Passover celebration of the Old Covenant. It also leads us into the very heart of the paschal mystery of the New Covenant: the liberation of God's people from sin.

Using the expression 'wandering Aramean', the author of Deuteronomy refers to Israel's wanderings in search of the promised land. The term 'wandering Aramean' gives us the image of someone who is looking for the way to a safe haven, to a land where he will no longer be a foreigner and sojourner. He is looking for a place of true freedom that he can call home.

It is in God that we find our home. God hears the cries of his people and rescues them from slavery in Egypt. God leads them into the promised land and establishes a covenant with them. He becomes their God, and they become his people.

But due to numerous transgressions against the covenant, Israel is led into exile. And, again, the Lord acts. He promises the chosen people a new covenant that will be sealed by the blood of his very own Son Jesus on the cross. We, as the church, are the people of the New Covenant. In us, God leads his people who had been wandering in search of salvation into the promised land.

Thus, the church is the new Israel. Through Christ and in Christ, she is given the grace and strength to fulfil the call of the New Covenant between God and man. Not through obedience to the Mosaic law does the church stand as the people of God, but rather through faith in Christ the Saviour who is our passover. He liberates us from slavery to sin and leads us into the joy of an abiding relationship with God our Father.

He Must Deny His Very Self

Psalm 91 is like a resounding echo of the experience described in the exodus of the Israelites. In fact, it is recited in the Easter liturgy. It is a song of absolute confidence in God, who delivers and gives security to whomever places himself under his protection: 'You who dwell in the shelter of the Most High, who abide in the shadow of the Almighty, say to the LORD: "My refuge and my fortress, my God, in whom I trust" ' (Ps. 91.1–4).

On his way towards God, every believer, like the wandering Aramean, is a sojourner who passes through a time of risks and dangers. As the psalmist says, 'You shall tread upon the asp and the viper' (v. 13). But the Lord delivers the one who believes and leads him to salvation, to intimacy with himself – the goal of all sojourners here on earth. The Gospel of Luke clearly shows us that the church, guided by Jesus as her Lord, begins the messianic journey – the way that leads towards true liberation (Luke 4.1–13).

The New Covenant of Christ offers us liberation from evil – from death and from sin. The way towards that liberation begins with our victory over the tempter. For temptation leads to sin, so overcoming temptation means overcoming sin at its very root.

Jesus overcame the tempter by denying himself and holding fast to God's truth in the face of temptation. He teaches us to do the same. Yes, we must attack sin at its very root! And the root which we must cut away with the axe is our own selfishness and pride: 'Whoever wishes to be my follower must deny his very self' (Luke 9.23).

Not on Bread Alone

We must be radical with sin. If we do not strike with the axe at the root of selfishness, it will surface again and again. We cannot make progress in the ways of God without making this decision.

The way has been so dramatically laid out for us in Jesus' temptations in the desert. We see him reject the deception of selfish ambition and pride to fully obey his divine call. By renouncing all ambition he perfectly fulfils the word of God and submits to the Father's will.

Obeying Scripture as the Word of God, Jesus overcame the temptation of *independence from God* when he told the tempter 'Not on bread alone shall man live' (Luke 4.4). He rejected the temptation to *work wonders on his own* when Satan insinuated, 'If you are the Son of God, throw yourself down from here' (Luke 4.9). He also rejected *vain ambition and lust for power* when the tempter offered him earthly kingdoms. 'I will give you all this power,' the evil one told the Christ (Luke 4.6). By overcoming these three temptations, which the people of Israel had fallen into while wandering in the desert, Jesus gave us an example of how we are to act when confronted by deceptions.

The Lenten season is an especially important time for listening to the Word of God and submitting to its demands by denying our old self. Then, we are transformed into new creations that live not according to our own will but according to God's will. Through the example and the victory of Jesus, we, too, can have victory over temptation and sin in our lives.

Call on the Name of the Lord

Israel used to look back to the night of the exodus, and that memory served to encourage her to trust in the God who saves.

The church, together with the Apostle Paul, looks back to Easter night. There she finds encouragement for saving faith whose source is the paschal mystery of Christ: 'For if you confess . . . that Jesus is Lord, and believe in your heart that God raised him from the dead, you will be saved' (Rom. 10.9).

With these words, St Paul exhorts us to become ever more aware of our need to be saved. We need to call on that deliverance which comes through the mystery of Christ's death and resurrection: 'Everyone who calls on the name of the Lord will be saved' (Rom. 10.13).

Human Needs and Our Call in Christ

'Not on bread alone is man to live, but on every utterance that comes from the mouth of God' (Matt. 4.4). This is a key passage for us during the season of Lent. Jesus reminds us that God and his word need to have priority in our lives over the things of this world. God calls us during Lent to give up earthly things so we can focus more on him and his kingdom.

At the same time, we need to remember that Jesus also instructed us to pray to God our Father 'to give us this day our daily bread'. Even though it is true that man does not live on bread alone, we see it is *also* true that he lives on bread. Man's physical and material needs must be met, too. God our Father wants to provide for all of our needs.

Thus, we are called to defend the rights of the weak, the poor, the handicapped, and all those who live on the margins of our society. God want us, in Christ, to help meet their material and physical needs and not just to be concerned about our own needs. We are called to reach out to all in need with God's love and care.

But the issue at hand goes much deeper than a call to help those in need. It reaches to the heart of the human, cultural, and spiritual heritage that rightfully belongs to every man, woman, and child in God. We are called to protect and promote that heritage in Christ. At the same time, we need to remember the clear hierarchy of values: the things of the Spirit must have first place in our hearts.

Be Converted

From Ash Wednesday throughout Lent these words of the liturgy resound in our hearts: 'Remember that you are dust, and to dust you shall return' (Gen. 3.19). As we humble ourselves, we can embrace the seriousness of God's call: 'Reform your lives and believe in the gospel!' (Mark 1.15).

May these words accompany us all the days of Lent. May they shape our way of thinking. May they make us yearn for more prayer and for intimacy with Christ in the inner room of our conscience. May they make us understand also the need for self-denial and fasting. May these words of Ash Wednesday be for us both a demand of the heart and a rich blessing as we receive God's help. May they direct our attention towards the needs of others, both our friends and families and those who are far away. May they urge all of us to perform works of charity and mercy.

Lent is upon us again. Now is the 'acceptable time' to turn to God. Now is the 'day of salvation'. Yet much of it depends on our response.

Called to Renew the Covenant

'The Lord made a covenant with Abram' (Gen. 15.18). Through the Lenten season we are called in a special way to intimacy with the God who covenants himself to us. The God of our faith is Creator and Lord of the universe. He is the God of infinite majesty; and, at the same time, he is the God who lowers himself to make a covenant with man.

'Again and again you offered to man a covenant' – these are the words we proclaim in the fourth eucharistic prayer. These words go back to our forefathers, even to Noah.

The covenant with Abram, of which the liturgy speaks, marks a new beginning for the story of God's people: 'Look up at the sky and count the stars . . . Just so . . . shall your descendants be' (Gen. 15.5). Those descendants are, in fact, very numerous. Perhaps one half of all mankind, if not more (Jews, Muslims, and Christians), claim the spiritual fatherhood of Abraham, whom St Paul calls the father of our faith (Rom. 4.11).

During Lent, we are called to renew that covenant with God which had its beginning in the faith of Abraham. This covenant reaches its fulfilment in Christ. The gospel witnesses to that in an eloquent way. Every year during Lent the church leads us up to Mount Tabor. There – before the eyes of Peter, James, and John – appears the full revelation of the covenant, leading from Abraham to Jesus of Nazareth, the Messiah. We see Moses and Elijah with Jesus. They represent the law and the prophets, milestones in God's covenant with the descendants of Abraham. And all of God's revelation revealed through the law and the prophets leads us to the one of whom the Father says, 'This is my Son, the Chosen One. Listen to him' (Luke 9.35).

The Fulfilment of the Covenant

Christ ushers in the fullness of revelation: it is in him that God fully reveals himself. In Christ, God establishes the new and eternal covenant with mankind.

However, the fulfilment of the covenant did not take place on Mount Tabor, even though the apostles desired to remain there and to build three booths – one for Christ, one for Moses, and one for Elijah (Luke 9.33). Mount Tabor was merely the place where the fulfilment of the covenant was summed up in the person and mission of Christ as the Son of God. But the mountain where the covenant will be fulfilled is not the mount of transfiguration but the Mount of Calvary where Christ will be glorified in utter self-abasement before God and men.

And now God, who makes a covenant with Abraham, reveals himself in utter self-sacrifice. The descendants of Abraham, born through faith, will be gathered by the word and by the power of the covenant sealed in the blood of the Lamb of God. That covenant will endure to the end of time.

During the Lenten season, the church guides us towards the mount of transfiguration and prepares us for the mount of crucifixion. In fact, it is in Christ's crucifixion that transfiguration must find its fulfilment. Yes, all of us are called to his crucifixion by the word and the love of the God who is faithful to his covenant.

We Have Our Citizenship in Heaven

During the Lenten season, we are called in a special way to enter the paschal reality. This reality is found in Christ. At the same time this reality is for us. It must embrace us just as the cloud surrounded Peter, James, and John on the mount of transfiguration (Luke 9.34).

The promise of the New Covenant is fulfilled through this paschal mystery which is extended to man. In it we see perfectly fulfilled God's commitment to lead Abraham and his descendants into the promised land. This land became for many generations the Israel of the Old Covenant. Yet it is but a shadow and type of the land God has given us in Christ.

For the God of the New Covenant does not limit his promise to any single earthly country or to any physical dwelling. And no earthly dwelling can contain God's saving action for those gathered together in Christ. This is what Paul writes concerning this mystery: Brethren, 'we have our citizenship in heaven; it is from there that we eagerly await the coming of our Savior, the Lord Jesus Christ. He will give a new form to this lowly body of ours and remake it according to the pattern of his glorified body, by his power to subject everything to himself' (Phil. 3.20–21).

Who Is God?

Just as Moses is called while he is tending his flock in the desert, so we, too, are called by God in the desert. God calls each of us by name just as he calls to Moses: 'Moses! Moses!' (Exod. 3.4).

God commands us as he orders Moses: 'Remove the sandals from your feet, for the place where you stand is holy ground' (Exod. 3.5).

Remove unbelief from your heart! Root out pride from your mind and your will! The time of Lent for the church is a *holy time*. It is a powerful time. It is a time when God is present to us in a special way.

Lent commands our heart and our conscience to turn back to the God who made himself known to Moses in the desert. He is the God of Abraham, the God of Isaac, the God of Jacob. He is the God of infinite majesty, who also seeks out man to establish a covenant with him.

Behold, he reveals himself in the form of a burning bush that is not consumed (Exod. 3.2). The omnipotent God of love reveals himself to the eyes of Moses in the form of a burning bush.

This is God, the transcendent one. Man cannot behold him with his naked eye while living on earth. Moses hides his face because he is afraid to look at God (Exod. 3.6). Then he hears God's voice: 'Come no nearer!' (Exod. 3.5). Moses is both fearful of and attracted to the one who speaks from the burning bush. God's presence envelopes him. He is overwhelmed by God's holiness and is profoundly changed by this encounter.

19th March
The Solemnity of St Joseph
Your Father and I

The church regards St Joseph, 'an upright man', as the one who was before men the father of Jesus of Nazareth. That is why we hear these words in the gospel: 'You see that your father and I have been searching for you in sorrow.'

These words were uttered by Jesus' mother after three days of seeking the twelve-year-old Jesus when she found him 'in the temple sitting in the midst of the teachers, listening to them and asking them questions' (Luke 2.46).

All of us recognise this event narrated by the Evangelist Luke. Today's liturgy brings it to our attention. It is the only event of Jesus' adolescence recorded by the Gospels. It is a significant event, since that twelve-year-old pilgrim from Nazareth found himself in such a position among the teachers in the temple at Jerusalem. 'All who heard him were amazed at his intelligence and his answers' (Luke 2.47).

At the same time, this event throws a particular light on the mystery of the fatherhood of Joseph of Nazareth. We see that Mary, when she rebukes the Son ('Son, why have you done this to us?'), says: 'Your father and I have been searching for you.' And Jesus replies, 'Why did you search for me? Did you not know I had to be in my Father's house?' (Luke 2.49). Mary refers to Joseph's fatherly concern. The twelve-year-old Jesus points to the Fatherhood of God himself.

Hoping Against Hope

The liturgy leads us to look at the fatherhood of man, of Joseph, through the Fatherhood of God himself.

That is why we address our thoughts to the promise made to Abraham, which reveals in a certain way the beginning of God's great covenant with man. We see that 'hoping against hope, Abraham believed and so became the father of many nations, just as it was once told him' (Rom. 4.18).

Abraham's fatherhood was based on faith. It was based on hope 'against hope'. And it was through faith that he became the father of numerous descendants, not in a physical but in a spiritual sense. . . . The fatherhood of Joseph of Nazareth is also based on faith. It is based on faith in a complete way.

By the work of the Holy Spirit, he believed in the mystery of the conception of God's Son in the womb of the Virgin who was his betrothed. By the work of the Holy Spirit, he became a witness to God's birth on Christmas night in Bethlehem. He became the most careful custodian of this mystery, and the custodian of the mother and of the Son. First in

Bethlehem. Then in Egypt where the Holy Family is forced to flee to avoid Herod's evil designs. Finally, in Nazareth, where Jesus grows up under his care and is continually at his side working at the bench as 'the carpenter's son' (Matt. 13.55; Mark 6.3).

Upon finding the twelve-year-old Jesus in the temple of Jerusalem, Mary says: 'Your father and I have been searching for you.' These words, so human, contain all the greatness of the divine mystery.

The foster fatherhood of Joseph of Nazareth finds its confirmation in this mystery. It also finds the unceasing source of its spiritual splendour. Here is Joseph who 'hoping against hope . . . believed'. The faith of Abraham finds in him an altogether special fulfilment.

Children Belong to God

In the bright figure of Joseph we are allowed to glimpse the profound link that exists between human fatherhood and divine Fatherhood – how the human is founded on the divine, drawing from it true dignity and greatness.

For man, begetting a child is above all 'receiving him from God': it is a matter of welcoming as a gift from God the creature that is made. That is why children belong to God first. Then they belong to their own parents. Indeed, this truth is rich in implications both for the children and for the parents.

Isn't this the place to find the greatness of the mission entrusted to the father and the mother – to be instruments of the heavenly Father in the formation of their own children? But here we also find the clear limit that parents must respect in rearing their children.

Parents can never feel that they own their children. But they must educate them with constant attention to the privileged relationship that they have with their heavenly Father. In all things they must be ultimately occupied with the Father – like Jesus – more than in their own earthly parenthood.

The Holy Family of Nazareth is rich in teaching not only for the parents but also for the children. St Paul tells us that 'every family in heaven and on earth takes its name' from the Father (Eph. 3.15). Let us all draw near to our heavenly Father.

The Riches of Conjugal Love

A fatherhood and a motherhood that desire to be worthy of the human person cannot in fact limit themselves to mere physical parenthood. Christian parenthood is above all a moral and spiritual reality. Several months are enough for bringing a man into the world, but a whole life is not long enough to fully raise him and educate him. In fact, there is a world of values that are both human and supernatural which the parents must transmit to their children. Then their action of giving life has a fully human dimension. And this requires time, patience, and an inexhaustible reserve of intelligence, tact, and love. It is a way that the whole family is called to follow together day after day. It is a gradual growth in which all members of the family are involved. It is not just the children. No, the parents who live out their fatherhood and motherhood responsibly discover unexpected and wonderful aspects of their conjugal or married love.

These more intimate aspects of married love allow us to glimpse that great horizon. We see that the love between man and woman transcends the experience of time and opens itself up to the perspective of the glorious resurrection of the body, where physical generation will have been superseded but the spiritual union of hearts will not diminish.

In this light, the figure of Joseph takes on an extraordinary eloquence. For in his virginal marriage to the Blessed Virgin Mary, he foreshadows in some way the full experience of heaven. He places under our very eyes the riches of a conjugal love built on the secret harmonies of the soul and nourished with the inexhaustible fountains of the heart.

This is a lesson which is very relevant to our age when the family is often in crisis precisely because the love it is founded on lacks this depth and richness. Instead, it is characterised by worry and by an over-emphasis on instinct and attraction. Instinct and attraction are important, but they cannot be the very foundation of married love for the Christian couple. Let us learn from the example of St Joseph.

I Had to Be in My Father's House

'Son, why have you done this to us? You see that your father and I have been searching for you in sorrow' (Luke 2.48). This is a sentence taken from the story of St Joseph, the husband of the Mother of God, who was before men the father of Jesus of Nazareth, of Jesus Christ, the Son of God. It is a sentence taken from the story of man – a very 'human' sentence in its contents. It is a rebuke. But, above all, it is a manifestation of concern. Fatherhood and motherhood are expressed precisely in this kind of concern from the moment of conception in the mother's womb through childhood and even adulthood. This fatherly and motherly concern is a reflection of divine providence.

And then comes another sentence taken from the story of Joseph: 'Did you not know I had to be in my Father's house?' (Luke 2.49). These words are uttered by Jesus, but they also belong to Joseph's story – to the story of Mary and Joseph. In the midst of the father's and the mother's concern, there are possibilities for the growing child, the possibility for a vocation that comes from God himself: 'I had to be. . . .'

Blessed be that fatherhood! Blessed be that human begetting that gives man back to God – to the Fatherhood of God himself!

God's Intimacy with Man

At the very heart of the Lenten liturgy, the mystery of God's infinite holiness is announced to us – that holiness of which Moses became a special witness. This mystery must accompany us during all the days of Lent up to the very end (John 13.1) when holiness and love will be proclaimed through Christ's cross and resurrection.

And yet, in order for the paschal mystery to yield its full fruit in our hearts and in our consciences, we must experience an encounter with God like the one Moses experienced at the base of Mount Horeb.

Who is the God who speaks to man at the base of this mountain? Moses asks his name and hears the answer: 'I AM who am' (Exod. 3.14). According to St Thomas Aquinas, God's answer can be interpreted to mean: 'I am he whose substance is existence.'

God speaks his own name to man. It expresses the intimacy of the covenant he makes with Abraham and his descendants. He, in effect, says to Moses: 'I am he who will liberate and save my people.'

God reveals to Moses his concern for every man and for his people as a whole: 'I have witnessed the affliction of my people in Egypt and have heard their cry of complaint against their slave drivers, so I know well what they are suffering. Therefore I have come down to rescue them from the hands of the Egyptians and lead them out. . . .' (Exod. 3.7–8). He is the one who *is*, the one who liberates. He is the Creator, the God of the covenant, the God who saves.

I Have Brought You out of Slavery

Through the liturgy, Lent recalls every year Moses' encounter with the living God at Mount Horeb. It teaches us about our own encounter with God. At the very root of our experience of faith we see that there must spring the unsearchable greatness of our God. God, who is beyond our senses and unfathomable to our minds, becomes present to us. Just as he revealed himself to Moses, so he reveals himself to us.

God's presence and power anointed Moses for service and his life was transformed. He had new-found power and authority. Yes, Moses felt deeply the oppression of his people in Egypt and desired their liberation from slavery. But he had not the strength to carry it out because weakness and sin proved his undoing. He had to save himself by fleeing to the land of Midian after killing an Egyptian.

Yet now God calls him by name and reveals to him his own name. Through this name, God's power is released in Moses, a power that will work mighty wonders. Moses returns to Egypt, stands before Pharaoh, and overcomes his resistance with the power of God. He also overcomes the weakness and faintheartedness of his people with this power. He delivers them from slavery in Egypt. Thus, Moses becomes the servant of the exodus, that is, of the passover of the Old Covenant. God reveals himself in that exodus as 'the one who liberates': 'I the LORD, am your God, who brought you out of the land of Egypt, that place of slavery' (Exod. 20.2).

God Restores Our Freedom

The passover of the Old Covenant foreshadows the new passover in Christ. During Lent, we prepare for this passover of the New Covenant. God, who during Israel's flight from Egypt reveals himself as the one who liberates from slavery, now reveals himself as the one who saves every man through the power of the cross and of the resurrection.

I, the Lord, am your God. Through Christ's sacrifice on the cross I can bring you out of the place of slavery. Do you not know what kind of slavery sin is? It leads to death. Do you not know what kind of slavery you are under when you misuse your freedom? It can only lead to death. Have we, modern men, chosen bondage and deceived ourselves by defending the appearances of a limitness freedom?

The restoration of our freedom from sin requires a great act of God. Every sin must be called by its name! God's saving grace must be released anew in our lives.

What we need is that convicting light that comes from the presence of the living God. It enables each one of us to enter the way that leads to true freedom in Christ.

I Do Not Deserve to Be Called Son

Through St Paul's second letter to the Corinthians, the church says to us: 'If anyone is in Christ, he is a new creation. The old order has passed away; now all is new! All this has been done by God, who has reconciled us to himself through Christ and has given us the ministry of reconciliation' (2 Cor. 5.17–18).

In light of these words, we consider the message of the parable of the prodigal son. God, who 'has reconciled us to himself through Christ', speaks in this parable through the figure of the father. He welcomes back his son when he returns home crying: 'I have sinned . . . I no longer deserve to be called your son' (Luke 15.21).

Becoming a New Man

All of us know quite well the parable of the prodigal son. It is full of truth about the relationship between God and

man. It is an unforgettable story because it moves us so
deeply.

In the encyclical *Dives in Misericordia* as well as in the
apostolic exhortation *Reconciliatio et Paenitentia*, this parable becomes a central point of reference for teachings
addressed to the church of our day. These teaching address
an issue which is always extremely important to the whole
evangelical message: the issue of man's conversion to God.
To be converted – as St Paul teaches – means to become a
new creation in Christ. God, like the father of the parable,
welcomes back all of his prodigal sons and daughters.
Thus, when a human being is born again in Christ, he
becomes a new man.

The Father has given us Christ his only begotten Son,
so that each one of us – even if he is a prodigal son –
might become a new man in Christ. Renewed in our
inmost being, we can find our way back to the home of
our Father. Such is God's unconditional love for us.

The Grace of Conversion

We read in the encyclical *Dives in Misericordia:* 'The parable
of the prodigal son expresses in a simple yet profound
manner the reality of conversion. This is the most concrete
expression of the work of love and mercy in the world.'
We see how the love and the mercy of God restore and
promote everything that is good. This love and mercy
even bring good out of every form of evil in our world.

God's unconditional love and mercy form the foundation of the messianic message of Christ. They speak to
us of God reconciling the world to himself in Christ.
We see Jesus also teaching his disciples to be loving and
merciful. This message never ceases to reveal itself in the
hearts and in the actions of Christ's disciples. Their love
for God and each other is never overcome by evil but
overcomes evil with good (Rom. 12.21).

Thus, the parable of the prodigal son shows us how

God's love and mercy transform the life of the sinner, how the old man passes away. Even deeply rooted sins and bad habits are uprooted by the grace of conversion. Christ has obtained this new life for man 'through the blood of his cross' (Col. 1.20). In Christ, the sinner becomes 'a new creation'. In Christ, he is reconciled to God the Father.

25th March
The Solemnity of the Annunciation of the Lord
'Kekharitomene'

Mary gives her assent to the angel. This passage in Luke, even in its brevity, is extremely rich in Old Testament sources and in the unheard-of newness of Christian revelation. The main character in this drama is a woman. She is the woman *par excellence* (John 2.4), chosen from all eternity to be the first indispensable collaborator with the divine plan of salvation. She is the *almah* (young woman) foretold by Isaiah (Isa. 7.14). She is the girl of royal lineage who responds to the name Myriam, Mary of Nazareth, a most humble and hidden village of Galilee (John 1.46). A genuine Christian newness has placed woman in an incomparably high dignity, inconceivable for the Hebrew mentality of that time, as well as for the Greco-Roman civilisation that rules the world.

It begins with the announcement addressed to Mary by Gabriel in the very name of God. He greets her with such lofty words that she feels afraid: *'Khaire – Ave –* Rejoice!' The messianic joy resounds on the earth for the first time. *'Kekharitomene – gratia plena –* full of grace!' Here is the immaculate, sculpted in her mysterious fullness of divine choosing, of eternal predestination, of glorious clarity. '*Dominus tecum* – The Lord is with you!'

God is with Mary, a member of the human family chosen to be the mother of the Emmanuel, of him who is 'God-with-us'. From now on and forever, God will be with mankind. There will be no turning back and no retraction. He has made himself one with mankind to save it and to give it to his Son, the Redeemer. And Mary is the living and concrete guarantee of this salvific presence of God.

The Son of God

From this conversation between the chosen Virgin and the angel of God, there continues to emerge for us other fundamental truths: 'You shall conceive and bear a son and give him the name Jesus. Great will be his dignity and he will be called Son of the Most High. The Lord God will give him the throne of David his father. . . . The Holy Spirit will come upon you and the power of the Most High will over-shadow you; hence, the holy offspring to be born will be called Son of God' (Luke 1.31–2, 35). Here comes the one who, from the line of Adam, enters into the genealogies of Abraham and David (Matt. 1.1–17): he is in the line of the divine promises but comes into the world with no need for the descent of human fatherhood, which he surpasses in the line of immaculate faith. The entire Trinity is involved in this work as the angel comes: Jesus, the Saviour, is the 'Son of the Most High', the 'Son of God'. Yes, the Father is also present to extend his shadow over Mary. And the Holy Spirit is present to come upon Mary to fertilise her womb with the seed of God.

'Here I Am'

The angel asks for Mary's assent to the coming of the Word into the world.

Mary's answer is the perfect echo of the Word's answer to the Father. Her 'Here I am' is possible inasmuch as it has been preceded and supported by the 'Here I am' of the Son of God. At the moment of Mary's assent, he becomes the Son of Man. We are celebrating the fundamental mystery of the incarnation of the Word. The letter to the Hebrews allows us to penetrate into the unsearchable depths of this lowliness of the Word, of this self-humiliation of his borne out of love for men unto death on a cross: 'On coming into the world, Jesus said: "Sacrifice and offering you did not desire, but a body you have prepared for me; holocausts and sin offerings you took no delight in. Then I said, As is written of me in the book, I have come to do your will, O God" ' (Heb. 10.5–7).

'A body you have prepared for me.' Today's celebration leads us directly to the date of Christmas nine months from today. With that mystical thinking that was grasped so well by our brothers and sisters of the church in the early centuries, it leads us, above all, to the passion, death, and resurrection of Jesus. The fact that the annunciation of the Lord falls within the Lenten season makes us understand its redeeming significance: the incarnation is closely linked to the redemption, which Jesus accomplished by shedding his blood for us on the cross.

I Have Come to Do Your Will

I have come to do your will, O God.' Why this obedience? Why this abasement? Why this endurance? The creed gives the answer: '*Propter nos homines et propter nostram salutem* – for us men and for our salvation.' Jesus descended from heaven to give man full access to heaven as a son in the Son. Jesus is to restore him to the dignity he lost because of sin. He came to bring to its fulfilment the original plan of the covenant. The incarnation confers forever to man his extraordinary, unique, and unspeakable dignity.

And it is from here that the path followed by the

church starts. As I wrote in my first encyclical:
'Christ the Lord indicated this way above all when –
as the Council teaches – "With the incarnation the
Son of God united himself in a certain way to every
man" (GetS, 22). The church acknowledges and sees
her fundamental task when she makes it possible for
that union with God to become a reality in the life
of men. The church desires to serve only this goal:
that every man may discover Christ anew. Then
Christ can lead the way down the road of life with
the power of that truth about man and about the
world which is contained in the mystery of the incarnation and of the redemption' (RH, 13).

The Word Offers Himself for Man's Salvation

The church does not forget. How could she? The
Word offers himself to the Father for man's salvation.
In that act of self-offering is contained already all the
salvific value of his messianic mission. All is already
in seed. In this mysterious arrival of the 'Sun of
justice' (Mal. 3.20) into the darkness of this world,
which has not accepted him (John 1.5), all is ready.
However, as the Evangelist John testifies, 'Any who
did accept him he empowered to become children of
God. These are they who believe in his name who
were begotten . . . by God. The Word became flesh
and made his dwelling among us, and we have seen
his glory: the glory of an only Son coming from the
Father, filled with enduring love' (John 1.12–14).

Let us accept him! Let us tell him too: 'Here I am,
I have come to do your will.' Let us be available for
the work of the Word who wants to save the world
also through the collaboration of all of us who have
believed in him. And with him, let us love every
man. Darkness seems to want to prevail all the time
– greed in wealth, a selfishness which is indifferent
to the sufferings of others, mutual mistrust, enmities

among peoples, pleasure seeking which darkens
reason and perverts human dignity – all the sins that
offend God and go against the love of neighbour.
We must give, even in the midst of so many false
testimonies, the testimony of faithfulness. We must
uphold, even among so many perverted values, the
value of the good which overcomes evil with its
intrinsic force.

Be Reconciled to God!

St Paul tells us: 'God, in Christ, was reconciling the world
to himself, not counting men's transgressions against
them' (2 Cor. 5.19).

The reconciliation that takes place between the father
and the prodigal son has been fulfilled through the work
of Christ. The God of the everlasting covenant reveals
himself in Christ as the God of reconciliation. This truth
is essential to Christianity. Man is called to be reconciled
to the Father in Christ.

In the second letter to the Corinthians, St Paul writes
not only that God 'has reconciled us to himself through
Christ' but adds 'he has given us the ministry of reconciliation' (2 Cor. 5.18). Then he goes on: 'This makes us
ambassadors for Christ, God as it were appealing through
us. We implore you, in Christ's name: be reconciled to
God!' (2 Cor. 5.20).

The ministry of reconciliation – a fruit of God's reconciliation to man in Christ – is a fundamental part of the
saving mission of the church. This mission gives the
church the power to reconcile men to God through the
forgiveness of their sins.

'But' – in the words of the exhortation *Reconciliatio et
Paenitentia*, ch. 11, n.7 – 'St Paul even allows us to enlarge
our vision of Christ's work to cosmic dimensions when
he writes that in him the Father has reconciled to himself
all things, those in heaven and those on earth (Col. 1.20).'

The Precious Price of Our Salvation

Christ the Redeemer paid the just penalty for our sins. 'In the time of wrath he was taken in exchange' (Sir. 44.17 RSV). He is 'our peace' (Eph. 2.14). He is our reconciliation.

That is why his passion and death represented sacramentally in the Eucharist is rightly called the liturgy of the 'sacrifice of reconciliation'. 'See the victim whose death has reconciled us to yourself' (Eucharistic Prayer III). Reconciliation to God and our brothers and sisters is essential. Jesus himself teaches that brotherly reconciliation must take place before the sacrifice is offered (Matt. 5.23).

Paul writes: 'We implore you, in Christ's name: be reconciled to God!' (2 Cor. 5.20). Today the church repeats with great spiritual fervour this exhortation of the apostle. She calls all of us to true holiness in Christ. As Paul continues, 'For our sakes God made him who did not know sin, to be sin, so that in him we might become the very holiness of God' (2 Cor. 5.21).

Man's call to reconciliation with God is not merely a message or even a cry. Even though the message is as powerful as that of John the Baptist on the banks of the Jordan and that of the prophets of the Old Covenant, it is a mighty work! It is more than just a message. It is a work born of the love of the Father and the Son. It is a sacrifice. It comes at a great price. We have been purchased at a precious price. Let us glorify God and thank him for his mercy (1 Cor. 6.20; 7.23).

Water Will Flow From the Rock

'Strike the rock, and the water will flow from it' (Exod. 17.6), the Lord Yahweh tells Moses in the desert. From that hard rock the Israelites receive life-giving water for their journey towards the promised land. So, too, from the heart of Christ who thirsts on the cross we receive the living water that sustains us on our journey of faith.

As in the time of the exodus, so today men thirst for this saving water that comes from Christ. The church proclaims this truth to all who will listen. She is present in the world to help men believe that Jesus is the Son of God, so that through faith they may have life in his name. She instructs all who will listen in this life and thus builds up the body of Christ. The church will never cease to devote her energies to this supreme aim: to bring all to the saving knowledge of Jesus Christ.

So That I Shall Not Grow Thirsty

Christ offers the water of eternal life to the Samaritan woman by the well of Sychar. Tired from the journey, he sits down at the edge of the well. The disciples have gone off to the city to buy food. Jesus asks a Samaritan woman who has come to get water to give him some to drink. She is surprised that a Jew would ask for something from a Samaritan woman. For centuries the Jews and Samaritans had lived at enmity with each other. Yet Jesus shows her he does not harbour prejudice and the Jewish opinion that it is improper for a rabbi to talk publicly to a woman. He gives no thought to the distinction of nation and race, or even to the distinction between man and woman.

He asks her for water and then leads her to the living water of eternal life. The expression 'living water' in the language of the prophets indicates the blessings of salvation in the messianic age (Isa. 12.3). But the woman, unable to understand that concept, thinks Jesus means a miraculous water which will forever quench her bodily thirst. In this way Jesus has awakened in her the desire for his gift: 'The woman said to him, "Give me this water, sir, so that I shall not grow thirsty and have to keep coming here to draw water" ' (John 4.15).

The Need for Salvation

In the inspiring Gospel passage about the woman at the well, personal revelation and saving help come from Jesus. He starts with a concrete situation the woman can understand. Then he leads her to examine her life in the light of the truth, for only in truth can we encounter Christ.

When the Samaritan woman turns to Jesus with the words 'Give me this water,' he does not hesitate to lead her to it. He leads her to conversion by revealing to her who she is and what she has done. 'Go, call your husband' (John 4.16), is his response to the woman. He invites her to examine her conscience and to search the depths of her heart. She tries to hide her sin and deceive Jesus. But he leads the woman to confront her sin and her need to be saved. Convicted, she asks him herself about the way to salvation. Through this examination of conscience, she is able to face the sin in her life and see her need for salvation.

Come and See

How has the living water leaping up to eternal life changed the life of the Samaritan woman? If we study the spiritual growth of the woman, we can see that her encounter with Christ has borne great spiritual fruit. In fact, we can find in her a true conversion which leads her to recognise Jesus as the Messiah: 'Come and see someone who told me everything I ever did! Could this not be the Messiah?' (John 4.29).

The Samaritan woman proclaims Jesus as the saving Messiah to her neighbours and friends. She tells them of her conversion and Jesus' saving power. He 'told me everything I ever did'. She shows forth a new strength and joy which leads her to announce to others the truth and the grace she has received. 'Come and see,' she tells them. In a certain way, she becomes a messenger of Christ and of his gospel of salvation, like Mary Magdalene on Easter morning.

We, too, are invited to drink of this living water that can cleanse our hearts and change our lives. We, too, can be messengers of the gospel. Like the Samaritan woman, we need to let Christ lead us in a sincere examination of conscience, so we can turn from sin and be filled with joy. Then we will want to share the good news of our salvation in Christ.

You Shall Not Take the Name of the Lord in Vain

> I, the LORD, am your God, who brought you out of the land of Egypt, that place of slavery.
> . . . You shall not take the name of the LORD, your God, in vain . . .
> Remember to keep holy the sabbath day . . .
> Honor your father and your mother . . .
> You shall not kill.
> You shall not commit adultery.
> You shall not steal.
> You shall not bear false witness against your neighbor.
> . . . You shall not covet your neighbor's wife . . . nor anything else that belongs to him (Exod. 20.2, 7–8, 12–17).

The church proclaims the ten commandments given to the sons and daughters of Israel at Mount Sinai. This is the divine law which lays down God's instructions for right behaviour. These norms for living reveal to us God's mind about moral good and evil. They are the moral law.

The Observance of the Commandments

Through obedience to the commandments man becomes good. He takes on God's character. By disobeying them he commits evil. Thus, the commandments give us a yardstick for judging our conduct and our very lives. Our dignity as men who can choose between right and wrong is directly linked to our obedience to God's moral law.

Obedience to the moral law is not simply a personal issue but a social issue. The law shows us how God wants us to live with others. It holds up to us a standard of life. It shows us how to preserve dignity and respect for others and for ourselves. In that way, it liberates man from bondage to evil. This is no accident. The giver of these ten commandments is Yahweh God who has brought the children of Israel out of the land of Egypt, that place of slavery.

Breaking with Sin

During Lent we remember the ten commandments because this is the season when Jesus Christ calls us to examine our conscience. From the beginning of Lent, the Lord has called us to conversion and reconciliation. This call involves obedience to God's moral law found in the ten commandments. For to be converted means to break with evil and abandon patterns of sin. It means to decide anew to obey God and do what is right.

We know that Jesus Christ came to fulfil all of the commandments God gave his people on Mount Sinai. He charged men to observe them. He told them that observance of the commandments is fundamental for reconciliation with God and eternal salvation.

That is why the liturgy proclaims: 'LORD, you have the words of eternal life. The law of the LORD is perfect. . . . The precepts of the LORD are right, rejoicing the heart . . . The ordinances of the LORD are true, all of them just;

They are more precious than gold, than a heap of purest
gold' (Ps. 19.7–11).

The season of Lent is the time to return to the commandments of God. In their light, we begin to examine
our conscience and renounce any sin that has taken root
in our lives.

The Summons to Reconciliation

The church calls us to be reconciled to God. The gospel
reminds us that reconciliation is a matter of the heart. A
right attitude towards ourselves and God is central to the
life of faith. If we are true disciples and witnesses of Christ,
we cannot live without seeking inner reconciliation with
God. We cannot remain in sin or half-heartedly follow
the road to the house of the Father, who is wholeheartedly
awaiting our return.

Through the parable of the prodigal son, the Lord Jesus
has shown us the power and beauty of reconciliation by
appealing not only to our minds but also to our imagin-
ations, our hearts, and our consciences. How many men
in the course of the ages, how many men in our day, find
again in this parable their own personal story!

I Will Arise and Go to My Father

For man to arise and go the Father (Luke 15.18 RSV), he
must recover what he lost through sin. He must begin to
realise, like the prodigal son, that by living in sin he
has deprived himself of the Father's protection and love.
Anew, he must behold the loving countenance of the
Father on whom he has turned his back.

Yet he has broken all ties with the Father by sinning
and squandering his inheritance. He does not deserve to
be welcomed home. Reconciliation can only start when
the prodigal son really wants to return. Then, the love
and kindness of God the Father can overcome the way-

ward son's sense of guilt and unworthiness. As he looks into the eyes of his loving Father, he can begin to receive the words of forgiveness.

The son approaches the Father's estate and thinks, 'I no longer deserve to be called your son.' But the Father is waiting, filled with patience and joy. He has altogether forgotten the wrongs committed by his son. He yearns to receive the son as he approaches with a contrite heart. 'Father, I have sinned. I no longer deserve to be called your son' (Luke 15.21).

In this Lenten season, each one of us – even the greatest of sinners – can return and confess our sin. We need to call our sin by name and walk towards the arms of our waiting Father.

Let us begin our journey homeward. Let us examine our conscience, confess our sin, repent, and then determine to live a new life. These are the stages of conversion.

The Father's Unconditional Love

The father awaits the return of the prodigal son with great love and anticipation. He forgives all of the son's wrongdoing and is filled with compassion.

'While [the son] was still a long way off, his father caught sight of him and was deeply moved. He ran out to meet him, threw his arms around his neck, and kissed him. The son said to him, "Father, I have sinned against God and against you; I no longer deserve to be called your son."

'The father said to his servants: "Quick! bring out the finest robe and put it on him; put a ring on his finger and shoes on his feet. Take the fatted calf and kill it. Let us eat and celebrate, because this son of mine was dead and has come back to life. He was lost and is found" ' (Luke 15.20–25).

God the Father reaches out to each of us as sinners with this kind of unconditional love. He has compassion on us

when we return to him with truly contrite hearts. He
shows us the tenderness of his fatherly love.

Faith in Christ

Jesus confirms the importance of obeying the divine law
of the Old Covenant proclaimed on Mount Sinai. But his
mission goes far beyond that of the moral law of the Old
Covenant. 'Yes, God so loved the world that he gave his
only Son, that whoever believes in him . . . may have
eternal life' (John 3.16).

Faith in Christ is something more than mere obedience
to the law, even if this obedience is dictated by that sincere
'fear of the Lord' to which Psalm 111 refers. Believing in
God means to recognise in Christ God's unconditional
love for us. God's love is summed up in his marvellous
gift of his only Son. That is why all of the moral law of
the New Covenant reaches its very peak and its essence
in the commandment of love. We can fulfil God's will by
observing all of the divine commandments. But to the
God who has revealed himself in Christ as love we can
only respond through love! That is why our Lenten examination of conscience must focus on the demanding call to
love God and our neighbour. This is also the main way
that Christ leads us to conversion. The call to love is
meant to be a continuous call to conversion of the heart.
Just as we need to pray constantly, so conversion is a
lifelong process for the believer.

The Answer to Everything

During Lent, the church does not limit herself to proclaiming the moral law of the ten commandments. Instead, she
proclaims for us – together with St Paul – 'Christ crucified'
on Mount Calvary.

Long ago the Jews demanded signs and the Greeks
demanded wisdom before they would believe in God's

saving action (1 Cor. 1.22). Men of today behave like the Jews and the Greeks of apostolic times. Indeed, their demands go even beyond that. Sometimes we even find a much more bitter criticism and opposition to God's teaching and to the commandments. And yet the church remains faithful to the statement of the Apostle Paul: 'We preach Christ crucified' (1 Cor. 1.23).

In him we find the answer to everything! Every criticism and every opposition to the divine teachings and commandments pales when it faces the eloquence of Christ crucified. The cross of Calvary 'is wiser than men' and 'more powerful than men,' as St Paul writes (1 Cor. 1.25).

Let Us Listen to Our Conscience

'I, the Lord, am your God, who brought you out of the land of Egypt, that place of slavery' (Exod. 20.2). God, who delivered Israel from Egypt, constantly delivers man from his sins. The way of the divine law – the ten commandments and the commandment of love – leads towards our deliverance.

Christ finds himself on the road towards that deliverance of man when he says, 'Destroy this temple . . . and in three days I will raise it up' (John 2.19). He means 'the temple of his body' (John 2.21). He is speaking about the resurrection.

During the season of Lent, let us search our conscience in the light of God's commandments so we can put aside our sin.

Let us renew in ourselves that hope which is linked to Christ's resurrection, for it signals the beginning of our complete deliverance from evil – from sin and from death.

The liberation from Egypt – from that place of slavery – was in fact a foreshadowing of our liberation from sin through the blood of Christ.

Blessed Is He Who Comes

'Blessed is he who comes in the name of the Lord!
Hosanna in the highest' (Lenten Antiphon). These words
are proclaimed with enthusiasm by all of the people who
have arrived in Jerusalem for the great feast of Passover.
They ring out as the crowds greet Jesus' arrival for the
feast.

They are proclaimed with great vigour by the children
of the Jews as the liturgical text says. Thus, the involve-
ment of young people in Jesus' triumphal entry into Jerusalem has always been an important part of the church's
celebration of Palm Sunday. Jesus continues to call to the
youth of our day. He says, 'Come! Hail me as your King
and Lord.'

Let us all look to Christ in this spirit – this is the Christ
who enters Jerusalem astride a colt, fulfilling the words
of the prophet. The apostles put their cloaks on that
donkey for Jesus' entry into the holy city. And when he
draws near the hill that slopes down from the Mount of
Olives, the entire crowd of disciples exults, young and
old alike. They 'rejoice and praise God loudly for the
display of power they had seen' (Luke 19.37).

Palm Sunday
Constrained to Silence

We see Jesus of Nazareth arrive in Jerusalem. His arrival
is accompanied by the excitement of the pilgrims who
have come to celebrate the Passover. 'Hosanna to the Son
of David!' (Matt. 21.9) they cry.

Yet we know that in a few moments the excitement
will be stifled. Right now among the crowd, some Phar-
isees ask Christ to prevent his disciples from praising him
(Luke 19.39).

Jesus' reply is very significant: 'If they were to keep

silence, I tell you the very stones would cry out' (Luke 19.40). Yes, let us behold him 'who comes in the name of the Lord' (Matt. 21.9) in the perspective of Holy Week. 'We must now go up to Jerusalem . . . the Son of Man . . . will be delivered up to the Gentiles. He will be mocked and spat upon. They will scourge him and put him to death . . .' (Luke 18.31–3).

That is how the praises of the crowd on Palm Sunday will cease. The very Son of Man will be stifled by the silence of death itself. And when, on the eve of the Sabbath, they bring him down from the cross, they will place him in a tomb and roll a stone across the tomb's entrance and seal shut his grave.

But three days later this stone will be rolled away. The women who come to the tomb will find it empty. Peter and John will also find it empty. That is how that stone that was rolled away will 'cry out' when everyone and everything else has become silent. It will cry out. It will proclaim the paschal mystery of Jesus Christ. And it is from that stone that this mystery will be revealed to the women and the apostles, who will carry it on their lips to the streets of Jerusalem and later to every byway and thoroughfare of the known world. Thus, from generation to generation, the 'stones will cry out'.

Monday of Holy Week
The Divine Economy of Salvation

What is the paschal mystery of Jesus Christ? It consists of the events of these last days of Lent, especially the last days of Holy Week. These events have their human side to them which is set down in the accounts of the passion of our Lord in the Gospels. It is through these events that the paschal mystery takes on a truly human aspect. It becomes our history.

Yet these events also have their divine aspect. St Paul writes about this divine dimension of Christ as the God-man: 'Though he was in the form of God, he did not deem equality with God something to be grasped at. Rather, he emptied himself and took the form of a slave, being born in the likeness of men' (Phil. 2.6–7).

This aspect of the divine mystery is called the incarnation: The Son – who shares the same nature as the Father – becomes man. He becomes God's humble servant, the servant of Yahweh, as the book of Isaiah says. Through this humble service of the Son of Man, the divine economy of salvation reaches its greatest height and achieves fullness.

St Paul continues to tell us of this mystery, 'He was known to be of human estate, and it was thus that he humbled himself, obediently accepting even death, death on a cross!' (Phil. 2.7–8).

This aspect of the divine mystery is called the redemption. The obedience of the Son of Man, his obedience unto death on a cross, outweighs and cancels out our debt of sin.

Tuesday of Holy Week
Life Is in God

The paschal mystery is the single divine reality of the incarnation and the redemption revealed to man by God. It is revealed by God to the very heart and conscience of each one of us. Every one of us is present in that mystery through the inheritance of sin, which from generation to generation leads men to death. Every one of us finds in that reality the power for victory over sin.

The paschal mystery of Jesus Christ is not exhausted in Christ's life-giving sacrifice of himself. It cannot be obscured by the great stone that was rolled across the entrance of the tomb after Jesus' death on Golgotha.

On the third day this stone will be rolled away by the power of God, and it will begin to 'cry out'. Its cry resounds with these ringing words of St Paul: 'Because of this, God highly exalted him and bestowed on him the name above every other name, so that at Jesus' name every knee must bend in the heavens, on the earth, and under the earth, and every tongue proclaim to the glory of God the Father: Jesus Christ is Lord!' (Phil. 2.9–11). Redemption, then, also means exaltation.

Christ's exaltation – his resurrection – gives us an absolutely new perspective on human history. Human existence had been under the tyranny of death because of the inheritance of sin. But Christ has given us the perspective of life conquering death. Death is part of the reality of the visible world. But life is found in God. The God of life speaks to us through the cross and resurrection of his Son.

Wednesday of Holy Week
The Faithful Witness

'Grace to you and peace . . . from Jesus Christ the faithful witness' (Rev. 1.4, 5 RSV).

Jesus Christ, the faithful witness of the invisible God, challenges us with the power of his discourse in the upper room during the liturgy of Holy Thursday. These are the words that institute the New Covenant in the blood of his sacrifice. These are words which reveal to the utter depths the mystery of God who is love.

We prepare for this great feast which will make present to us once more the reality of the Last Supper. When we start this great feast we begin the Holy Triduum, the holiest cycle of the year. During this holy time, we celebrate the three great feasts of Holy Week: Holy Thursday, Good Friday, and the Easter Vigil. This special time makes present to us that love with which God has loved the world: 'He had loved his own in this world, and would show his love for them to the end' (John 13.1).

Before we enter into this holy time, the church celebrates the morning liturgy of Holy Thursday. It is the liturgy of holy expectation, and also the liturgy of the great preparation. It is called the Mass of the Chrism. In this mass, the first reading is taken from the prophet Isaiah, and Jesus quotes the text later in Luke's Gospel: 'The Spirit of the Lord is upon me; therefore he has anointed me' (Luke. 4.18; Isa. 61.1). Jesus of Nazareth refers back to these words of Isaiah at the very beginning of his messianic mission.

Holy Thursday
The Anointed and His Call

'Anointing' means the working of the Holy Spirit, the bestowing of his power. It is God's gift of himself through grace, which is the way to our holiness and sanctification. And this anointing must be fully accomplished by God. Jesus of Nazareth is fully revealed as the Messiah and the Christ, the anointed one who is called to save.

His call in the Holy Spirit will reach its height in the Eucharist. It will become the sacrament of the church for all ages. In this sacrament Christ will become the source of anointing and of mission in the Holy Spirit for all those who welcome his words of institution – the word and the sacrament.

That is why the church blesses the holy oils during the morning liturgy of Holy Thursday, especially the chrism. The oils are the sign of sacramental power which has as its source Christ's sacrifice. This is the power of the Spirit of truth, of the comforting Spirit, the Paraclete.

This morning liturgy is one of preparation: We see those things that will become the fruit of Christ's saving sacrifice revealed and expressed through sacramental signs.

A Royal Nation of Priests
'To him who loves us and freed us from our sins by his own blood . . . to him be glory and power forever and ever! [He] has made us a royal nation of priests in the service of his God and Father' (Rev. 1.5–6). Christ has

made us priests. He has given us external signs which make up the sacramental order of the church. They serve its saving mission on earth. He has also given us 'internal signs'.

A special internal sign is impressed on the soul of each one of us. That sign is a spiritual seal. It is an indelible mark through which the Holy Spirit enables us to participate in Christ's priesthood. It is a special participation, both ministerial and hierarchical, so that in us may remain the likeness of him who is the only 'priest forever, according to the order of Melchizedek' (Heb. 5.6; 7.17; Ps. 110.4).

Therefore, we anticipate in a special way the time of the Last Supper, for then both the Sacraments of the Eucharist and Ordination were instituted by Christ. Thus, we desire – together with all our brothers in priesthood all over the world – to renew today the vows and promises which we made on the day of our ordination. We desire that God renew in us the grace of the Sacrament of Ordination. That grace has become our life, our vocation, our charism, and our ministry in the church. Let us embrace it.

You Will Have No Share in My Heritage

'You shall never wash my feet!' (John 13.8), Peter insists. The institution of the sacrament of the Last Supper is tied to the washing of the feet of the apostles. 'Jesus – fully aware that he had come from God and was going to God, the Father who had handed everything over to him – rose from the meal and took off his cloak. He picked up a towel and tied it around himself. Then he poured water into a basin and began to wash his disciples' feet' (John 13.3–5).

At that very moment he meets Peter's resistance. The Gospel reminds us of that. Peter resists Christ, firmly telling him: 'You shall never wash my feet!'

Peter opposes Christ in a similar way at an earlier point in the Gospels. After Peter confesses his faith in Jesus as the Son of God, Jesus foretells his own passion. At that moment Peter begins to protest, saying: 'May you be spared, Master! God forbid that any such thing ever happen to you!' (Matt. 16.22).

If he is the Son of the living God, how can he speak of passion, of death on a cross? God is the Sovereign of all things. He is the Lord of heaven and earth. How, then, can he be overcome by men? How can men inflict death on him?

On that occasion Jesus rebukes Peter harshly. Probably there is no one else to whom he has spoken so severely as he does with Peter in those circumstances.

But at the Last Supper Jesus does not rebuke Peter. He simply admonishes him gently. He persuades him: 'If I do not wash you . . . you will have no share in my heritage' (John 13.8). And Peter yields to his Master.

No One Knows the Son But the Father

Why does Peter oppose Jesus the first time? Why does he oppose Jesus when he foretells his passion and death on a cross?

Perhaps because he has been given the knowledge of Christ's divinity; 'You are the Messiah, . . . the Son of the Living God!' (Matt. 16.16). He had been given the knowledge of God's unsearchable mystery – all those things which have been hidden from the powerful and the wise are now revealed to the little ones (Matt. 11.25).

However, 'no one knows the Son but the Father' (Matt. 11.27). It is the Father who has revealed the Son's divinity to Peter.

But that is exactly why Peter reasons: How can he say – he who is the Christ and the Son of God – that he will be put to death, condemned to death by men? Is not God the absolute Lord of all that exists? Is he not the absolute Lord of life?

And how can the Son of the living God and the Lord of all behave like a servant? How can he bend his knees before the apostles and wash their feet? How can he kneel down at Peter's feet?

Peter is defending his own image of God before himself, before the twelve, and before Christ.

Good Friday
To Forgive Sins

How many men in the world have defended and continue to defend their own image of God? How many peoples, how many traditions, cultures, and religions? God is the most perfect being, the supreme and unsearchable being; he is the absolute Lord of all things.

It is impossible that he could become man. It is impossible that he would serve and that he would wash the apostles' feet. It is impossible that he could die on the cross. But this is man's perspective.

God's perspective is quite different. To put it quite simply – this God is love. As love he has created man in his image and likeness. As love he has established a covenant with his people. As love he has become man. He has loved the world so much that he has given his only Son, so that man may have eternal life (John 3.16).

As love, he wants to go to the cross to forgive the sins of the world and to establish the new and eternal covenant in his blood. As love he institutes the Eucharist.

God Cannot Cease to Be Love
Love intends nothing else but the good that it desires to do, the good it wants to serve.

For the sake of this good, he who is all-powerful is willing to become weak like a man who is destined to die. He is willing to become weak and defenceless like bread: 'This is my body to be given for you. Do this as a remembrance of me' (Luke 22.19).

Is man capable of accepting a crucified God? Is he capable of accepting a eucharistic God? Such is the question posed at the very heart of the Holy Triduum, these three great feasts of Holy Week.

With the question, we receive the answer. Yes, man is capable of accepting or denying this God of infinite love. In fact, his thoughts can turn against God and deny his existence. And yet God, above all of this, 'cannot deny himself' (2 Tim. 2.13). He cannot cease to be himself. He cannot cease to be love.

Lord, to Whom Shall We Go?

'Lord, to whom shall we go? You have the words of eternal life' (John 6.68). Christ, to whom shall we go? There is no other day in the year when we come as close to the cross as on Good Friday.

In the cross, O Christ, we have a memorial of your death and resurrection. The cross is the last word of your mission. The cross is the word of eternal life.

This word has been uttered once and for all between heaven and earth, between God and man. God has not revoked this word. This word remains. This is what the prophet Isaiah says, and these are the words of the liturgy on Good Friday: 'Yet it was our infirmities that he bore, our sufferings that he endured, while we thought of him as stricken, as one smitten by God and afflicted. But he was pierced for our offences, crushed for our sins . . .' (Isa. 53.4–5).

'We had all gone astray like sheep, each following his own way; but the Lord laid upon him the guilt of us all . . .'(Isa. 53.6).

'When he was cut off from the land of the living, and smitten for the sin of his people, a grave was assigned him . . .' (Isa. 53.8).

The Word of the Father

Who is he? He is man, one among the millions of men who have passed through this earth. But can a man carry upon himself the sins of all?

Who is he? He is the Word of the Father. He is the firstborn of all created things. 'In him everything in heaven and on earth was created' (Col. 1.16). Through him 'all things came into being' (John 1.3). He is the Son of the same divine essence as the Father. He, who eternally embraces in himself all created things, can become sin for our sake before his Father. He can carry it upon himself. He alone. And only in him can we men who bear the weight of sin become 'God's justice'.

Pope Pius XII said: 'The sin of our century is the loss of the sense of sin.' These words have been repeated by the synod of bishops which drafted the document on the Sacrament of Reconciliation and Penance: 'The sin of our century is the loss of the sense of sin.' Man commits sin without calling it by name and repenting. But such is not the way of liberation. That is merely the way of counterfeit truth. True liberation can only come by confronting the truth.

Holy Saturday
The Truth Will Set You Free

The one who died on the cross says: 'You will know the truth, and the truth will set you free' (John 8.32). For that very reason he went to the cross. In the cross is summed up the truth of man's sin, of the sin of the world. And no matter how much mankind tries to reject that truth, no matter how much mankind tries to erase the sense of guilt and sin in the consciences of people today, the cross will always bear witness to that truth.

'Yes, God so loved the world that he gave his only Son, that whoever believes in him may not die but may have eternal life'(John 3.16). The Word is crucified! The Son, who has come into the world 'did not come to condemn the world but to save it' (John 12.47).

O man of the twentieth century! Do not flee from the judgment seat of Christ's cross! The cross is the judgment seat of salvation. The cross is the word of eternal life. This word of salvation was uttered once and for all between heaven and earth, between God and man. God has not revoked this word. This word does not fade away.

Easter

Easter Sunday
O Truly Blessed Night

O blessed night.

This is how the church sings during the Easter Vigil, watching by the tomb of Christ. In this tomb is placed his body, bruised and torn, brought down from the cross in haste because of preparations for the feast of Passover. That was still the passover of the Old Covenant on Good Friday.

O *truly* blessed night!

This is how the church sings during this vigil, which precedes the passover of the New Covenant. In every land and nation, the church is gathered expectantly waiting to adore the power of the Most High: 'The right hand of the LORD is exalted, the right hand of the LORD has struck with power' (Ps. 118.16). This is the same power which was revealed at the beginning of the creation of the world. God said: 'Let there be!' and thus he 'created the heavens and the earth' (Gen. 1.1,3).

He manifested the same power in delivering Israel from Egypt. This is the power which led the chosen people through the Red Sea, sparing them from the hand of Pharaoh.

The church, gathered together in its watch by the tomb of Christ, meditates on the events in which the power of God is shown forth: the creating power and the saving power of God.

This night is truly blessed for in it the light of Christ shines again. In that light life will conquer death. Behold, in the words of Psalm 118, he who 'was dead' speaks to

us: 'I shall not die, but live, and declare the works of the
Lord . . .' (v. 17).

'The right hand of the LORD is exalted.'

O Happy Fault

The church gathered by the sepulchre of Christ on this
blessed night even considers sin under a new light, as she
dares to sing: 'O happy fault, that has won for us so great
a Redeemer!' We can truly say of the things that take
place this night that 'by the Lord has this been done; it is
wonderful in our eyes' (Ps. 118.23).

We are invited in a special way through the church to
receive this revelation of the divine power, of the creating
and saving power of God. The paschal mystery of our
Lord Jesus Christ is always present in the sacrament of
the church. The power of his death and resurrection does
not cease to work in the souls of men.

By the work of the same divine power, which creates
and saves, the church is born anew in the resurrection of
her crucified Lord: 'The stone which the builders rejected
has become the cornerstone' (v. 22).

All of us have been born from that stone: we are all
living as members of the church. We are all sustained by
the life-giving breath of Christ's resurrection. '[We] must
consider ourselves dead to sin but alive for God in Christ
Jesus' (Rom. 6.11).

Passing Through Death Towards Life

The Hebrew word for Passover or Easter means 'passing
through'. It is a passing through death towards life, just
as Israel passed through death towards life when they
slaughtered the passover lamb in Egypt. Because of the
blood of the passover lamb, the angel of death passed
over their homes and did not slay their firstborn sons.
However, that was only a passing towards another life on
this earth – from the slavery in Egypt towards the freedom
of the promised land.

The Passover or Easter of the church signifies the passing towards the eternal life that comes from God.

No promised land in this world could ensure such freedom and such life. And yet the passover of Christ was fulfilled on this earth. It was on this earth that death was destroyed by death. It was on this earth that Christ was crucified and placed in the tomb. Yet at dawn, 'after the sabbath', the tomb appeared empty.

The first cause of death is sin. All the tombs scattered all over the face of the earth speak about the death of generation after generation of human beings. All the tombs of the dead bear witness to sin, to the inheritance of sin in man.

But Christ passed from death to life in his paschal mystery. This means that he destroyed the inheritance of sin at its very root through his obedience unto death. Thus, the Passover or Easter of Christ also means a passage through the history of the sin of mankind from the very beginning. It starts with Adam for from that point 'through one man's disobedience all became sinners' (Rom. 5.19).

Easter Monday
The Redeeming Death

The church professes in the creed: 'He suffered, died, and was buried. On the third day he rose again.'

Before rising from the dead, Christ touched with his saving death the sin of man in all the generations of those who have died. He visited them with the redeeming power of his death, with the life-giving power of his death. O death, I will be your death! declares the Christ.

We, too, who are living have been immersed in his death as St Paul writes (Rom. 6.3). The death of Christ, the redeeming death, the life-giving death, has destroyed the inheritance of sin which is in every one of us. In fact, 'we . . . were baptised into Christ Jesus' (Rom. 6.3). And Paul continues, 'Through baptism into his death we were buried with him, so that, just as Christ was raised from

the dead by the glory of the Father, we too might live a
new life' (Rom. 6.4).

Easter Tuesday
Seeing the Christ

As the story of the apostles teaches us, God raised Jesus
up and he was seen 'not by all, but only by such witnesses
as had been chosen beforehand by God' (Acts 10.41).
When Jesus appears, he gives the apostles the task to
announce the gospel and to witness to all men about Christ
who is crucified and risen from the dead. Christ will be
present wherever the glad tidings of these eyewitnesses
are received and believed. Only a few people have seen
the risen Lord, but all men are called to believe in him.
Because, according to the witness of the Scriptures, all
men are called to salvation and therefore to faith. That is
why Christ rebukes the attitude of the unbelieving
Thomas and calls blessed all those who will discover
Christ solely through the witness of the message of faith:
'You became a believer because you saw me. Blest are
they who have not seen and have believed!' (John 20.29).

Easter Wednesday
Intimacy with Christ

We are also called to believe in Christ through the preaching of the church. As his body, we are called to proclaim
his redeeming death and his resurrection, and his constant
presence among us. Jesus himself reassures us: 'And know
that I am with you always, until the end of the world!'
(Matt. 28.20). Faith does not refer so much to a past event;
rather, it declares the Lord who lives and is present among
us. It means, above all, an abiding friendship and fellowship with Christ. We must have an intimate union and

familiarity with him in which Christ becomes ever more deeply rooted in us.

We need to believe and grow at the same time. Our aim, then, is to be close to Christ and to preserve our friendship with him. Then he can shape and form our lives. This leads us to grow in intimacy with Christ, to get to know him better, and to firmly move ahead in our journey with love and faithfulness to him.

Easter Thursday
Victory Over Sin

Let us give thanks for the resurrection of Jesus Christ. Let us give thanks for his glorification by the Father. This is he who emptied himself, 'obediently accepting even death, death on a cross!' (Phil. 2.8).

Yes, the work of the redemption of the world is accomplished in his resurrection. From the stone cold tomb the seal of death has been removed. On the hearts of men the seal of life has been stamped. Christ has been offered in sacrifice as our passover (1 Cor. 5.7).

Let us give thanks for the sacrifice of Jesus which reaches to the very throne of the Father. Let us give thanks for the Father's love which has been revealed in the resurrection of the Son. Let us give thanks for the breath of the Spirit which gives life. This breath is received by the apostles, gathered at Jesus' instruction in the upper room. Christ will come into their midst, even though the doors are closed. He will say to them: 'Receive the Holy Spirit. If you forgive men's sins, they are forgiven them' (John 20.22–3).

It is from the resurrection of Jesus that we have forgiveness for our sins. In his cross is our conversion. In the resurrection is our victory over sin. Christ has rescued us, delivering us from evil. He has forgiven our sins. He has reconciled us to God and to our brethren. He has given us his own life, thus opening to us the gates of eternal life which has no end.

Easter Friday
Witnesses of the Resurrection

'This Jesus God raised up, and of that we all are witnesses' (Acts 2:32 RSV).

The testimony of faith about the risen Lord is a commitment which binds together in a concrete way all the members of the people of God. The Council has made this call an explicit summons to all of the laity. The Council sums up with this exhortation the mission which rightfully belongs to every member of the laity because of their incorporation into Christ through Baptism: 'Every lay person must be a witness before the world of the resurrection and life of the Lord Jesus' (LG, 38).

To witness means essentially to attest to the certainty of some truth which, in some way, is the result of personal experience. The holy women were the first witnesses to the Lord's resurrection (Matt. 28.5–8). When they came to the tomb, they did not see Jesus, but they became certain of his resurrection because the tomb was empty and the angel told them he had risen. That was their initial encounter with the mystery of the resurrection. Their experience of the Lord acquired more value as Jesus appeared to the apostles and to the disciples on the road to Emmaus.

Easter Saturday
The Christian Is a Living Gospel

Every Christian – as he explores the historical record of Scripture and tradition and comes to a deep, abiding faith – experiences that Christ is the risen one and that he is therefore the eternally living one. It is a deep life-changing experience. No true Christian can keep it hidden as a personal matter. For such an encounter with the living God cries out to be shared – like the light that shines, like the yeast which leavens the whole mass of dough.

The true Christian is truly a living gospel. That does not mean he is a disciple of a doctrine which is far away in time and foreign to the reality of life. He does not repeat powerless formulas. No, he is convinced and tenacious in asserting the relevance of Christ and the unceasing newness of the gospel. He is always eager before anyone and at any time to give reason for the hope which he harbours in his heart (1 Pet. 3.15).

Second Sunday of Easter
Everything Written about Me Had to Be Fulfilled

When the apostles and disciples of the Lord receive the Holy Spirit, they begin to speak publicly about Christ. They announce him to men, starting in Jerusalem. In their preaching, they refer to the body of commonly known facts: the *kerygma* or basic gospel message.

'You handed [him] over and disowned [him] in Pilate's presence when Pilate was ready to release him' – these are Peter's words to the inhabitants of Jerusalem. 'You disowned the Holy and Just One and preferred instead to be granted the release of a murderer [that is, Barabbas]!' (Acts 3.13–14).

After mentioning Christ's passion, Peter then starts to describe the resurrection: '. . . You put to death the Author of life. But God raised him from the dead, and we are his witnesses' (v.15).

Peter is the only one who speaks. But he speaks not only for himself but in the name of the whole apostolic college. He tells the crowds, 'We are his witnesses.' And he adds: 'Yet I know, my brothers, that you acted out of ignorance, just as your leaders did' (Acts 4.17).

From the description of the events themselves and the testimony about the resurrection, St Peter now does some exegesis of the Old Testament. He explains how Christ as the Messiah fulfilled the law and the prophets. Christ himself had prepared his disciples to give an exegesis of his death and resurrection. We have the proof of this in the Gospel of Luke. The risen Lord says to his disciples: 'Recall those words I spoke to you when I was still with you: everything written about me in the law of Moses and the prophets and psalms had to be fulfilled' (Luke 24.44).

'He said to them: "Thus it is written that the Messiah must suffer and rise from the dead on the third day. In his name, penance for the remission of sins is to be preached to all nations, beginning at Jerusalem. You are witnesses of this" ' (Luke 24.46–8).

Easter Weekday
The Testimony of the Apostles

And the evangelist adds: 'Then he opened their minds to the understanding of the Scriptures' (Luke 24.45). From Peter's speech in the Acts of the Apostles, we see how effectively Christ opened up the minds of the apostles to the truth of the gospel.

In fact, after presenting the events linked to Christ's death and resurrection, Peter declares to the inhabitants of Jerusalem: 'God has brought to fulfillment by this means what he announced long ago through all the prophets: that his Messiah would suffer. Therefore, reform your lives! Turn to God, that your sins may be wiped away!' (Acts 3.18–20).

In these words of the apostle we find a clear echo of Christ's words. We see how the risen Lord has transformed the minds and lives of the apostles by imparting his truth.

This is the story of our faith. We learn how the first

generation of Christ's witnesses – the apostles and the disciples – passed on the *kerygma*, the basic gospel message. It springs directly from the testimony of those eyewitnesses of Jesus' death and resurrection.

What does it mean, then, to be a Christian? It means to continue to receive and accept the witness of the apostles, the eyewitnesses of our salvation. It means to believe in Christ with the same faith which was born in them from the works and the words of the risen Lord.

This is what the Apostle John writes: 'The way we can be sure of our knowledge of him is to keep his commandments. The man who claims, "I have known him," without keeping his commandments, is a liar; in such a one there is no truth. But whoever keeps his word, truly has the love of God been made perfect in him' (1 John 2.3–5).

The apostle is speaking of a living faith. Faith is living when it bears the fruit of good works. These are the works of love. Faith is alive through God's love in us. Love is expressed in the observance of the commandments. There can be no contradiction between the knowledge of 'I have known him' and the actions of one who confesses Christ. Only he who completes his faith with good works remains in the truth.

Easter Weekday
Being a Christian

The Apostle John speaks to those who receive his first letter with the affectionate words 'my little ones' and invites them to refrain from sinning (1 John 2.1). Yet he also writes: 'But if anyone should sin, we have, in the presence of the Father, Jesus Christ, an intercessor who is just. He is an offering for our sins, and not for our sins only, but for those of the whole world' (vs. 1–2).

In the words of his letter written by the end of the first century, John the Apostle and Evangelist proclaims the same truth that Peter had proclaimed shortly after the

Lord's ascension. It is the basic truth about conversion
and the remission of sins through the power of Christ's
death and resurrection.

What does it mean to be a Christian?

Being a Christian – today just as in those days – means
to continue to accept the witness of the apostles, the eyewitnesses. It means to believe with the same faith which
was borne in them from the works and words of Christ
and then confirmed by his death and resurrection.

We, too – we who belong to the present generation of
those who confess Christ – must seek to have the same
experience as the two disciples on the road to Emmaus.
Let us pray, 'Lord Jesus, make us understand the Scriptures; let our hearts burn inside us as you talk to us' (Luke
24.32).

Let our hearts burn! Faith cannot be only cold, hard
facts calculated and weighed by our intellect. No, faith
must be quickened by love. It must come alive through
the good works which reveal God's truth in us.

So we, too, inherit from the apostles the witness they
gave, even if we are not direct eyewitnesses of the resurrection. We become witnesses to Christ ourselves. Being
a Christian must mean being a witness for Christ.

Easter Weekday
I am the Resurrection and the Life

We are in the midst of the paschal solemnity in which a
profound spiritual experience has made us taste deeply of
our faith in the risen Christ, 'our Passover' (1 Cor. 5.7).
He has been sacrificed for us, but death has not vanquished
him. His mission did not end when hanging upon the
cross he said: 'Now it is finished' (John 19.30). In fact, at
that very moment, the fulfilment of God's saving plan
opened a new epoch in human history. Christ, himself,
consecrated this new epoch through his resurrection from
death. His was the appointed hour to fulfil God's perfect

plan for our salvation. Christ is risen just as he promised. Death could not hold him down, because he is the eternal life of God given for us. For example, he says about himself: 'I am . . . the life' (John 14.6). And he proclaims on another occasion: 'I am the resurrection and the life' (John 11.25). With him, then, the all-powerful principle of divine life has entered our world. Yes, and through Christ's sacrifice, this divine life has been poured out upon all peoples and – in a certain way – throughout the entire universe. A certain vitality and freshness has invigorated all created things from the moment of his triumph on the cross. We, ourselves, are now no longer the slaves of 'fear and death' (Heb. 2.15). Christ has liberated us forever!

Easter Weekday
Peace

The gospel leads us to the upper room in Jerusalem, which has become the first place of the history of the New Israel, of the people of God in the New Covenant. We have been here before, on the very day of the resurrection. That was the first day 'after the sabbath', the first day of the week. The apostles knew already that Jesus' tomb was empty because earlier the women, and then Peter and John, had visited the sepulchre. On the evening of the same day, Jesus himself comes to them. He appears in their midst even though the doors of the upper room are still closed. He appears and greets the apostles, saying: 'Peace be with you' (John 20.19). He shows them 'his hands and his side' (John 20.20) – the wounds caused by the crucifixion.

And behold, it is as if from these wounds – from these pierced hands, from his feet, and from his side – he draws those things which he above all desires to tell them in this first encounter after the agony of Calvary.

Easter Weekday
The Paschal Joy, Full of Thanksgiving

'Sing joyfully to the LORD, all you lands; serve the LORD with gladness; come before him with joyful song . . . for her is good: the LORD, whose kindness endures forever' (Ps. 100.1–2, 5).

The paschal joy we share must be full of thanksgiving. The church invites us to behold with the eyes of faith all the benefits of God from the very beginning. 'Know that the LORD is God; he made us, his we are; his people, the flock he tends' (v. 3).

We rejoice with a paschal joy because the world is not a forsaken, patternless void. We rejoice with a paschal joy that God has created the world; he has created us. He has created man in the midst of a beautiful visible world. We rejoice and give thanks because this man is created in God's own image – even though he has so much in common with the world in which he lives.

We rejoice and give thanks because, through this unique likeness to divinity, man belongs to God. He is especially God's as his Son. Christ's resurrection reconfirms this holy ownership. We are the Lord's. His holy blood has purchased us and ransomed us from the penalty of sin and death.

Easter Weekday
Sunday *in Albis*

'The stone which the builders rejected has become the cornerstone' (Ps. 118.22). The church derives its very life from Christ's resurrection. This reality is borne out in the liturgy. For this is the Easter season. We have a tradition called Sunday *in Albis Depositis*, for instance. The name takes its origin from a rite which was practised for a long time in the church on the Saturday following Easter

Sunday. Later it was remembered on the Sunday after Easter. On that day the catechumens returned the white robe which they had received at their Baptism during the Easter Vigil. At Baptism, they had left behind their old clothing to indicate that their souls had been cleansed by Christ. Now they returned their white baptismal robe after Easter week to symbolise their commitment to preserve that baptismal innocence in their daily lives.

In the baptismal rites we use now, the baby is clothed in a white robe which indicates – today as in times past – that Baptism does not merely mean an outer change. No, it is a transformation that reaches to the roots of our being. The call to renew our own Baptism means to put off the old man as if it were worn-out clothing, so we can receive the clothing of incorruptibility offered to us by Christ (St Gregory of Nyssa, *De Bapt.*, PG 46, 420 C). Christ purifies and regenerates us. He clothes us in himself by incorporating us into his very body. And thus, sons in the Son, we walk in newness of life. We lead a redeemed existence as is fitting. 'God's chosen ones, holy and beloved, [clothe] yourselves with heartfelt mercy, with kindness, humility, meekness, and patience' (Col. 3.12).

Third Sunday of Easter
The Apostolic Church

The early chapters of the Acts of the Apostles underscore how through the ministry of the apostles – especially of Peter – 'more and more believers, men and women in great numbers, were continually added to the Lord' (Acts 5.14).

We see the events of the first days after the resurrection which gave birth to the church. The Holy Spirit had been poured out upon the apostles in the upper room. Now through the ministry of the apostles in Jesus' name thousands come to a saving knowledge of the Christ.

These events form the foundation of a future which is

yet far away. They usher in the age of the apostolic church, whose mission is to proclaim the testimony and the saving power of the resurrection to each new generation. This important work continues in our own day right up to the present.

And throughout all these generations, the same timeless truth is declared: 'The stone which the builders rejected has become the cornerstone.' This truth expressed under the veil of a metaphor possesses wonderful prophetic power. It confirms that the building up of the church is God's work from the first to the last day of the history of the church and of mankind. It confirms this even in our own day and on what a deep level!

Jesus of Nazareth is rejected by those to whom the construction of 'God's dwelling among men' (Rev. 21.3) in the Old Covenant had been entrusted. And in this way, the rejected Jesus – through his cross and resurrection – was revealed as 'the cornerstone' of that building. It is precisely on him that this building is supported. It is on him that it stands throughout the generations. It is from him that it develops.

Easter Weekday
As the Father Has Sent Me

Jesus said: ' "As the Father has sent me, so I send you." Then he breathed on them and said: "Receive the Holy Spirit. If you forgive men's sins, they are forgiven them; if you hold them bound, they are held bound" ' (John 20.21–3).

From that very first day, the church lives in the power of the new and eternal covenant. She lives in the power of the saving death and resurrection. Thus, she is given the power over evil directly from the Christ, who is the source of her life.

We are led once again to the upper room. This is the eighth day after the resurrection. Jesus comes for the sake of Thomas, one of the twelve. Together with them, he has been called to be a witness of the resurrection. But he doubts the reality of the resurrection. He had not been with the others eight days earlier when the risen Lord had come to the apostles. He must see for himself. Then Jesus comes for the second time. He comes to convince doubting Thomas. He offers him ample evidence of his resurrection.

Thomas is convinced of the resurrection when he sees Jesus and his wounds with his own eyes. He doubts no more and makes a tremendous profession of faith with these powerful words: 'My Lord and my God!' (John 20.28).

Yes, the church lives Christ's resurrection from her very first days. She lives in the paschal mystery of her master and bridegroom. From this mystery she receives twofold power – the power of testimony and the power of grace that saves men. The age of the church begins only after Pentecost. And yet Pentecost has its start in the resurrection. In fact, in the very first appearance to the apostles on the day 'after the sabbath', the risen Lord tells them: 'Receive the Holy Spirit' (John 20.22).

Easter Weekday
The People of God

If men did not belong to God as Christ's witnesses and disciples, they would be completely subject to this fallen world. Our entire life as men would lead towards death. Through death, the world of matter would take total possession of our wonderful dignity as human beings, making of us the mere 'dust of the earth'. Without faith in Christ, this would be our only perspective on life. Human existence would be very bleak.

Christ's resurrection frees us from such an earthbound perspective. It frees us from the dominion of death. That is why our Easter joy is above all a joy that springs from the mystery of creation. Therefore, we rejoice because the Lord is God, because he has made us, because we are his.

We rejoice with Easter joy because we are the people of God, the flock he tends. During the Easter season, the figure of Christ the Good Shepherd emerges clearly. He says about himself: 'I am the good shepherd. I know my sheep, and my sheep know me' (John 10.14).

Easter Weekday
Seek the Things That Are Above

'Seek the things that are above' (Col. 3.1 RSV). We celebrate the resurrection of the Lord. The one who speaks is Paul the Apostle. He, in a particular way, has experienced the power of the risen one: 'If . . . you have been raised with Christ, seek the things that are above. . . . Set your minds on things that are above, not on things that are on earth . . . your life is hid with Christ in God' (Col. 3.1–3 RSV).

The message of Easter is testimony. Those who give witness are the ones who have found the empty tomb, the ones who have experienced the presence of the risen Lord. 'What we have seen with our eyes, what we have looked upon and our hands have touched' (1 John 1.1) – like the hands of doubting Thomas – 'we proclaim . . . to you' (1 John 1.3). 'This life became visible; we have seen and bear witness to it' (1 John 1.2). It became visible when all things seemed to have sunk into the darkness of death.

A large stone had been rolled in front of the tomb. It had been sealed shut. Yet life became visible again! Yes, the message of Easter is a testimony and a challenge. Christ has come into the world for our sake. He has been crucified. Yet through his death he gives us life. And this means our life is now hidden with Christ in God (Col. 3.3).

Easter Weekday
God Does Not Resign Himself to Man's Death

'This is the day the Lord has made' (Ps. 118.24). This day always confirms for us a special truth: God does not resign himself to man's death.

Christ came into the world to show us this important truth, a truth that reveals the Father's love. Christ died on the cross and was laid in the tomb to bear witness to this amazing fact: God does not resign himself to man's death.

In fact, 'He is the God of the living, not of the dead' (Matt. 22.32). Death has been challenged in Christ. Christ has conquered death with his own death.

This is the day the Lord has made. This is the day of God's great conquest – his conquest of man's sin and death. Does man resign himself to his fate? Is he conquered by death?

Or is he willing to partake of this great conquest?

Man resigns himself to death when he only yearns for the things that are of the earth. When he only seeks those things, he courts death. The earth itself does not contain the seeds of immortality.

Yes, tragically, man does resign himself to death. He not only accepts it, he inflicts it. Men constantly inflict death on other men. Often they inflict it on unknown men, on innocent men, on men who are not yet born.

Man not only resigns himself to death. No, he has frequently made it the very fabric of his existence. Are these not the ways that deal out death to our fellow human beings: violence, the bloody seizure of power, selfish accumulation of wealth, fighting against misery by feeding on hatred and on the desire for vengeance, intimidation and outrage, torture and terror? And yet man, even though he resigns himself to death, is terribly afraid of it.

Easter Weekday
To Live in Truth and in Love

Why is it that Christ, right after the words 'Receive the Holy Spirit', speaks about the remission of sins? He says, 'If you forgive men's sins, they are forgiven them; if you hold them bound, they are held bound' (John 20.22–3). Christ says this because the remission of sins presupposes the knowledge and confession of sins. And both of these involve the effort to live in truth and in love.

True knowledge and confession of sins brings the force of truth and love to bear in our lives. It makes us new men and transforms the world.

The opposite of this happens when men falsify the truth and merely simulate love. Then we have obliterated the dividing line between good and evil. That is how men label as humanism what is actually sin.

Unfortunately, it is very easy to give examples of this kind of evil. In our day terrorism is condemned as a crime and a violation of man's fundamental rights. Manslaughter is condemned as wrong and inhumane in civilised countries. But taking the life of unborn human beings is called 'humanism' and is considered a 'proof of progress'. This is called freedom. But true freedom respects the dignity of the human person!

My dear brothers and sisters, I am not saying this to accuse anyone. I say this to show my own suffering for the life of the unborn, for the dignity of the human person.

Let us not delude ourselves! All of us must confront and renounce sin in our lives. Only 'the truth will set us free' (John 8.32). Only the truth has the strength to transform the world and bring about genuine progress and real Christian 'humanism'. And let us not say that the demands of truth, conscience, and human dignity are merely a 'political' choice. They are actually the supreme demands of being truly human. Let us not demean any more those things on which man's life or destruction depend. They are the very stuff of his humanity.

Easter Weekday
Choosing Life

Is today's man willing to participate in God's great conquest of death? A challenge is before him. It is more pressing and more complex than any other – the great challenge of peace. Choosing peace means choosing life. Building peace means to participate with courage and with responsibility in the saving work of the God of the living. God calls man to oppose death wherever death appears today.

Where death appears as the fruit of selfishness, of division, and of violence, men must oppose it. Where blood is spilled because of military conflict and guerrilla warfare, where the temptation to resort to terrorism and reprisal is great, in nations where the dignity of the human person is trampled upon and the person's rights and liberty are denied – men must oppose it.

I want to invite all men of all religious convictions, all men of good will, to pray especially for peace. Let us reaffirm our commitment to victory over the fear of death and claim the victory of life, the victory of the risen Christ.

Fourth Sunday of Easter
Redemption Starts with the Cross

Redemption starts with the cross and is accomplished in the resurrection. The Lamb redeemed the sheep. The innocent Christ reconciled sinners to the Father.

Behold, man has been released from death and restored to life. Behold, man has been set free from sin and restored to love. All of you who are still caught in the darkness of death, listen: Christ is risen! All of you who have lived under the weight of sin, listen: Christ has conquered sin in his cross and resurrection. Surrender your life to him!

O men of the modern world! Submit yourselves to him and to his power! The more you discover in yourself the old ways of sin, the more you become aware of the horror of death on the horizon of your life, submit yourself all the more to his power to save.

Easter Weekday
The Final Victory

Christ rose from the dead at a precise moment in time. yet he still waits for his resurrection to transform all men as he breaks into the lives of each individual and into the history of all peoples. But the transformation of society and individuals through the resurrection depends on the co-operation of men.

In this resurrection there is always an ebb and flow. Men break the bonds of sin and death. They rise in Christ as he did that Easter morning so many centuries ago. Yes, wherever there is a heart that overcomes selfishness, violence, and hatred – wherever there is a heart that reaches out to someone in need – Christ is risen from the dead, risen today. Wherever someone pursues true justice and peace, death is defeated and Christ's resurrection is reaffirmed. Whenever a person dies who has lived believing, loving, and suffering for Christ, there is the resurrection.

This resurrection, which is meant for all men, is the final victory. It is God's answer to man's sorrow and trials. It is not death but life. It is not despair but hope. And it is to this hope that the church invites all men today.

To us, to all men, she repeats the unbelievable yet true announcement: Christ is risen! May the whole world rise with him! Alleluia!

Easter Weekday
Peace Be with You

During the Easter season we return to the upper room. We remember the events of the first day of the week, of Easter Sunday.

Jesus comes in – even though the door was shut – stands in the midst of his disciples, and says to them: 'Peace be with you. As the Father has sent me, so I send you' (John 20–21). And after he says these words, he breathes on them and says: 'Receive the Holy Spirit' (John 20.22).

This is Jesus' first appearance to the apostles after the resurrection. Jesus comes. He is still the same, and yet he has changed. He is the same man who suffered the passion, for he shows the apostles the nail prints in his hands and the wound in his side. But he has changed. The closed door is no obstacle to his glorified body.

He has been transformed by the resurrection. He now manifests the power of the life-giving Spirit in his body. Jesus comes in the power of the Spirit, and he gives the Holy Spirit to the apostles. Our Lord gives the Spirit, thanks to the wounds of his passion.

Easter Weekday
I Am the Good Shepherd

'I am the good shepherd' (John 10.11). The figure of the Good Shepherd is linked to the paschal season. In light of the events of Christ's passion, the church reads once again about Jesus as the Good Shepherd, as she has over the centuries.

'The good shepherd lays down his life for the sheep' (v. 11). This is the central idea of the parable of the Good Shepherd, which is now fully realised through the sacrifice of Christ on the cross. He offers his life as a sacrifice for men. That is why he is the Good Shepherd!

The earliest pictures of the catacombs show us how

deeply the early Christians appreciated the truth of the Good Shepherd. This truth is rooted in the Old Testament. For instance, Psalm 100 declares, 'The Lord is God; he made us, his we are; his people, the flock he tends' (Ps. 100.3).

For the chosen people, the image of the shepherd who knows and cares for his sheep was a familiar one from the very beginnings of their history. And all that took place between the shepherd and the sheep became a figure, a metaphor for Israel's relationship with God.

Easter Weekday
The Flock He Tends

In biblical times, the shepherd is not just a leader but a friendly and attentive guardian. He is concerned about the life of his flock. He leads the flock to the pastures and springs. He protects it from predators and wild animals. He guards it from dangers. The shepherd is a saviour. It is easy to trust in him with a simple heart – as we must now do with Christ – because his care provides safety and abundance of life. It is easy to grasp in him the authority and sovereignty of God who takes the initiative. Extending goodness and grace, he is concerned for man and becomes his steadfast support. Yes, we are his. He made us. We are his people. We are the flock he tends.

Christ says, 'my sheep' (John 10.14). Then he explains why he calls his disciples 'mine', because 'my Father . . . has given them to me' (John 10.29 RSV).

Every man has been given to the Son by the Father in a special way. The Son himself has become man to take on the Father's shepherding concern for all men. A shepherd's concern is synonymous with God's fatherly providence in the Scripture. This providence becomes a living reality for us through the Son, through the Christ.

Easter Weekday
He Lays Down His Life for the Sheep

The Good Shepherd is the most unique expression of
God's saving providence, of his fatherly concern for man.
In his mercy, the Father decided that Christ should come
to lead his sheep to the fullness of life, a life rich and fertile
as running water and green pasture. The Word emptied
himself and saved us, making us like to him in such a
powerful way that every Christian, together with St Paul,
can say: 'The life I live now is not my own; Christ is
living in me' (Gal. 2.20).

However, let us not forget that the comforting presence
of the Redeemer does not exempt us from taking up our
cross. It is a consoling grace which unites us to God,
making us live and suffer according to his will for our
neighbour's sake.

We see, then, that Christ carries out a providential mission on behalf of those whom the Father has given him.
He is the Good Shepherd.

Easter Weekday
My Sheep Hear My Voice

Christ's mission consists of a particular knowledge, the
saving knowledge of his own. 'My sheep hear my voice.
I know them' (John 10.27). This is a knowledge that
comes through faith and trust. In fact, the shepherd is the
only one whom the flock trusts. That is why they follow
him. He knows the just value of each one of them, and
he knows each one of them in God's eyes. The shepherd
carries in himself an understanding of each one. Only he
is able to pay the price for each one. And the price is the
hard wood of the cross: he 'lays down his life for the
sheep'.

This precious price is united to the shepherd's intimate

knowledge of each of his sheep. He knows that they are destined to share eternal life in him: 'They follow me. I give them eternal life' (John 10.27–8).

Fifth Sunday of Easter
No One Shall Snatch Them from Me

We must place before our eyes God's foreknowledge and our infinite worth before God to understand the parable of the Good Shepherd: 'They shall never perish. No one shall snatch them out of my hand. . . . There is no snatching out of [my Father's] hand' (John 10.28–9). These are very forceful words. In a certain way, the whole drama of redemption is reflected in them.

Christ says: 'My Father, who has given them to me, is greater than all . . . I and the Father are one' (John 10.29–30 RSV). Through the cross and the resurrection, the divine unity of the Father and the Son is fully revealed. This unity is expressed in the creation of man. It is expressed in God's saving providence. It is expressed in redemption.

Redemption is in a certain way God's complete commitment to make sure that what he has created in his own image and likeness will not be taken away from him. He guarantees that the salvific work of eternal love will be accomplished among men.

The church bears witness to this love. She bears witness to the work of man's redemption in Christ. She bears witness to the resurrection through which the mission of the Good Shepherd has been carried out in the deepest way possible. We receive the same witness in the Acts of the Apostles when Paul and Barnabas recall the words of Isaiah: 'I have made you a light to the nations, a means of salvation to the ends of the earth' (Acts 13.47).

Easter Weekday
The Cornerstone

The Christ is the cornerstone. 'This Jesus is the stone
rejected by you the builders which has become the cornerstone' (Acts 4.11). Those who have not accepted the witness of the good news and have condemned Christ to
death on the cross have rejected this stone. Those who
seek to organise the world and its social life without him
and against him, don't they reject him again? And yet this
rejected stone – so many times rejected – is the cornerstone.

Only on him can the building of our salvation stand.
Only in him can the building of true order and peace
within man and among men find a secure foundation.
Only by him can man be spiritually renewed and grow
to the full measure of his eternal destiny. And only
through him can the world of men become ever more
fully human.

Easter Weekday
Goodness and Kindness Follow Me

Psalm 23 paves the way for our understanding of the
parable of the Good Shepherd. It is a psalm which is very
familiar to all of us.

The imagery in the psalm is so rich, belonging to two
different settings. First of all it speaks about 'pastures',
which signify the safety and spiritual nourishment sup-
plied to us by the Lord; about 'waters', which quench our
thirst; of 'paths', which remind us that we are moving
toward a destination; and about 'the dark valley', which
represents the difficulties we encounter on our journey.
These images are drawn from the relationship between
the shepherd and his flock.

But in the second half of the psalm there are other

images which recall a scene of joyous fellowship. That is
why the psalm speaks about a 'table' which is spread,
meaning the abundance which is offered to us in communion with the Lord; about 'oil', referring to his warm
hospitality; and about an overflowing 'cup', since the Lord
is always kind and generous towards us.

The entire psalm, especially the last verse, reminds us
of the great contentment and peace we have in Christ the
Good Shepherd. 'Only goodness and kindness follow me
all the days of my life; and I shall dwell in the house of
the LORD for years to come.' Christ leads us in the paths
of 'goodness and kindness' during his earthly life, so he
can finally arrive at 'the house of the LORD' and prepare a
place for us.

Easter Weekday
The Sheepgate

In the liturgy, Christ calls himself not only 'the shepherd'
but also 'the sheepgate' (John 10.7). In this way, Jesus uses
two different metaphors which are particularly expressive.
The image of the 'shepherd' is contrasted to that of the
'hired hand'. It serves to underscore the deep concern of
Christ for his flock to the point of laying down his life
for our salvation: 'The good shepherd lays down his life
for the sheep' (John 10.11). The letter to the Ephesians
follows the same theme: 'Christ loved the church. He
gave himself up for her' (Eph. 5.25). It is our task to
acknowledge him as our only Lord and to follow 'his
voice' (John 10.4), not giving the same allegiance to a
mere hired hand, who ultimately 'has no concern for his
sheep' (John 10.13) but only for his pay.

This reflection helps us understand the other image, that
of the 'door' or 'sheepgate'. Jesus says: 'Whoever enters
through me will be safe. He will go in and out, and find
pasture' (John 10.9). The shepherd leads us to safety and

rest. We can go in through the sheepgate and find that safety and rest.

Easter Weekday
I Am the Vine, You Are the Branches

To understand the reality of the church as the people of God, we need to read the allegory about the vine and the branches attentively and then ponder its meaning in our hearts. 'I am the vine, you are the branches. He who lives in me and I in him, will produce abundantly, for apart from me you can do nothing' (John 15.5).

These branches represent not only individuals but peoples of every age and every generation. They transcend time and death itself as the people of God are gathered together in Christ. This great people of God make up one body because of Christ. They are one through him, with him, and in him as branches of the same vine. And this vine is a living organism that gives us all a oneness of life in Christ. It is from the vine that the branches always draw their life.

Easter Weekday
Each Branch Is Sustained by the Vine

In the unity of the vine, every branch has its place. Yes, the life of Christ flows to each branch and nourishes it. When he says: 'I am the true vine and my Father is the vinegrower', he is also saying: 'He prunes away every barren branch, but the fruitful ones he trims clean to increase their yield' (John 15.1–2).

Christ goes on to say: 'You are clean already, thanks to the word I have spoken to you' (v. 3). When he says 'you', although in the plural, he is addressing every human 'you' in the singular. He is thinking about each branch.

The Lord continues: 'Live on in me, as I do in you' (v.

4). And soon afterwards he says: 'No more than a branch can bear fruit of itself apart from the vine, can you bear fruit apart from me.'

Christ says 'you' and he means 'each one of you'. Also the image he develops centres on the one vine. In him alone do the branches find life. And they each find life in him. Multiplicity does not become mass. Each branch is sustained by the vine. It has its own unique point of contact. The same is true of the relationship between every person and Christ. In fact, through our relationship with Christ, we also come in contact with the Father.

Easter Weekday
Easter for Youth

Easter is a personal encounter with Christ. Like the apostles, we realise the risen Christ is a reality. Easter is also an invaluable resource for each young person's journey through life. Jesus enlightens us about our future and invites us to receive his call with the eyes of faith. In the risen Lord we encounter true freedom, for God gives himself in Christ to man and saves him. He saves us from destruction, from death, from despair, from problems, from resignation to evil.

The resurrected Christ restores us to the truth and a richness of life by conquering sin. That is true freedom. Christ becomes the foundation of this new freedom. Every young person who has known Christ is called to live out that freedom wholeheartedly.

Young people cannot remain indifferent to these great values on which the destiny of mankind depends. They cannot be passive about society or themselves. The knowledge of true freedom gives the young responsibility and encourages all of us to give real meaning to our actions. Freedom is not an object that can be discarded, the way so many things are in our consumer society. It is a radical commitment. It is a call to live out the truth.

Sixth Sunday of Easter
The Comforter Will Come

In the upper room, Jesus has spoken to the apostles about his departure. He has explained why he must leave. 'If I fail to go,' he says, 'the Paraclete will never come to you, whereas if I go, I will send him to you' (John 16.7).

After these words, Jesus leaves his disciples. He leaves this world in the most painful way that can be imagined. He is judged like a criminal, like an impostor. He is condemned to death and crucified. It is easy to understand how Christ's passion became traumatic for the apostles. Humanly speaking, it was a great disappointment.

But now he appears to them. He is among them. He is opening their minds and hearts to understand his mission and purpose. He opens their minds to the Scriptures which point to him.

But they need the Paraclete, the Holy Spirit, to truly understand. And behold, Christ gives him to them. Even before 'sending' the Holy Spirit on Pentecost, he gives him to the apostles on the day of the resurrection. He says: 'Receive the Holy Spirit.'

In this way the Holy Spirit is given to the apostles as a fruit of Christ's saving work on the cross. The entire paschal mystery is sealed by this great gift of the Holy Spirit.

Easter Weekday
He Makes All Things New

'See, I make all things new!' (Rev. 21.5). There are some particular places we are led to visit during the Easter season. The first of these places is the upper room in Jerusalem. The upper room becomes a hiding place for the apostles in which the Easter beginnings of the church mature. Soon afterwards it becomes the place of a new exodus – the exodus of the people of God of the New Covenant into the world. In this holy place, the words of Revelation are engraved: 'See, I make all things new!'

Christ's farewell address is also linked to the upper room. It is significant that right after Judas' departure from the upper room at the Last Supper, Christ speaks about how God the Father will glorify him. He also tells how he, himself, will be glorified. He speaks these words just as the traitor prepares for his betrayal and arrest in the garden.

Humanly speaking, one would not expect such a discourse. All that is about to happen will be in human terms a denial of Christ's glory. He will be ridiculed and abased. But Jesus' words are beyond human understanding. We recognise in them the divine mystery of Christ. In the cross of Christ, God will be glorified as love and truth, as justice and mercy. God the Father will also glorify Christ, and the sign of this glory will be his resurrection on the third day. That is why Jesus speaks these words at the Last Supper. They are so unusual and at the same time so full of another truth: the divine truth of salvation. In these words, he 'makes all things new'.

Easter Weekday
Entering into the Reign of God

During the Easter season, the liturgy turns in a special way to the Acts of the Apostles. We follow the apostolic journey of Paul and Barnabas to various cities throughout the Roman Empire where the gospel is first announced and the church is born.

This gradual development of the gospel and the church is the fruit of the paschal mystery that took place in Jerusalem. Those events, which are all linked to the upper room, continue the same saving work of Christ. Now we see this work go forward through the preaching of the gospel and the life of the church in the Acts of the Apostles.

Is is only possible because of the power of the crucified and risen Christ and the power of the Holy Spirit whom he has sent. As the apostles tell us, 'We must undergo many trials if we are to enter into the reign of God' (Acts 14.22). In fact, that way is shown to all Christians by Christ. The church is being born in the hearts of the disciples, in the new communities, in every place where God's Spirit is at work. It is being born and bearing fruit because of the great paschal mystery: the Lord's death and resurrection. That is how it has been down through the centuries. We are still linked to the heritage of this salvific birth of the church after almost 2,000 years.

Easter Weekday

If You Truly Loved Me You Would Rejoice

The Lord Jesus prepares his disciples for his departure from earth. He says: 'I go away . . . If you truly loved me, you would rejoice to have me go to the Father, for the Father is greater than I' (John 14.28). The church reads these words once again as she draws near the fortieth day after Christ's resurrection – Ascension Thursday.

Yet Christ does not simply say 'I go away', but actually says 'I come back to you.' The departure only signals the conclusion of his messianic mission on earth. It is not a separation from Christ. Christ's messianic mission ends with the coming of the Holy Spirit and with the birth of the church.

In the church, Christ is always present and always at work in the power of the Spirit. He leads us home to the Father. The mission of the church is to lead mankind to this final destiny which every man has in God.

Thus, Christ's departure does not cause confusion or anxiety. It is full of peace. The Saviour says: ' "Peace" is my farewell to you, my peace is my gift to you" (John 14.27). Every day we repeat these words during the euch-

before Communion. And he adds: 'Do not
⌐ or fearful. I go away for awhile, and I come
ⁿu' (vs. 27–8).

As ┐ision Thursday
Full Authority in Heaven and on Earth

'Full authority has been given to me both in heaven and
on earth' (Matt. 28.18). It is the fortieth day after the
resurrection. It is the day when new life in Christ reveals
its spiritual dimension beyond time – the day of the ascension. On this holy day, the complete authority and power
of the risen Christ has been revealed. It is 'authority in
heaven and on earth'. Christ possesses that authority and
power eternally, for he is the Son of the same divine
essence as the Father. Jesus of Nazareth as a man has
conquered through his cross, and God the Father has given
him all power and authority. It is the authority that comes
from the power of redemption.

Through this authority Christ gives the apostles his last
command on earth: 'Go, therefore, and makes disciples of
all the nations. Baptise them in the name of the Father,
and of the Son, and of the Holy Spirit. Teach them to
carry out everything I have commanded you. And know
that I am with you always, until the end of the world!'
(Matt. 28.19–20). It is the apostles' mandate to preach the
gospel: 'As the Father has sent me, so I send you' (John
20.21).

When we hear these words, full of the power of Christ's
redemption, our thoughts turn to the twelve who were
the first ones to hear them.

We cannot separate this mandate of Ascension Thursday
from its fruit in the life of the church and in the history
of nations and of peoples. That fruit is the salvation of
souls.

Easter Weekday
The Spirit of Truth

'When the Paraclete comes, the Spirit of truth who comes from the Father – and whom I myself will send from the Father – he will bear witness on my behalf. You must bear witness as well, for you have been with me from the beginning' (John 15.26–7).

Now we return to these words of Christ. And we return to the upper room in Jerusalem, where those words were spoken. The promise contained in those words must come true in the same upper room on the day of Pentecost. Christ's words lead us from the events of Easter to Pentecost. They are like a bridge.

The Holy Spirit comes constantly to Christ's disciples as the Comforter who is sent by the Father. He comes as the Spirit of truth to bear witness to Christ.

Easter Weekday
Faith Transforms Man

The mission of the Holy Spirit is linked to that of the Son. On the one hand, the Spirit prepares the whole messianic mission of Christ, and draws from it a new beginning. The Holy Spirit comes to us again from the cross and the resurrection. His witness leads us into God's mystery as the Blessed Trinity. It also gives us a knowledge of our salvation. We now know that God is love. We know that the love of God has transformed man and changed the world: 'My Father is at work until now, and I am at work as well' (John 5.17), Jesus tells us.

This work of the Father, fulfilled through the Son, is carried out at the same time before the eyes of men. It becomes a part of God's saving plan. And these men – especially the apostles – are witnesses to Christ. Theirs is a human witness, based on hearing, on seeing, on touching (1 John 1.1), based on encounters with the living God.

This human witness builds up the church from the very beginning – the church as the community of the disciples of Christ. This is the community of faith which sets its eyes on the mystery that had remained hidden in God for many ages (Eph. 3.9). Therefore, this human, apostolic witness is organically linked to the witness given on Christ's behalf by the Comforter, the Spirit of truth. It is rooted in him. It is from him that it draws its transforming power. And this transforming power gives men faith in the Christ.

Seventh Sunday of Easter
Go and Make Disciples

We turn to Christ's words on Ascension Thursday: 'Go . . . make disciples.' We find a striking echo of this call when the Apostle Paul writes: 'Preaching the gospel is not the subject of a boast; I am under compulsion and have no choice. I am ruined if I do not preach it!' (1 Cor. 9.16). Paul then explains: 'If I do it willingly, I have my recompense; if unwillingly, I am nonetheless entrusted with a charge' (v. 17).

Therefore, I am 'ruined' if I do not preach the gospel because this mission is empowered by the resurrection of Christ. It is the price which the Son of God has paid for man. We have been purchased at a precious price (1 Cor. 6.20; 7.23).

These penetrating words of Paul show us how great the power of the crucified and risen Christ really is. These words continue to bear witness to the power of the apostolic mandate of Ascension Thursday.

Easter Weekday
Towards the Glory of the Father

On the fortieth day 'he was taken up to heaven' (Acts 1.2). The liturgy celebrates this blessed event. The real place of Christ's exaltation, of his glory, is not the earth but the bosom of the Father. Heaven indicates some place altogether different from the earth.

It is perfect communion with God, that God who subsists in the unity of the Father, the Son, and the Holy Spirit. This is the God who 'fills the universe in all its parts' (Eph 1.23) as 'the Father of glory'.

The place of perfect fellowship and communion with God is where Christ is exalted. It is there that he receives adoration as the eternal Son of the same essence as the Father and also as Lord of the redeemed creation. In fact, the Father 'has put all things under Christ's feet and has made him, thus exalted, head of the church, which is his body: the fullness of him who fills the universe in all its parts' (Eph. 1.22–3).

Christ, the Lord of redeemed creation, is exalted in the resurrection and glorified in the ascension. He continues to work with the same divine power which was revealed through him on earth. This power, sealed in the Easter mystery, leads mankind and all creation towards the glory of the Father.

Its fruit is the whole treasure of glory inherited by the saints. It is also the immeasurable scope of his power in us who believe (Eph. 1.18–19). Thus, the Solemnity of the Ascension of the Lord speaks to us about the call to glory, which man and all creation must find in God through Christ who ascended into heaven.

Easter Weekday
The Fullness of All Things

At the Last Supper, Christ speaks to the apostles very clearly about the coming of the Spirit. After the resurrection he turns back to that announcement and to that promise 'of which you have heard me speak. John baptised with water, but within a few days you will be baptised with the Holy Spirit' (Acts 1.4–5).

Then the apostles ask him: 'Are you going to restore the rule to Israel now?' The apostles still do not understand. Like their fellow Jews, they still think Christ will save them from political oppression and tyranny.

Jesus' answer is the same as always: 'The exact time is not yours to know. The Father has reserved that to himself' (Acts 1.7). There are certain times in earthly history: the times of peoples and of nations, of their rule and their downfall. But the time Jesus is thinking about is different: 'You will receive power when the Holy Spirit comes down on you; then you are to be my witnesses in Jerusalem, throughout Judea and Samaria, yes, even to the ends of the earth' (Acts 1.8).

Jesus is describing a time which is different, a history which is different, a kingdom which is different from the earthly one of Israel. The Holy Spirit will lead you out into the streets of Jerusalem and then send you to the far corners of the earth. You will preach to all peoples, to all languages, cultures, and races, to all continents.

The psalm speaks in the same vein: 'All you peoples, clap your hands, shout to God with cries of gladness, for the LORD, the Most High, the awesome, is the great king over all the earth. God reigns over the nations' (Ps. 47.2–3, 9). The kingdom which 'does not belong to this world' is revealed once again in these words. We are reminded of Ascension Thursday as Christ is exalted as the great king in the heavens.

This kingdom is realised through the history of all the

peoples and all the nations. It is realised in Christ as the fullness of all things.

Easter Weekday
I Will Not Leave Your Orphaned

'I will ask the Father and he will give you another Paraclete – to be with you always: the Spirit of truth . . . I will not leave you orphaned; I will come back to you' (John 14.16–18).

With these words Jesus prepares the disciples for his departure as the time of his messianic mission on earth draws to a close. When he says 'I will not leave you orphaned; I will come back to you', these words tell of the days after the resurrection when he will spend forty more days with the disciples. These words also refer to the Holy Spirit.

The risen Christ does not leave his disciples 'orphaned'. He does not leave the church 'orphaned'. No, he gives us the Holy Spirit.

Easter Weekday
Guest of Human Souls

Christ calls the Holy Spirit 'another Paraclete' or Comforter, because he brings – in a different way than Christ does – the same good news of salvation and of grace. All that Christ has revealed in word and deed and has confirmed through the resurrection – this is the same work that the Spirit of truth will manifest. He will remain forever with the church as the breath of the Father and of the Son, as the gift from on high, and as 'the sweet guest of human souls'. The Second Vatican Council has shown us this work of the Spirit through the whole history of the church. Its fruits are truth, love, and light. They develop in men through the breath of the Spirit.

Easter Weekday
The Promise of the Holy Spirit

'The Paraclete, the Holy Spirit whom the Father will send in my name, will instruct you in everything, and remind you of all that I told you' (John 14.26). Christ utters these words on the eve of his passion and death on the cross as he says farewell to the apostles. We recall these words during the season of Easter. This very season is the time when the promise of the Holy Spirit will be fulfilled in a complete way.

On the evening of the resurrection, Christ already gives the Holy Spirit to the apostles gathered in the upper room. He tells them, 'Receive the Holy Spirit' (John 20.22). He brings the Spirit to the church as a gift. The Holy Spirit, himself, will be revealed in the events of Pentecost as a gift given to the church. During these days and weeks, all of us should have a special awareness of the link between Easter and Pentecost. Let us pray that God will continue to pour out his Holy Spirit upon his people.

Easter Weekday
He Will Instruct You in Everything

Christ tells the apostles about the Holy Spirit: He 'will instruct you in everything, and remind you of all that I told you'. The apostolic teaching of the church is always rooted in this vigilant presence of the Spirit of truth. It is he who ensures the truth of the gospel. He watches to make sure that the church will hand on from one generation to another all that she has heard from Christ.

Protecting and guiding the development of tradition, the Holy Spirit is the invisible source of revelation for the church. He will 'remind you', says Jesus. Tradition is our heritage. It is 'remembering' all that Christ has told the church: the whole heritage of revelation and of faith.

'Holy tradition and holy Scripture are bound closely together and communicate one with another. For both of them, flowing out from the same divine well-spring, come together in some fashion to form one thing and move towards the same goal', Vatican II teaches (DV 9). In them, we see the presence of Christ, our Good Shepherd, down through the centuries.

Pentecost to Trinity Sunday

Pentecost
In the History of Man and of the World

'When the Paraclete comes, the Spirit of truth who comes from the Father – and whom I myself will send from the Father – he will bear witness on my behalf. You must bear witness as well for you have been with me from the beginning' (John 15.26–7).

We go back to these words of Christ. And we go back to the upper room of Jerusalem where these words were spoken. The promise mentioned in this passage must be fulfilled in the same upper room on the day of Pentecost. Christ's promise to send his Spirit takes us from Easter to the events of Pentecost. It forms a bridge between the two great feasts.

The Holy Spirit comes constantly to the disciples of Christ as the Comforter sent by the Father. He comes as the Spirit of truth to bear witness on behalf of Christ who sends him from the Father.

The mission of the Holy Spirit is linked to that of the Son. On the one hand, he prepares the whole messianic mission of Christ, and ushers in a new beginning. The Holy Spirit comes to us because of the cross and resurrection. His witness leads us into the mystery of God as the Blessed Trinity. It leads us into an appreciation of the economy of our salvation. Due to this witness we know that God is love. We know that he has performed a mighty work of love that has changed the course of human history.

Faith in Christ Transforms Man

'My Father is at work until now, and I am at work as well' (John 5.17). This work of the Father, which is accomplished through the Son, is seen by men. It has become a part of our history. And these men – the apostles first of all – are witnesses to Christ. Theirs is a human witness, based on hearing, on seeing, on touching (1 John 1.1).

This human witness has built up the church from the very beginning – the church as the community of Christ's disciples. The community of faith sets its eyes on the mystery that was hidden in God through the ages (Eph. 3.9). Therefore, this human and apostolic witness is organically linked to the witness given to Christ by the Comforter, the Spirit of truth. It is rooted in him. It is from him that the church obtains the transforming power of Christ. This is how faith in Christ transforms man.

Inner Light

The Holy Spirit acts as an inner light, which leads the sinner to recognise his own sin. As long as man keeps his eyes closed to his own guilt, he cannot be converted. The Holy Spirit produces in the soul the light of God, which convicts the conscience so the sinner can be freed from the blindness which hides from his sight the guilt of sin. That is why those who took part in condemning Jesus by demanding his death suddenly discovered under the scrutiny of his light that their behaviour was sinful.

The Holy Spirit also produces repentance and confession. He helps us understand that divine forgiveness is available to sinners, thanks to Christ's sacrifice. Such forgiveness is accessible to everyone. Those who have heard Peter's discourse in the second chapter of the Acts of the Apostles ask: 'What are we to do, brothers?' How can the sinner leave his sin behind? The way out would be impossible for him if the way of forgiveness were closed! But this way is wide open; one only needs to tread upon it. The Holy Spirit develops in man feelings of trust in the divine love which forgives. It leads him to redemption in the Saviour Jesus Christ.

Spirit of Love and of Unity

From the day of Pentecost, the reconciliation of all people in God is no longer a distant dream. It has become a reality, destined to grow constantly as the church reaches out with the saving gospel. The Holy Spirit, who is the Spirit of love and of unity, brings about the aim of Christ's redeeming sacrifice through the reunion of the children of God who were scattered.

Two important points become clear as the Spirit brings God's people together. By leading men to cling to Christ, the Holy Spirit brings them into the unity of the church as the body of Christ. In this way, he reconciles people to each other in brotherhood, even though they are separated from each other by geography and culture. Thus, he makes of the church a perpetual source of unity and reconciliation. The Holy Spirit even reconciles those who remain outside the church in a certain way. He inspires in all the desire for a greater unity and encourages men's efforts to overcome the many conflicts which still divide the world.

Make Room in Your Hearts

Live in the faith and hand it on to your children. Bear witness to it in your life. Love the church as a mother. Live in her and for her. Make room in your hearts for all men. Forgive one another and be peacemakers wherever you are.

To non-believers, I say: 'Seek God, for he is seeking you.'

And to those who suffer, I say: 'Be confident. For Christ, who has gone before you, will give you strength to face sorrow.'

To the youth, I say: 'Make a good investment of your life, for it is a precious treasure.'

To everyone, I say: 'May the grace of God accompany you every day.'

And greet your small children in my name as soon as they wake up. How I would like this 'good morning' to be for them the announcement of a good life, for your consolation and for mine, and for the consolation of the whole church!

Renew the Earth

'May your Spirit come down and renew the earth.' Is it only the apostles who are supposed to pray like that? Only that small community, united to Christ in the most personal way? Only they?

It is the whole earth that prays in the same way. All things created, even when they have no voice or words, raise up this cry: 'How manifold are your works, O Lord! . . . The earth is full of your creatures. . . . If you take away their breath, they perish and return to their dust. When you send forth your spirit, they are created, and you renew the face of the earth' (Ps. 104.24, 29–30). 'It is the Spirit that gives life' (John 6.63). It is he who renews the face of the earth.

May your Spirit come down upon us!

The Revelation of the Son of God

Man prays. Thus, he becomes the voice of all created things. The apostles pray gathered together with Mary in the upper room at Jerusalem. The church prays in the name of all creation.

Creation, in fact, was made subject to futility (Rom.

8.20) because of sin, which is opposed to the life-giving Spirit. And, behold, before our very eyes man's work is progressing in the marvellous fields of science and technology. This work unveils in a unique way the riches that are hidden in creation. But it also reveals the sin which lurks in human hearts and which spreads among societies as part of our history.

That is why a fear is growing in the world. Many fear that creation and man's work may be made subject to an even greater futility as we experience crises and threats of ever increasing proportions. That is why all of creation – through the prayer of all mankind more than through the works of man – cries out for the sons of God. Paul tells us, 'The whole created world eagerly awaits the revelation of the sons of God' (Rom. 8.19).

Let us pray to the Lord like this: 'Allow us, Lord, to speak in all the languages of the modern world: languages of culture and of civilisation; languages of social, economic, and political renewal; languages of justice and of liberation; languages of information systems and of the mass media. Allow us, Lord, to announce everywhere your manifold works. May your Spirit come down! Renew the face of the earth through the revelation of the sons of God!'

Trinity Sunday
Glory to the Trinity

Glory to you, O Blessed Trinity! Today we sing with the whole church the glory of the Blessed Trinity: Father, Son, and Holy Spirit.

We sing glory to God, who is one in the unity of his divinity. To God, who is one in the unsearchable mystery of the divine Trinity. One in the unity of his divinity. One in the unity of communion in one divine essence among the three persons. Glory to the Trinity. We sing glory to God 'who is and who was and who is to come' (Rev. 1.4).

'When he comes, . . . the Spirit of truth, he will guide you to all truth' (John 16.13).

Yes, when he comes he will guide you. Precisely because he not only 'is' but also 'has come' – precisely because of this – he has brought us closer to the mystery of the life of the Blessed Trinity. The God who is absolutely above us in majesty and power has become the God of our salvation. 'And we have seen his glory' (John 1.14).

From now until the First Sunday in Advent (see p. 1) readings for 'Ordinary Time' may be used (pp. 140–294), except for those feasts which have a Special Reading (pp. 130–39).

Other Feasts with Special Readings

2nd February: The Feast of the Presentation of Jesus in the Temple
King of Glory

God is present at the very heart of all human cultures because he is present in man – who is created in his image and who is the architect of culture. He has been present in every person who has contributed through his experience and aspiration to form those values, customs, and institutions which make up the cultural heritage of the whole earth.

And the king of glory wants to enter these cultures in an even fuller way. He wants to enter every human heart that is willing to open to him: 'Lift up, O gates, your lintels; reach up, you ancient portals, that the king of glory may come in!' Yes, at the feast of the Presentation, God enters his temple as 'the king of glory'.

But – 'Who is this king of glory?' (Ps. 24.7–8). Today's feast gives us the answer. We behold Mary and Joseph who carry an infant into the temple at Jerusalem. It is the fortieth day after his birth.

And they present him to the priests in the temple to fulfil the command of the law. But with their obedience they are fulfilling much more than the law. All the prophecies of old are being fulfilled since Mary and Joseph are carrying into the temple 'the light of all nations'.

God enters the temple not as a potentate or mighty one but as a small child in his mother's arms. The king of glory does not arrive in a great demonstration of human strength and power, not with great pomp and noise. He does not enter causing terror or destruction. No, he enters the temple as he entered the world, as an infant. He enters in silence, in poverty, and in the company of the poor and the wise.

Power Is in Simplicity

God comes as a little child – God, the Creator of all, the omnipotent Lord of heaven and earth, the king of glory. God's first entrance into the temple of his people is wrapped in the mystery of helplessness. Yes, his power is concealed in simplicity and in the defencelessness of a babe.

His coming is completely wrapped in mystery. Unexpectedly, out of the very centre of the mystery, a voice speaks. It is Simeon, for the Gospel of Luke says, 'the Holy Spirit was upon him' (Luke 2.26).

These are surprising words to be said concerning an infant. Yet Simeon's prophecy is true. And the words of the psalm are fulfilled. He who had entered the temple of Jerusalem as an infant shall become the light and the salvation of the whole world. In this way, he comes bearing light and salvation. He comes as the king of glory.

But, how will this king establish his own 'reign of glory' on earth? How will Jesus, who had been born in Bethlehem, become the light and salvation of the world? Simeon responds to this question when he speaks about 'a sign that will be opposed' (Luke 2.34).

These words reveal the whole messianic way of Christ from his birth to his death on the cross. Even though he is the light of the nations, Jesus is destined to be also for all ages a sign of rejection, a sign that will provoke hostility, a sign of contradiction.

That had been true for the prophets of Israel before him. It was true of John the Baptist and would be true for the lives of those who would follow Jesus. He accomplished great signs and wonders. He healed the sick, multiplied and distributed bread and the fish, calmed the storms, and even brought the dead back to life.

The crowds rallied to him from all places and listened to him with attention because he spoke with authority. And yet he encountered hard opposition from those who refused to open their hearts and their minds to him.

Ultimately, the most tangible expression of this contradiction is found in his suffering and death on the cross. Simeon's prophecy proved true.

It proved true about the life of Jesus, and it is true about the lives of his followers in all lands and in all times.

29th June: The Feast of the Apostles St Peter and St Paul

We Celebrate Their Lives

O Roma felix – O happy Rome!

Today's liturgy proclaims the martyrdom of the Apostles Peter and Paul. And through the memory of their deaths, we celebrate their life today. Death, in fact, is not just the end of life. It is also its fulfilment at the end of time, at the end of history. It is like God's last seal stamped on the whole earthly existence of man.

Therefore, the death of the Apostles Peter and Paul proclaims at the same time the story of their life. This life – the life of each of them – was all the more extraordinary because of their relationship to Christ, who called them to follow him. He called Simon, son of Jonah, who was a fisherman in Galilee and gave him the name Peter. That is 'rock'. He also called Saul of Tarsus, who was a persecutor of Christians. And he made him Paul, the apostle of the gentiles, 'the instrument I have chosen' (Acts 9.15).

The life of both of them is so extraordinary because of the power of the Holy Spirit who allowed them to bear witness to the crucified and risen Christ: 'He will bear witness on my behalf. You must bear witness as well' (John 15.26–7).

The cruel death that each of them underwent in Rome in the days of Nero was the last word of this witness. It came from the fullness of that witness, their martyrs' blood. Precisely because of this death of theirs as martyrs, their life lives on in a special way in the memory of the church. It lives on above all in God, who 'is the God of the living, not of the dead' (Matt. 22.32), in God in whom all of us live.

The Truth About Love
O Roma felix!

If today's liturgy speaks thus about Rome, it does so precisely because of the death of the apostles.

Be happy, Rome! You have seeded the martyrs' blood that consolidates the apostolic witness of life. See, you have become a new stage in 'the marvels of God' (*magnalia Dei*). To you, capital of the Caesars, was led Simon Peter, a poor fisherman of Galilee, guided by the invisible hand of the Lord of history. To you, came afterwards, Paul – the indefatigable apostle of that Christ who is the Bridegroom of the church. A poet, Norwid, remarked that the Latin name for Rome, if read backwards, forms the Latin word for 'Love' (ROMA – AMOR)

O Rome, ancient capital of the world! We see that love manifest! You proved cruel towards many generations of Christians. You put to death as martyrs the first apostles of Christ. But Christ brought forth the love of the gospel from that witness.

Yes, in your name, the truth about love is consolidated – that love which is greater than all cruelties, tortures, and persecutions. That love is greater than death itself!

That is why the liturgy speaks about you, *O Roma felix*. And today we rejoice at the fact that you were chosen by the Lord of history and the Bridegroom of the church.

Moreover, all of us pray 'that your faith may never fail' (Luke 22.32). Repent! And be converted to Christ! And once converted, 'strengthen your brothers'.

15th August: The Solemnity of the Assumption of Mary into Heaven

Hail Mary!

Hail Mary! You who were *assumed into heaven.*
We greet you with the angel: you are full of grace!
The Lord is with you (Luke 1.28).
We greet you with Elizabeth:
blest are you among women,
and blest is the fruit of your womb;
blest are you who believed
the divine promises (Luke 1.42, 45).
We greet you with the words of the Gospel:
blest are you because you have listened to God's word
and have put it into practice (Luke 12.27).

You Are Full of Grace!
We praise you, favourite daughter of the Father.
We bless you, mother of the divine Word.
We venerate you, dwelling of the Holy Spirit.
We invoke you, mother and model of all the church.
We behold you, fulfilment
of the hopes of all mankind as the mother of the Saviour.

The Lord Is with You
You are the Virgin of the annunciation,
the yes of all mankind to the mystery of salvation.
You are the daughter of Zion
and the ark of the New Covenant
in the mystery of the visitation.
You are the mother of Jesus born in Bethlehem,
she who has shown him to the simple shepherds
and to the wise men from the east.
You are the mother
who presents her Son at the temple,
accompanies him to Egypt,

and takes him to Nazareth.
Virgin Mother of Jesus,
of the hidden life and of the miracle at Cana,
sorrowful mother of Calvary
and glorious Virgin of the resurrection,
you are the mother of Jesus' disciples
in the anticipation and the joy of Pentecost.

You Are Blessed,
because you have believed in the word of the Lord,
because you have hoped in his promises,
because you have been perfect in love,
for your faithful love to Elizabeth,
for your motherly kindness to Jesus in Bethlehem,
for your strength in persecution in fleeing to Egypt,
for your perseverance
in your search for Jesus in the temple,
for your simple life in Nazareth,
for your intercession at Cana,
for your motherly presence at the cross,
for your faithfulness in awaiting the resurrection,
for your steadfast prayer at Pentecost.

You Are Blessed,
for the *glory of your assumption into heaven*,
for your motherly protection of the church,
for your constant intercession
for all mankind.
For all this, we honour you, Blessed Virgin!

4th October: The Feast of St Francis of Assisi
Saint Francis of Assisi

The figure of St Francis of Assisi gives a Christian flavour to our human adventure. Bringing the evangelical beatitude of peace, he reconciles the divided soul to the church and to society.

The life and personality of the 'Poverello' of Assisi are extraordinarily rich in the ways of Christian holiness. There is no doubt that one of the inspired passages that St Francis lived out in depth and which he continues to make resound in the consciences of modern men is his urgent and fervent desire for peace. After wholeheartedly choosing the vocation to which God called him, he and his first followers went through the cities, through the villages. They stopped in the squares and neighbourhoods where he used to repeat the simple but sublime words, 'Peace and good', which were intended not just to be a desire but a commitment that should involve his listeners, often rent by divisions and bitter struggles: region against region, city against city, village against village, family against family. In medieval Italy, a word arose and resounded: a humble and modest, but strong word – strong with the power of the gospel – of this man of God. He was a man enamoured by Lady Poverty, a man who lived in an intense and unique way his brotherhood with everyone he met.

A New Man Given by Heaven

The humble Friar was seen and judged by his contemporaries as 'the new man, given by Heaven to the world' (FF 1212). And in the spirit of Christ, he even wanted to become available as a mediator between Christendom and Islam, to the point of paying a visit to the Sultan of Egypt, Melek-el-Kamel. He desired to announce to him – as a genuine prophet – the message of the incarnate Son of God.

We can truly say that St Francis was not only a messenger. No, more than that he was a builder and an architect of reconciliation and peace: 'The Lord revealed to me', he says, 'the greeting we were to use, saying: May the Lord give you peace' (FF 121). His biographer Thomas of Celano portrays thus the actions of the 'Poverello': 'In all of his sermons, before communicating the word of God to the people, he expressed the desire for peace saying:

"May the Lord give you peace!" This peace he announced always sincerely to men and women, to all he met or all who came to him. In this way he often succeeded, through the grace of the Lord, in making men who were the enemies of peace or of their own salvation become sons of peace and desirous of eternal salvation' (FF 359).

The chronicles of those days tell us that St Francis brought harmony to the city of Arezzo, which had been rent by inner quarrels. It is well known that during the last year of his life, he succeeded in obtaining peace between Bishop Guido II and the Podesta of Assisi, Oportulo.

1st November: The Feast of All Saints
All Saints

'I heard the number of those who were . . . marked [with the seal]' (Rev. 7.4). These words of the book of Revelation of St John the Apostle are found in today's liturgy. On the feast of All Saints, the church in every corner of the earth venerates those in whom salvation has been accomplished in a full way. They are those who, according to John's Revelation, 'cried out in a loud voice, "Salvation is from our God . . . and from the Lamb!" ' (Rev. 7.10).

In fact, they are marked with the blood of the Lamb. They bear in themselves the seal of redemption, which is the fountain of life and holiness. 'Everyone who has this hope based on him keeps himself pure, as he is pure' (1 John 3.3).

God is holy – thrice holy, infinitely holy. And he calls men to holiness. Today the church rejoices in all those who have carried this vocation to its fullness, those who participate forever in God's holiness. That is why, once again, a prayer flows from the depths of our heart – the prayer that is lifted up to heaven on this great feast:

'O almighty and everlasting God, who give to your church the joy of celebrating in this feast the merits and the glory of all the saints, grant to your people through the common intercession of so many brothers of ours, the abundance of your mercy.'

With the recitation of the Angelus we address in a particular way her whom the church venerates as queen of all saints: 'Blest are you among women!' 'The Holy Spirit will come upon you and the power of the Most High will overshadow you' (Luke 1.42, 35). In you we desire to adore God, in the highest degree, for the gift of holiness offered to men in Jesus Christ. And you deign to preside over our prayer for the departed, with which the church completes, in a certain way, the joy of the Solemnity of All Saints.

2nd November: The Feast of All Souls
All Souls

Man Succumbs to the Things of the Earth
'The Lord's are the earth and its fullness' (Ps 24.1). They belong to the Lord of the universe. He is their Creator. In the midst of this universe is the earth. In it is man, created in God's image – created as male and female.

To man the Creator said, 'Fill the earth and subdue it' (Gen. 1.28). Throughout history, man fills the earth and subdues it. However, man, at the same time, succumbs to the things of the earth. He succumbs to it through death. All the cemeteries of the world bear witness to this. Man returns to the earth from which he was taken (Gen. 3.18). Today the church meditates on the mystery of death which is the common lot of man on earth. And yet the earth belongs to the Lord! 'The Lord's are the earth and its fullness.'

Can he who has been created in the image of God himself belong to the earth forever? Only and exclusively to the earth? Can the earth remain his only destiny? Must everything end with the fact that man becomes the dust of the earth?

All the cemeteries of the world contain in themselves this great and eternal question. If the earth is God's, then with greater reason – can he not be God's? He who has been created on the earth in God's own image and likeness?

Indestructible Life

In today's liturgy, we listen to the words of John the Apostle who writes thus in his first letter: 'See what love the Father has bestowed on us in letting us be called children of God! Yet that is what we are. The reason the world does not recognise us is that it never recognised the Son' (1 John 3.1). Man really is a son of God, adopted as a son in the eternal Son, the incarnate Word.

This man whom the earth seems to snuff out entirely through death by turning him back into dust – this very man if he has died in the grace of Christ – bears in himself the reality of indestructible life – of divine life!

All the cemeteries of the world contain this great mystery. Here are the sons of God, the sons and daughters in the eternal Son who in time became man. He became one of us. By the work of the Holy Spirit, he was born of the Virgin, died on the cross, and rose again from the dead. This is our faith that we profess.

All the cemeteries of the world share in Christ's cross and resurrection. The earth has been visited by the mystery of the Son of God. The earth has been visited by the mystery of the redemption. Death does not deprive us of humanity to turn us back into the 'dust of the earth'. Death restores us to God in Jesus Christ.

We Are God's Children

'We are God's children now; what we shall later be has not yet come to light. We know that when it comes to light we shall be like him, for we shall see him as he is' (1 John 3.2). We are living in the economy of divine revelation. God has spoken to us in his only Son. God, through this Son, accomplishes in us the mystery of sonship which is new life. Death ends irrevocably the life of each one of us. Here ends all the knowledge we can draw from the world. But revelation goes further – 'What we shall later be has not yet come to light.'

Death opens for human existence the dimension of eternity. What man bears in God's image and likeness rediscovers its own prototype: 'We shall see him as he is.' Hence, we look at all the cemeteries of the world as the place of man's death: 'It is appointed that men die once' (Heb. 9.27). At the same time, it is a place where men, our brothers and sisters, go up before the Lord's presence. It is the place where justice and mercy speak, the place of judgment.

'Who can ascend the mountain of the LORD? Or who may stand in his holy place? He whose hands are sinless, whose heart is clean . . . He shall receive a blessing from the LORD, a reward from God his saviour' (Ps. 24.3–5). 'It is appointed that men die once, and after death be judged' (Heb. 9.27).

In You, O Lord, Man Enjoys Eternity

And, behold, on this day remembered by the whole church, we pray for the deceased. We who are still pilgrims in this world unite ourselves to all those who have already left this world – to all those who rest in the cemeteries of the world. 'Such is the race that seeks for him, that seeks the face of the God of Jacob' (Ps. 24 [23].6).

May they be granted the pleasure of seeing his face! May they 'see him as he is'! May the revelation of man in God be accomplished in them in all its fullness!

Such is our prayer on the day of All Souls! Such is our prayer on the feast of All Souls – a prayer of intercession and simultaneously a prayer of praise. Blessed are you, O Lord, because yours is the earth and the fullness thereof. Blessed are you because man does not belong ultimately to the earth, because he is not subject to it. He enjoys eternity in you!

Readings for Ordinary Time

The Great Family of Man

Peace and brotherhood are necessary for the life of the local community, wider social groups, and the nation itself. The quality of life in a nation or that of any community depends on the presence or absence of peace and brotherhood. When there is an atmosphere of peace, extraordinary energies for good are released which give people joy and foster creativity, helping them reach full maturity and work together as sons and daughters of a loving God. Where a genuine brotherly spirit of co-operation exists the rights of the weak and of the defenceless are not trampled upon. The dignity and welfare of all are cared for and promoted. And there can only be peace where justice, freedom, and genuine respect for man's nature are fostered.

But the modern world is already accustomed to a lack of brotherhood and to ways that lead to violence, discrimination, and injustice. The world in which we face these problems proves trying to our own humanity. The quality of our communities and nations is threatened. It is a challenge that every nation in the world must face.

We need to see that the whole of mankind makes up a family. This is man's great family with all of its diversity. The cause of ensuring peace, international justice, and genuine solidarity among all peoples in the whole world is a growing aspiration of our time. It is expressed by the leaders of the nations and of international organisations. Programmes for peace are supported in various ways by almost all political parties in the world. Popular movements and public opinion support the same cause. In every country, people are tired of conflicts and divisions. The world longs for harmony and peace.

The Home of Men

The church of the twentieth century constantly appeals for justice and for true human development. In bishops' conferences, in local churches, and in many other ways, the church works towards harmony and brotherhood. Above all, she depends upon the contribution that Christian families give in their witness of Jesus' call to share brotherly love.

She does not cease to pray that God would give mankind a new spirit. That men's stony hearts would be changed into hearts of love. That there would be a true and lasting peace in so many areas of conflict in our world.

Indeed, the world is the home of individuals, of peoples, of nations, and of all mankind. The human race is more numerous than ever and is reaching a scientific and technological level of development that it has never known before. So we need to make ethical progress. We need to make progress in the things of the spirit. We need to make fully *human* progress.

At the same time, the earth – the home of men – belongs to God. The liturgy proclaims it in the words of the psalmist: 'Give to the LORD, you families of nations, give to the LORD glory and praise; give to the LORD the glory due his name! . . . Tremble before him, all the earth; say among the nations; The LORD is king. He has made the world firm, not to be moved; he governs the peoples with equity . . . for he comes to rule the earth. He shall rule the world with justice and the peoples with his constancy' (Ps. 96.7–10, 13). May this voice, which comes from the very heart of the church, join with the cry of prayer of all human families and praise the Creator of life and the source of love. May this voice become ever stronger. May it not remain unheard in heaven and on the earth!

Faith Must Be Lived at Home

The Christian home is not merely a community of human life. The precious gift of human life must be incorporated into and enriched by the very life of Christ. The family is rightly committed to preserve human values, but it must also focus on cultivating Christian values.

The members of the family can be tempted to think that only priests and religious have been entrusted with responsibility for the church. But this is far from being true. It is precisely at home that the children learn for the first time what it means to be 'sharers of the promise . . . in Christ Jesus . . . through the preaching of the gospel' (Eph. 3.6). As the Second Vatican Council teaches: 'Christian spouses are co-operators with grace and witnesses of faith to each other, to their children, and to other members of the family. They are for their children the first heralds of faith and Christian education; they form them in the Christian life by their word and by their example. They help them use prudence in choosing their vocation. They favour greatly priestly and religious vocations if their children are so called' (AA, 11).

The Christian family is the first place where vocations are developed. It is a seminary or a novitiate for the children. Let us get rid of the false idea that Christianity is practised only in church. Whatever takes place in the liturgy must be transferred to daily life. It must be lived at home. Then the home will become a place in which life in Christ grows and matures. Such a home is a true expression of the church.

For the Benefit of Society

The exercise of justice, which forms the basis of social life, does not limit or restrain the freedom of the human person when it corresponds to the nature of man and is not arbitrary. No, it aids him and guides him in making his own choices correspond to the common good. Marriage and family life are such natural institutions. They are rooted in the very being of the human person. Their specific good results in the benefit of the whole society. Their life aids us in making good and right choices.

In fact, the pastoral constitution *Gaudium et Spes* of Vatican II remarks, 'God did not create man a solitary being; from the beginning "male and female he created them" (Gen. 1.27). This partnership of man and woman constitutes the first form of communion between persons. Man, in fact, by his innermost nature, is a social being, and if he does not enter into relationships with others he can neither live nor develop his gifts' (n. 12).

Family and married life, which are the foundations of society, are the institutions which the whole civil and religious community must serve. If one understands that 'this society of man and woman is the first form of communion of human persons', one can fully perceive that every action that serves married and family life gives vigour to and benefits all communities and, ultimately, all of human society.

The True Good of Society

We see that the family as the 'first society' has its own natural demands and cannot be manipulated by ideologies or by the particular demands of society. In fact, it is society's duty to uphold and support the family by establishing laws and laying down moral values that will build up the common good. Any law or moral value that does not build up the family cannot be good for society as a whole, since the family is society's basic building block. What harms the family harms all of society. Every society that begins to tear down the family eventually realises this truth.

Public authorities and the scientific community need to see that the genuine demands of man and of society call for a collaboration between the civil and religious spheres to support the rights of the family. 'In pursuing its own salvific purpose,' the Second Vatican Council teaches, 'not only does the church communicate divine life to man, but in a certain sense it casts the reflected light of that divine life over all the earth, notably in the way it heals and elevates the dignity of the human person, in the way it consolidates society and endows the daily activity of men with a deeper sense and meaning' (GetS, 40). Therefore, in defending the Christian vision of marriage and of family life, the church also builds and reinforces the whole civil community with good, stable moral order.

In fact, obedience of the faithful in following church doctrine on marriage and the family helps ensure that those moral virtues which make justice possible – namely, faithfulness, respect for the person, a sense of responsibility, and mutual understanding – are reinforced for the good of all society.

The Health of the Family

We see that the rights of the family are not a merely spiritual and religious issue which civil society can ignore. The church promotes the fundamental values of the family and so responds to her mission. But civil authorities also bear the obligation to promote and safeguard those rights which help promote and support marriage.

The destiny of the human community is closely linked to the health of the family as an institution in society. When civil power ignores the values that the Christian family brings to society and when it behaves indifferently as a spectator of those ethical values, it leads to the breakdown of the family in society. At the same time, a permissive attitude about procreation outside the bounds of marriage may seem to solve some immediate problems. But, in the long run, it is very destructive to the nature and dignity of marriage. Such a society will reap bitter fruit!

The First School of Social Virtue

There are many other aspects of the life of the family which are good to recall. For instance, we must never forget the rights of the woman, the child, or the older person. Then there are also the rights of the family as a whole which I refer to in the apostolic exhortation *Familiaris consortio*. They have been compiled by the Holy See in the 'Charter of the Rights of Families'.

Even though all of these rights are important, I think it is timely to underline the duty parents have to educate their children. It is an important task of theirs to form in their offspring a full maturity in all the fundamental values of life. 'This educational function', Vatican II says, 'is so important that, if it is not present, it can hardly be substituted for. In fact, it behoves the parents to create in the midst of the family an atmosphere animated by love and piety towards God and towards men, which favours the full education of the children both in a personal and in a social sense. The family is therefore the first school of social virtues, of which all societies are in need' (GetS, 3).

Man's Work

Every man and every woman is a pilgrim on this earth – a pilgrim in search of truth, a pilgrim in search of God! And everyone is called to this pilgrimage. All of us are pilgrims, members of the people of God that the Creator and Father is leading towards full holiness in him. He is leading us towards himself through the experiences and trials of this life.

To teach us the way of life that leads to union with God, the Father has given us his Son. He has made his Son the cornerstone so that we can grow towards salvation

(1 Pet. 2.6–8). In fact, in Jesus Christ, we too become living stones 'built as an edifice of spirit, into a holy priesthood, offering spiritual sacrifices acceptable to God' (1 Pet. 2.5). These spiritual sacrifices are linked to all that makes up our life. They are especially linked to man's work, for work is the fundamental dimension of human life on earth.

The Dignity of Work

I would like to reflect on the value and dignity of human work. Jesus Christ was the son of a carpenter. He worked for most of his life on this earth plying the same trade of Joseph, his foster father. Through his carpentry, Jesus proclaimed that in daily life we are called to the dignity of work. The work of man is a participation in the creative work of God himself. Whether we work in a factory, in an office, in a hospital, in the fields, or in the home – we all participate in God's own creative activity, and this gives value and significance to all of our work. 'The criterion for determining the value of human work is not first of all the kind of work that one carries out, but the fact that the one who does it is a person' (LE, 6). It follows that all human work, no matter how humble it may seem, must be fully respected, protected, and justly rewarded. Then all families – indeed, the whole community – may live in peace, in prosperity, and make progress towards a better life.

Man Earns His Bread by the Sweat of His Brow

Work brings joy and satisfaction, but it also calls forth effort and brings exhaustion, especially after a long and hard day of work. Fulfilment and joy flow from work because it allows man and woman to exercise dominion over the earth which God has entrusted to them (Gen.

1.26–8). In fact, God said to the first man and to the first woman: 'Be fertile and multiply; fill the earth and subdue it. Have dominion over the fish of the sea, the birds of the air, and all living things that move on the earth' (Gen. 1.28).

However, the kind of work we do may not be what we prefer. Or perhaps it is dangerous. For instance, there are those who work the mines in the depths of the earth. Sometimes our work can also be hard, monotonous, and frustrating. Such is our human condition. It is written in the Bible that because of man's disobedience he has to earn his bread by the sweat of his brow. Also because of his disobedience, when man cultivates the ground, it does not yield its fruit easily (Gen. 3.16–19). Yet for the worker who puts his trust in God, the effort and fatigue he experiences are accompanied by the joy of knowing that he is partaking in the very work of God the Creator.

For those of us who are Christians, Jesus is the perfect model and inspiration for our work. In his work, Jesus remained in deep communion with his heavenly Father. Therefore, we need to meditate on the way Jesus carried out his daily work during the many years he spent in Nazareth. This is a great example for us all. Jesus' witness in his work as a carpenter fills us with joy and encourages us to persevere in our own humble service to man whatever our calling or profession.

The Dignity of Work Comes from God

We must not forget the reason why Jesus came into the world. Jesus came in order to accomplish the work of salvation. How did he accomplish it? Through his suffering and death on the cross and through the victory of his glorious resurrection. All of human work, no matter how insignificant it may appear to be, shares in this work of salvation. As I said in my encyclical on man's work: 'By enduring the fatigue of work in union with Christ who was crucified for us, man collaborates in some way with the Son of God in the redemption of mankind. He shows himself to be a true disciple of Jesus. He carries his cross every day through the work which he is called to carry out' (LE, 27).

The church strives to be faithful to Christ's example and witness by harbouring a unique concern for the welfare of workers. The famous encyclicals of the popes, beginning with Leo XIII's *Rerum Novarum*, have always defended the worker's right to fair pay and to just working conditions.

The teaching of the church is based on the principle that every human person is created in God's image and has a unique dignity given to him by God. Consequently, nobody must be used as a mere means of production, as if the person were a machine or a beast of burden. The church rejects any social and economic system which leads to the dehumanisation of workers. Besides her concern for just working conditions, the church insists on fair pay for workers, a wage that takes into account the needs of the workers' families. 'A just wage for the work of an adult person who has family responsibilities is whatever will be enough to establish and maintain a family in dignity and ensure its future' (LE, 19).

I Am Close to the Unemployed

I feel particularly close in my heart to so many unemployed people who want to work but cannot find a job. Perhaps it is because of discrimination based on religion, class, race, or language. Unemployment and underemployment create frustration and a sense of uselessness. They cause conflict in families and lead to anguish and sometimes unspeakable pain. Besides weakening the social fabric of society, they threaten the dignity of man and woman in the family. We must make new initiatives to solve this serious problem. Those initiatives will demand co-operation on a national and international level. It is extremely important that programmes designed to solve the problem of unemployment inspire respect and understanding between employers and those who are looking for jobs.

The Gospel of Work

Work is first a vocation for man. It is a sign of his nature as a rational being endowed with an intellect and with a will. He is created in God's image and is called to subdue all of creation.

In our response to this vocation, our model is Jesus. He worked during his first thirty years at home with St Joseph in the humble occupation of a carpenter in the small town of Nazareth. The feast of St Joseph on March 19th links then two different figures: the Son of God born of the Virgin and his legal father. They both laboured alongside each other as carpenters.

There is something we can learn from this humble profession and quiet time in the life of Christ. Those first thirty years of work and quiet discipline, in a certain sense, formed the warp and woof of the Saviour's growth in age, in wisdom, and in grace. God the Son as the Son of Man took upon himself the essential task of subduing the earth, a task which God had entrusted to man since the dawn of time.

The home of Nazareth and the workshop of St Joseph and Jesus are the heart and the focus of the *gospel of work*. This model of work shows us that more than the kind of work performed our attention should be on the persons who carry it out. Thus, we get a very clear picture of the religious and human value of work.

Man Is the First Priority in Work

The Christian vision of reality focuses on man and his dignity as a person created in God's image. That is why

I want to insist that man is always the first priority in work. This leads us to a very important point of ethics. Even though it is true that man is called and destined to work; nevertheless, work is first of all for man and not man for work. In the final analysis, the goal of any kind of work done by man – even if it is a simple service or a very monotonous and menial task – is always man himself (LE, 6).

Man is the axis around which the entire organisation of work must move. Work is a great thing. But man is incomparably greater. Man is sacred. And this sacredness is inviolable. It requires respect in every work situation for the human person.

Sacredness is the root from which all human prerogatives spring. We witness the mystery of the individual person: all those things which make man a full member of the social fabric. Any enterprise of work that wants to foster a morally healthy environment must respect this understanding of man.

In fact, business measures its own level of morality and ethics – often also its effectiveness in the marketplace – by the attitude it has towards human beings.

Technology, capital, profit, and everything that contributes to monetary success are things to be appreciated and rewarded inasmuch as they respect the dignity of man in the workplace. They must always be subordinate to man who is the first priority in any work situation.

Man Is Called to Value His Own Dignity

Man is called to value his own dignity in his work.

Unfortunately, various circumstances in the workplace seem to be conspiring against this important goal. Heavy work schedules, long hours, an overemphasis on the competence or productivity of workers, and various aspects of mechanisation are all taking their toll. They sometimes end up making work the master of man instead of man the master of his work.

Man begins to have the impression that he lives for work instead of working for a living.

I have been asked how this kind of situation should be faced. The problem involves the worker, his family, and the conditions in which he works. I believe I can basically answer this question. I am taking it from a significant statement which the Second Vatican Council has made its own: 'It is what a man is, rather than what he has, that counts' (GetS, 35). This is a maxim of the highest order.

Everyone must constantly seek in himself the truth of who his is. He must discover in his heart his natural bent or orientation in work. He must recognise his own limits and try to overcome them as much as possible. He must recognise his resources and gifts and make them bear fruit for God and others. The more we become really aware of who we are, the more we understand how to balance and harmonise our rights and duties as human persons.

Being a man is the basis on which both doing things and having things must be judged. It is the point of reference towards which all our activities must point. It is the basis for ensuring that no part of us becomes harmful to another part. All aspects of the person must be integrated. For example, the obligations placed on work in the life of a factory worker should help him grow in personal maturity in his family life and in the contribution that he makes to the community.

The Family Is a School of Work

I know that many businesses are run by families. The duty to support the family through making contributions to its human and social needs is a constant theme in the church's teaching. Since Leo XIII, the notion of a salary has always been linked to the size of the worker's family to meet the demands of justice. The same must be said in other areas of social life.

In the encyclical *Laborem Exercens*, I underline the central point of the family and work relationship: 'The family is both a community made possible by work and the first essential school of work for every man' (n.10). I also indicate in my encyclical the growing sense of urgency about motherhood. 'In our time, there is a social re-evaluation of motherly tasks, of the fatigue they cause, and of the need children have for care, love, and affection so they can develop as responsible persons who are morally and religiously mature and psychologically balanced' (n.19).

The close tie between family and work makes it even clearer that man works to live. The weariness of our body and mind after work is part of life. And man's life is sacred. Faith tells us that this life is a very great gift of God.

We must be consistent in valuing life in an absolute way from conception in the mother's womb to our natural death. The seed of life is as sacred as the last breath. Both demand the highest respect and care.

Man Is the First Factor in Work

Man is always the most important factor in any situation of work from start to finish. Thus, the degree of civilisation of a people is measured by their attitude towards those at the lower end of society who are in difficult work situations, facing underemployment or unemployment. In fact, one of the tragic dramas of our age is the high level of unemployment, especially among the young. How do we view and treat our unemployed?

We need to realise that forced inactivity is an evil situation. It creates an immobility which tends to paralyse hope itself. Dreams and ideals are threatened and sometimes left in shambles. The young person finds himself deprived of the opportunity to establish a family. We see in it incredible moral and psychological devastation. It requires our earnest reflection and urgent attention.

I repeat with strong emphasis that unemployment 'is in any case an evil; and when it takes on certain dimensions, it can become a real social calamity' (LE, 18). Unemployment is 'a plague' (ibid., n.8). A plague develops in weak or sick organisms. When a society finds itself prey to such a thing, it should seriously question its own health.

I urge you to use every means to examine and study this grave problem so we can begin to solve it. For instance, sociology and economics certainly have much to say about unemployment in light of the enormous technological transformations that have changed the modern working conditions of man.

In our search for answers, we must always remember that man is the first factor we must consider. His contribution to work is and will always be essential on the road to genuine progress. No machine – no matter how ingenious – can ever substitute for his intelligence.

Support for the Worker

When we stress the overriding value of man in the work place, it becomes clear that he cannot be sacrificed for the sake of more efficient automation. No, modern places of work must carefully safeguard man's right to work by implementing change of this sort only after very careful planning. With good will and foresight, many of those displaced by technological change can be re-trained and re-absorbed into the work force.

In this kind of a situation, the real meaning of the human person and his dignity must be the priority in any agreement or any change of job with the worker. Employers should try to be in a position to guarantee adequate employment to all their workers. I propose this approach especially to trade union organisations, whose task is the defence and promotion of the workers' rights. Trade unions cannot restrict their vision to only one category of worker. They must be concerned about the dignity of all men in the work place.

The Global Nature of the Problem of Work

The global nature of the problem of work is pressing in on us with an urgency that cannot be ignored any more. That is one of the perspectives of *Laborem Exercens*, which concurs with the need for international co-operation through treaties and agreements. 'It is necessary that the basis of these treaties be a call for more work for men. Understood as a fundamental right of all men, work gives the same rights to all those who labour, so that the standard of living of working men in all societies may show less often those shocking disparities in wage which are unjust and that can provoke even violent reactions' (LE, 18). Therefore, national governments face a task of enormous proportions.

Workers can also contribute to this great objective. They can do that through representation in international organisations where they have an active voice, such as the International Labor Organisation.

In the sphere of their own country, workers are expected to stimulate public opinion. In democratically ordered societies, this can contribute to policies that are conceived not on prejudices but on the basis of man's right to adequately support himself and his family. We must capture the vision of the common good of the whole human family, which demands that we overcome the gross disparities among nations in employment and economic wealth.

Together through this wide-ranging action, a *raison d'être* can be found for 'micro-achievements' of co-operation, experiments that show what we can do with this kind of vision for the world.

Man Does Not Live on Bread Alone

There is in life a clear hierarchy of values. We exalt work. It is just. We exalt man in his relationship to work. This is even more just. But man needs something that is beyond himself. He needs his daily bread, and yet he does not live on bread alone.

Man is always looking for something else, motivated by his inner life. The riches which are hidden in the inner recesses of his heart are innumerable. The sense of goodness, of beauty, of generosity, of nostalgia and hope, the fascination of mystery, the ethical and moral sense, openness to justice, to freedom, to solidarity or co-operation – all these lie hidden in the heart.

Man becomes more of a man the more he succeeds in going beyond himself. Therein lies the horizon of the great spiritual values which go beyond sensible experience and make up the supernatural world.

Thus, my reflections today journey back to the religious heart of the *gospel of work*. When she draws near the worker and when she promotes dignity without distinctions of race, creed, nationality, and social class, the church is acting by virtue of the mission entrusted to her by Christ. Christ has been and he continues to be man's greatest ally and advocate. For us men and for our salvation – as we profess in the creed – he came down from heaven and became one of us.

Whoever believes in him finds at every turning point the light that can guide him. Under the cross of Christ, work is a way of human perfection and a supernatural call. It is a way to holiness. It never loses its meaning in this light.

As our Catholic laity mature in Christ – which is a fruit of the Council – an understanding of the spiritual nature of work is spreading. It is a spirituality which must be deepened by seeking to bring love, true brotherhood, and the peace of Christ into the work place.

The Product and the Tool of Man's Work

Technology and sophisticated machines are products and tools of human work. The real subject of work remains only man himself. A tool or an instrument cannot be raised to the level of the subject. It cannot be placed above the working man or user without overturning the order of reality. This would indeed be an unfortunate reversal of the means and the ends of work. The experience of modern times confirms that technology, if its use is not guided and enlightened by a higher moral order, can change from an ally into an adversary of man. An example of this is when automation in the factory supplants man and deprives many labourers of their jobs. Another example would be where the machine is exalted and man is reduced to merely serving it (LE, 5).

We are called to be masters of the earth and of change and not to be ruled by it. But this can only happen if we succeed in overcoming the break between ethics and economics which has prevented the great achievements of the modern age from working wholly for man's good.

Finding Ways to Understand Each Other

Whereas in the past the tendency was to present work as the only source and the only measure of man's value, in our days we see the emergence of a new so-called *functional* perspective. According to this view, work can only have meaning through earning income at an occupation. Precisely because of this it becomes more urgent than ever to recapture the conviction that 'work is a fundamental dimension of man's existence on earth' (LE, 4). But this must be qualified by the understanding that work is not the ultimate goal. No, it is always subordinate to man who is always the end and the goal of work (LE, 6).

From this truth, an important appeal goes out to all men: the appeal for co-operation and solidarity. In all things, men have always needed to extend help and co-operation to each other so they can grow together. Solidarity has its laws: it requires that no one lords it over the other. Instead, each party is willing to welcome the contributions of others in a constructive way. This applies for both individual businesses and for the entire production process. It also applies in a broad sense to all of social life.

The Benefits and the Duties of Work

We are able to see the complementary roles of everyone involved in work and production when we view it in the co-operative spirit of solidarity. Entrepreneurs and leaders have their function as decision-makers to safeguard the unity, co-ordination, and dynamism of business.

Independent workers take upon themselves the responsibilities, commitments, and risks of work in the free enterprise system. They bring flexibility and initiative to the whole production process and are adequately compensated by the principle that neither the state nor society can restrict the initiative and free choice of the individual (Instruction of the Sacred Congregation for the Doctrine of Faith, *Christian Freedom and Liberation*, n. 73).

Dependent workers, in turn, have the right to a just wage that provides an adequate standard of living for themselves and their families. They also participate with joint responsibility in the initiatives and decisions that affect the life of the business and, therefore, their own future. Besides, they operate in such a way that there is dignity and room for creativity in their work. Thus, they are able to feel like genuine *co-proprietors* at their place of work (LE, 14–15).

We know that every right carries with it a duty. This principle of justice and equity governs not only our reciprocal relationships but also the contribution that everyone is called to make to the common good. If we want a more just society and a better quality of life, all of us must know how to look beyond our own particular and immediate advantage. We must be willing to carry our own share of the responsibility so everyone can benefit from the common good that results.

Overcoming Trials with Dignity

Responding to a long-felt need, I have decided to form a special 'Pontifical Commission for the Pastoral on Health Workers'. The commission is called to encourage and co-ordinate the activities of the various health care workers serving the church, to study the programmes and initiatives for health workers in different countries, and to draw together implications for the pastoral work of health workers.

In my apostolic trips, especially to developing nations, I have seen that the world of health is a place of struggle for man. For example, technology tends to demand more attention, yet it does not always safeguard the person's rights.

Suffering, disease, and death are fundamental to human life. We must all work with one another to solve in a human way the problems that such realities entail. Helping the sick one to overcome his sickness with dignity is certainly the service that mankind expects from science, from technology, and from the use of medicine. But this is not possible without a clear vision of the need for absolute respect for the human being. After all, the human is the only creature who transcends material reality because of his spiritual nature. This must be our constant point of reference if we really want to avoid consequences in the medical field that could cause great social ills. We must respect the dignity of the human person, including his spiritual side.

Collaborators of Life

In the Christian view, man, created in God's image, is the highest expression of life in the universe. Man's goal is God, and the goal of the universe is man. Just as the Creator has set in motion the cosmic laws that govern the natural universe, so he has written in human nature the universal norms of behaviour, which are not open to sub-jective interpretations or changing views.

Yes, there are essential values and rights that are linked to the human dignity and eternal destiny of the individual person. They start with the right to life which should be defended throughout its existence. In fact, it is threatened now more than ever from the moment of its kindling to the hour of its passing. When we respect these norms we start to co-operate with life. Otherwise, we become agents of death. Let us say 'yes' to life!

A Journalist's Identity

The search for a new identity by journalists is an important development. In a certain way, it is an issue at all times. A journalist who wants to exercise his profession seriously – no matter what sector has been entrusted to him in the mass media – discovers that he is constantly asked to evaluate his work. He is called to become ever more aware of his function and his responsibility in the modern world.

In our day, such scrutiny is particularly urgent. In fact, journalism finds itself at the crossroads of changes that are transforming the way we live. The so-called technological revolution is on the cutting edge of these changes. It is making new demands on man. As a result, we need new resources and new difficulties spring up to challenge modern man. Important choices become imperative.

In the midst of these changes and choices, the journalist has the important duty to communicate them accurately and fairly. That way an informed and intelligent public will have the information they need to make the right choices. Thus, the journalist is an effective agent for the civil, spiritual, and moral good of man.

The Man of Truth

With all of the changes and problems that are emerging in our day, there cannot be anything less than respect for the truth – an absolute and total respect without any ambiguity. This is the call of the journalist. He must be faithful to the truth.

In fact, given the power and the speed of the mass media in transmitting news today, a journalist cannot help but feel the burden of his responsibility for society. Therefore, he must be a man of truth. The attitude he takes towards the truth is key to his identity as a reporter of the facts. His professionalism is rooted in his integrity as a person, his commitment to the truth. He must constantly juggle two loyalties in his work. Above all, he must be faithful to his own mission as a purveyor of the truth. Secondly, he must be faithful to the public trust he establishes with his readers or viewers.

The journalist must have the conviction to expose falsehoods and misconceptions with a forthrightness and a sincerity. Such a call is particularly important in dealing with our current problems. We need to squarely face the truth and lay aside falsehood if we are going to solve our problems.

Filled with the Divine Spirit

After leading the Israelites out of slavery in Egypt, Moses arranged for the construction of the tent, the first portable temple in the desert. So he assigned the task to men filled with the 'divine spirit'. And, after having called the artists by name, the Lord endowed them with wisdom. He gave them the gifts they needed to conceive their projects and carry out all the construction necessary for the sanctuary (Exod. 35.30–55; 36.1).

As we can see in this chapter of Exodus, what we now call sacred art has ancient and illustrious beginnings. From the depths of my heart I want to tell you that the believing artist must be aware that artistic talent is a gift from God. The artist must be grateful to God and devote himself to faithfully follow the vocation he has received. The Christian artist can trust that God will give him that 'divine spirit' which makes natural talent spiritually fruitful, especially when he is called to execute works of religious and liturgical art.

It is quite true that the genius of an artist can create eminent works that lie outside his religious faith. But, if alongside natural talent, the artist consciously seeks to live out the theological virtues – faith, hope, and love – they become a powerful encouragement for his work. His art becomes illuminated and informed by the mysteries of the Christian faith.

In this light, we can understand the exquisite detail of the medieval cathedrals. Outside the bounds of faith, we cannot fully understand it. Such is the case with the genius which informs the works of Giotto, Fra Angelico, Michelangelo, the poetry of Dante, the prose of Manzoni, the musical compositions of Pierluigi da Palestrina – to mention just a few.

Benefactors of Mankind

Artists are counted among the greatest benefactors of mankind. They are some of the most effective workers for mankind's salvation since they nourish man's sense of spirituality. When man contemplates art and its beauty, he abandons himself to it as a source of inspiration. His spiritual sense is heightened. Man feels and senses the fascination of pure spirituality. He glimpses God who is the origin and goal of all created spirituality.

Deeply aware of all this, the church 'has always favoured liberal arts, and has always sought their noble service . . . ; she has allowed the artistic forms of every age. Thus, she has formed through the course of the centuries an artistic treasure that is to be preserved with the greatest care' (SC, 43).

Also the arts of our time – of all peoples and nations – find freedom of expression in the church as long as they serve God with due reverence and honour.

The Value of the Spirit

In Christian art, the freshness and newness of religious experience have been eminently expressed through works which can be considered glorious manifestations of the spirit. With beautiful variety these works reveal the perception and awareness that believers have had of salvation throughout the centuries and up to our own day. It is tradition which gathers those diverse forms of art and then offers to all generations that which the church believes and hopes. Thus, it can be welcomed, understood, and lived out daily by the inspired believer.

The riches guarded in the practice and life of the people of God are revealed by art in such a worthy way that they allow one to glimpse in their harmony the value of the spirit, the passionate relationship between man and God, and the encounter with the Word made flesh.

It is a loving hand and heart – not deprived of suffering – which stamps on matter the face of pilgrim man and the reflection of the infinite majesty of the Creator. Thus, we stand before the great canvases and sculptures of Christian art down through the centuries.

The Inspiring Function of Sacred Art

The Incarnation has made possible the interpretation of the mystery of God through sensible signs, revealing God's presence to men. With this event, the Word has come to form part of history: the God-man has been seen, known, and loved. Christian art records Christ's visible humanity and his divine actions, while with the transparence of its language it opens up man to perceive some aspect of the unspeakable nature of God.

Beauty united to truth shines in every being, disclosing its intimate secret to the sons of men. Consequently, art is authentic when it is clothed in the signs of beauty and truth. It then becomes universal, legible, and understandable to man. Man receives it with joy, and his spirit draws from it encouragement for great and noble things.

The church holds in high esteem true art since she sees in it a fundamental expression of culture and of humanity. She is also convinced that faith can exercise and has often exercised on artistic creation an inspiring function that touches the heart and spirit of man. 'Among the noblest activities of human ingenuity,' teaches the Second Vatican Council, 'liberal arts are counted in full right, and specially religious art and its summit, sacred art. They, by their own nature, are related to infinite divine beauty, which must be in some way expressed by man's works. They are all the more orientated towards God and towards the increase of his praise and glory, inasmuch as they have been assigned no other goal than to contribute as effectively as possible with their works, to direct the minds of men towards God' (SC, 122).

Man Becomes More Human Through Music

Music has a universal language. It is able to arouse deep emotions, to transmit noble feelings, and to awaken states of mind corresponding to the musician's fervour. Mankind needs the beauty of music, which sounds the spirit, raises the soul, elevates the sensibilities, and helps to lift one's eyes to God with a feeling of joy. We could say that, in some way, man becomes more human and more Christian through the art of music.

I am saying this while I also think of the significant and unique associating value which music develops. Just as in the assonance of more notes harmony is created, so the practice of music in a group produces solidarity, unity of hearts, and friendship. It would not be possible to practise music without allowing yourself to become involved in a common movement, in a conscious tuning of intentions, in an agreement of sounds and of actions. In this sense, art can be considered an invitation to participate in a common and noble work which elevates and strengthens sentiment.

Such a way of thinking appears even more valid when music gives joy to feasts and celebrations of the community. In that way, people experience feelings of joy and of prayer, of enthusiasm, and of deep action – as music succeeds in inspiring service to God and others.

Music as art is therefore an appeal to meditate on beauty which springs from God, and an invitation to consider the harmony of creation. Thus, may all of us know how to praise God using music, following the wonderfully harmonised words of Haydn in the famous oratoria *The Creation*: 'Choirs of men, choirs of the worlds, voices, orchestras – may all resound: Praised be God for eternity!'

Valuing the Body

Through sports, we value the body. We achieve the best physical condition possible with remarkable results that bring great satisfaction. From our Christian faith, we know that, by Baptism, the human person in his totality and wholeness of body and soul becomes a temple of the Holy Spirit: 'You must know that your body is a temple of the Holy Spirit, who is within – the Spirit you have received from God. You are not your own. You have been purchased, and at a price! So glorify God in your body' (1 Cor. 6.19).

Sports are a struggle to win a contest and achieve some goal. But from our Christian faith we know that the 'incorruptible crown' of eternal life is more valuable than any earthly prize. It is God's gift, but it is also the result of a daily conquest in the exercise of virtue. And there is a really important contest, according to Paul. He tells us: 'Set your hearts on the greater gifts' (1 Cor. 12.31). Paul is telling us to set our hearts on the gifts that advance God's kingdom. Those gifts will reap a reward that will have eternal benefits for us if we persevere in running the race.

The Ethics of Sports

St Paul emphasises the inner spiritual meaning of sports: 'Athletes deny themselves all sorts of things' (1 Cor. 9.25). He is acknowledging that balance, self-discipline, soberness, and ultimately virtue are implicit in the practice of sports.

To be a dedicated sportsman you need to be honest with yourself and with others. You need loyalty and moral strength more than physical strength. You need perseverance, a spirit of co-operation and friendship, magnanimity, generosity, an openness of mind and heart – all of these are requirements of a moral order. But the Apostle

Paul suddenly adds: 'They [that is, athletes in Greek and Roman stadiums] do this to win a crown of leaves that withers, but we a crown that is imperishable' (ibid.). In these words we find an outline for an ethic of sports and even a theology that highlights all of its values.

A Treasure for the Young

Because old age is a stage of life which is lived out with great effort and love, we must give support and help to all those movements that reach out to the elderly to draw them out of a life of mistrust, of loneliness, and of resignation. We must help them become sources of wisdom, witnesses of hope, and workers of charity.

The first environment in which we need to help our senior citizens is the family. Their wisdom and experience is a treasure for young spouses. In their first difficulties of married life, they can find in their aged parents the confidants to whom they can open up and from whom they can seek counsel. The grandchildren, in turn, will find in the example and affectionate care of their grandparents a compensation for the absence of their parents, which is so frequent today for a number of reasons.

In society itself, we have always trusted in the counsel of mature persons who have the stability and the wisdom that we lack. Yes, we need our senior citizens to give us the benefit of their prudence and experience. They will help us build a wiser and a more balanced society.

Tasks of the Aged and Duties of the Young

By announcing to a young person his own faith in God, the senior citizen preserves a fruitful spirit which does not fade with the declining of health and strength: 'They shall bear fruit even in old age; vigorous and sturdy shall they be, declaring how just is the Lord' (Ps. 92.15–16). To the tasks of the aged correspond the duties of the young, particularly the duty to listen to them: 'Reject not the tradition of old men' (Sir. 8.9); 'Ask your father and he will inform you, ask your elders and they will tell you' (Deut. 32.7). Young people have also the duty to assist them: 'Take care of your father when he is old; grieve him not as long as he lives. Even if his mind fail, be considerate with him; revile him not in the fullness of your strength' (Sir 3.12–13).

No less rich is the teaching of the New Testament where St Paul presents the ideal of the life of the elderly with concrete words of advice on soberness, dignity, good judgement and stability in faith, in love, and in patience (Tit. 2.2). A very significant example is that of Simeon, who lived in anticipation and hope of seeing the Messiah. He proclaimed Christ as the fullness of life and the hope of the future for himself and for all men.

The Aged Person: A Teacher of Life

With increase in years, with declining strength, and with lingering sickness, the older person feels increasingly the physical frailty and, above all, the burden of life. These problems of old age cannot find meaning if they are not felt and lived by everyone as a reality of life. We are called to value the elderly person because of every man's dignity and because of the meaning of life, which is always a gift.

The Scripture often speaks about the elderly. It considers old age a gift that is renewed and must be lived every day in openness to God and one's neighbour.

Already in the Old Testament, the old man is considered, above all, a teacher of life: 'How becoming to the aged is wisdom . . . ! The crown of old men is wide experience; their glory, the fear of the Lord' (Sir. 25.5–6). The old person has yet another important task. He hands on God's word to the new generation: 'O God, our ears

have heard, our fathers have declared to us, the deeds you
did in their days' (Ps. 44.2).

The Work of Divine Renewal

'When he comes . . . the Spirit of truth . . . will give
glory to me, because he will have received from me what
he will announce to you. All that the Father has belongs
to me. That is why I said that what he will announce to
you he will have from me' (John 16.13–15).

That is what Christ said on the eve of his passion. He
was speaking about the Father, about himself, and about
the Spirit . . . The Spirit is he who, in the fulfilment of
the economy of salvation, 'takes from the Son'. He takes
what belongs to the Son and that which, in the Son,
belongs to the Father: 'All that the Father has belongs to
me.'

Man, the Image of God

Man, who is created in the image of God, is at once a
spiritual and a physical being. He is linked to the physical
world through his humanity, yet he also transcends the
physical world because he is spirit. Man is a person. This
truth about man is part of our faith. Scripture reveals that
God made man in his own 'image and likeness'. This truth
about man's nature has been constantly presented down
through the centuries by the Magisterium, the teaching
authority of the church.

The truth about man's nature does not cease to be exam-
ined intellectually through the study of philosophy or
other human sciences. We can see this in the study of
anthropology. We see that man is an incarnate spirit or a
spirit housed in a body. Or we should say he is a body
shaped in an immortal spirit. This can be inferred in some

way by studying the account of creation in the book of Genesis. We should especially examine the Yahwistic account which makes use of anthropomorphic images. In it, we read that 'the LORD God formed man out of the clay of the ground and blew into his nostrils the breath of life, and so man became a living being' (Gen. 2.7).

The Breath of Life

The development of this biblical text in Genesis allows us to understand clearly that man, thus created, is distinct from the whole visible world, especially from the world of animals. The 'breath of life' has made man capable of knowing the animals, of giving them names, and of recognising himself as different from them (Gen. 2.18–20). Even though the Yahwistic account of man's creation does not speak about the 'soul', it is still easy to infer from the account that man's life is such that it transcends the mere physical life of the animals. That life reaches beyond the material to the dimension of the spirit. Herein lies the essential foundation of that 'image of God' which Genesis 1.27 sees in man.

What Is Man?

Man is a unity. He is someone who is one within himself. But in this unity, a duality is contained. The holy Scriptures present both the unity (the person) and the duality (soul and body). One can think about the book of Sirach, which says, for example: 'the LORD from the earth created man, . . . and makes him return to earth again.' But Sirach also says: 'He forms men's tongues and eyes and ears, and imparts to them an understanding heart. With wisdom and knowledge he fills them; good and evil he shows them' (17.1–2, 5–6).

From this point of view, Psalm 8 is especially significant. It exalts man as a masterwork by addressing God with these words: 'What is man that you should be mindful of him, or the son of man that you should care for him? You have made him little less than the angels, and crowned him with glory and honour. You have given him rule over the works of your hands, putting all things under his feet' (vs. 5–7).

The Duality of Man

It is often stressed that biblical tradition highlights above all man's personal unity, using the term 'body' or 'flesh' to refer to man as a whole (Ps. 145.21; Joel 3.1; Isa. 66.23; John 1.14). This observation is accurate. But this does not deny that in the biblical tradition the duality of man is also present, sometimes in a very clear fashion. This tradition is reflected in Christ's words: 'Do not fear those who deprive the body of life but cannot destroy the soul. Rather, fear him who can destroy both body and soul in Gehenna' (Matt. 10.28).

Unity and Duality

The Bible allows us to consider man as a personal unity and, at the same time, as a duality of soul and body. This is a notion that has been expressed in the whole of tradition and in the teaching of the church. This teaching includes not only the Bible but also the theological interpretations of Scripture.

The analysis has developed under the influence of certain schools (such as that of Aristotle) of Greek thought. It has been a slow work of reflection which reached a fullness through the works of St Thomas Aquinas. We see this in the statements about man at the Council of Vienne in 1312. In the council documents, the soul is called the 'form' of the body: 'form of the human body, by itself and essentially' (DS, 902). This 'form' determines the very substance of man's being and is of a spiritual nature. Further, the spiritual 'form of man', the soul, is immortal. That is what was taught authoritatively by the Fifth Lateran Council in 1513: The soul is immortal, as opposed to the body which is subject to death (DS, 1440).

The school of thought founded by St Thomas Aquinas also teaches that because of the substantial union of body and soul, the soul yearns after death to be re-united to the body. And this theological understanding is confirmed by the revealed truth of the resurrection of the body.

Man, God's Image

Even though the philosophical terms we use for expressing the unity and complexity (duality) of man may be criticised at times, the unity of the human person and his spirit-body duality are fully rooted in the holy Scripture and in tradition. The view is often expressed that man is 'God's image' because of the soul. Yet traditional doctrine does not exclude the view that the body also participates in the dignity of 'God's image', just as it participates in the full dignity of the person as both spirit and body.

Evolution

In modern times, the theory of evolution has raised a particular difficulty with the revealed doctrine that man is created as a being made up of both a soul and a body. Many scientists who study the origins of man hold that not only is there a link between man and all of nature but that man also evolved from higher animal species. This problem of man's origins has created widespread public debate. It has been a primary concern of many scientists for over a century.

The answer of the Magisterium is found in Pius XII's encyclical *Humani Generis* of 1950. In it we read: 'The Magisterium of the church has nothing against the doctrine of evolution, inasmuch as it seeks the origin of the human body in a pre-existing and living matter – for the Catholic faith commands us to hold that the souls have been created directly by God – but in such a way that it is subject to research and discussion by the experts . . .' (DS, 3896). So from the point of view of doctrine, there is no difficulty believing that man's body evolved from higher animal species. But it is important to remember that evolution is only a theory. It states a probability or a likelihood that something is true. It is not a scientific certainty. On the other hand, the doctrine of faith teaches with certainty that the spiritual soul of man is created directly by God.

What this means is that it is possible the human body was prepared step by step for man, following an order established by the Creator. But the human soul cannot emerge from matter since it is spiritual in nature. And it is the very thing on which man's destiny ultimately depends.

Man Transcends the Universe

The Second Vatican Council speaks of man's origins in creation where it says: 'As a unity of soul and body, man synthesizes in himself by his very bodily condition the elements of the material world in such a way that these elements, through man, touch their vertex' (GetS, 14). And further along, the Council Fathers state: 'Man, however, is not mistaken when he acknowledges himself as being superior to bodily things and when he considers himself as something more than merely a small part of nature. . . . In fact, in his inner nature, he transcends the universe.' Thus, we see how the truth about the unity and the duality of human nature can be expressed in a language which is understandable to the modern world.

Man and Woman

'God created man in his image; in the divine image he created him; male and female he created them' (Gen. 1.27). Man and woman are created with equal dignity as persons who share the same unity of spirit and body. Yet they differ physically and psychologically. In fact, the human being bears the mark of both masculinity and femininity.

While this is a mark of difference, it is also an indication of complementarity; man and woman are meant to complement each other. This is what we can deduce from reading the Yahwistic account of creation. Man, as he sees the newly created woman, exclaims: 'This one, at last, is bone of my bones and flesh of my flesh' (Gen. 2.23). These are words of contentment and great joy as man beholds a being who is essentially similar to himself.

This is the richness of God's creation of mankind. There is psychological and physical diversity between the sexes, and yet they complement each other. Such is the unique heritage of Adam's descendants all throughout their history. It is from this reality that marriage takes its life. Marriage is instituted by the Creator from the very beginning: 'That is why a man leaves his father and mother and clings to his wife, and the two of them become one body' (Gen. 2.24).

Be Fertile

The text of Genesis 2.24 is matched by the blessing of fruitfulness recorded in Genesis 1.28: 'Be fertile and multiply; fill the earth and subdue it. . . .' We see that marriage and the family – which are part of the mystery of the creation of man – are linked to the commandment to 'subdue' the earth. This commandment is entrusted by the Creator to the first human couple.

Man is called to subdue the earth, but he must be careful. He has been called to subdue it, not to devastate it, for creation is a gift of God and deserves our respect. Man and woman are called to subdue the earth together. This relationship between man and woman must be based on mutual giving of the self. Out of this union is born the family and society.

Man is the image of God not only because he is male and female but because of the reciprocal relationship of the sexes. This relationship forms the soul and heart of the 'communion of persons'. It becomes a reality through the Sacrament of Marriage and bears a resemblance to the union of the three divine persons in the Trinity.

Along these lines, the Second Vatican Council tells us: 'God did not create man leaving him alone; but from the beginning "male and female he created them" (Gen. 1.27), and their union constitutes the first form of the "communion of persons." Man, in fact, is by his intimate nature a social being, and without relationships with others he cannot live or exercise his capabilities' (GetS, 12).

Man Among the Creatures

In the order of creation, man has a whole set of relationships: his relationship to the world, the relationship between man and woman, and his relationship with his fellows. Man's call to 'subdue the earth' shows us the relational character of man's life. He rules over the creation, rears up a family with his spouse, and forms a society with his fellows for the common good. These relationships are proper to the human person as God's image. They establish from the very beginning the role of man among the creatures. It is for this destiny that man has been called into existence as a subject (as a concrete 'I'), endowed with an intellect, a conscience, and freedom.

The ability to reason and to think radically distinguishes man from the whole world of the animals. Animals can only perceive things through their senses. But man's intellect enables him to discern and to distinguish between truth and falsehood. This opens up for him the fields of science, of critical thought, and of philosophy and theology. Because of the very nature of man, he perceives the truth in things. He stands in a relationship to the truth which determines his character as a creature with a spiritual destiny. The knowledge of truth encompasses all of man's relationships with the world and with other men. It lays an indispensable foundation for all forms of culture.

Man Is Able to Choose Between Good and Evil

Besides the intellect and its relationship to the truth, man has the will to choose. And this will to choose is integrally connected to the good. Human acts include both an act of the will and the ability to choose.

With this foundational understanding of man, the area of morals comes into focus. We see that man is able to choose between good and evil guided by the voice of his conscience. This conscience leads man to do good and causes him to pull back from doing evil.

Clearly, man's free will affects his relationship with the world, with his fellows, and makes him aspire towards the things of God. As we saw earlier, the same holds for man's pursuit of the truth. In fact, man's spiritual nature is integral to his abilities to reason and to choose freely. He finds himself from the beginning in a special relationship with God. The creation account in Scripture (Gen.

1–3) shows us that 'God's image' is revealed above all in the relationship of the human 'I' to the divine 'Thou'. Man knows God, and his heart and will are able to unite with God. Man is capable of union with God! Man can say 'yes' to God. He can also say 'no'. He is capable of welcoming God and his will, but he is also capable of opposing God and his designs.

The Law of Life

This mystery of man made in 'God's image' is presented in other books of Scripture. For instance, in the book of Sirach we read: 'The Lord from the earth created man, and in his own image he made him . . . and makes him return to earth again. He endows man with a strength of his own, and with power over all things else on earth. He puts the fear of him in all flesh, and gives him rule over beasts and birds. He forms men's tongues and eyes and ears, and imparts to them an understanding heart. With wisdom and knowledge he fills them; good and evil he shows them. He looks with favour upon their hearts, and shows them his glorious works. . . . He has set before them knowledge, a law of life as their inheritance; an everlasting covenant he has made with them, his commandments he has revealed to them' (Sir. 17.1, 2b–7, 9–10). Ponder upon this rich and profound passage from Sirach. Reflect upon it in your hearts and draw near to God.

Conscious and Free Choices

The Second Vatican Council expresses the same truth about man in words that are both timeless and relevant to today. 'Man can turn to good only in freedom. . . . The dignity of man requires him to act according to conscious and free choices. . . .' (GetS, 17). 'In his inner being, he transcends the universe: to those depths he returns when he enters his heart, where God, who searched the heart, awaits him; where, under God's watchful eye, he decides his own destiny' (GetS, 14). True human freedom is freedom founded in the truth. From the very beginning it has revealed the image of God in man. Yes, the truth sets man free to be fully himself in Christ.

The Covenant with God

We have just described a striking image of man as one who can know and reason to reach the truth at the heart of things. He can freely choose to do what is right and good. Thus, he is called to discern his fellows' true needs and establish justice. He is normally called to marriage where he gives himself freely to the other and establishes a communion of persons. Out of this unity comes the family and society.

But this is not all. He is also called to enter into a covenant with God. In fact, he is not only a creature of his Creator but also the image of his God. This special relationship between God and man makes a covenant possible. We witness this covenant in the account of creation in the first three chapters of Genesis. It is God's sovereign initiative as the Creator that establishes the covenant. And it remains unchanged throughout salvation history until God establishes the eternal covenant with man in Jesus Christ.

Openness to the Supernatural Life of God

Man can enter into a covenant relationship with God since he has been created in God's own image. This makes him capable of knowing the truth and choosing what is right and good. In fact, man's likeness to God is the basis for the call to participate in the inner life of God. Thus, God is able to reveal supernatural realities to men.

This is a great mystery that God has revealed to us. He has made us in his own image and likeness not only so that we can be fully human but so that we can share the divine life of God. What an undeserved grace and marvel! In other words, the Father, Son, and Holy Spirit have provided us with all the revelation and graces we need to share the very life of God. We have all we need to attain our full destiny in Christ and grow in God's supernatural life.

Divine Providence

'We believe in one God, the Father, the Almighty, maker of heaven and earth.' This first article of the Creed will never cease pouring out extraordinary riches for us. God the Father is Creator of 'all things seen and unseen'. He rules all created things with his divine providence.

Today with this reflection on creation, we begin a series of teachings on the topic of God's providence. This providence lies at the heart of the Christian faith and in the heart of every man called to faith. God is our almighty and wise Father. He is present and at work in the world. Through his divine providence, he provides for all of his creatures so they can live out their lives in his presence. He provides for us and our needs in a special way, since we are created in his image and likeness. God our Father desires that our journey be guided by his truth and his love as we head towards the goal of eternal life in him.

Why Has God Created Us?

'Why has God created us?' That is a question we pose in Christian catechesis or teaching on the Christian life. Enlightened by the great faith of the church, we are to repeat – both young people and adults – these words: 'God has created us to know him and to love him in this life and to dwell with him forever in the next.'

This is a great and sure truth about God. He is our heavenly Father who guides our lives with his gentle, loving touch. He wants us to be with him forever.

Paradoxically, we tend to be torn by doubt and double-mindedness at times. We are called to entrust our lives completely to this providential God. As the psalmist tells us: 'I have stilled and quieted my soul like a weaned child. Like a weaned child on its mother's lap, [so is my soul within me]' (Ps. 131.2). Yet we are afraid to abandon ourselves to God as our Lord and Saviour at times. Our mind may be darkened by problems. We forget about our Creator. Or we are really suffering and we doubt God's love for us as our Father.

Yet God's heart of providence is very close to us when we suffer. There are many examples in Scripture. For instance, Job does not hesitate to cry out to God, even in the midst of his suffering. Job shows amazing confidence in God. This confidence is not unfounded. The Word of God does indicate that the providence of God, his saving power, is poured out on his people in their hour of greatest need, for they are his children. Job, sick in his body and in his heart, exclaims: 'Oh, that today I might find him, that I might come to his judgment seat! I would set out my cause before him, and fill my mouth with arguments' (Job 23.3–4). Let us come today before our Father with our needs!

God's Action in the World

Let us remember that we are not alone when we try to understand God's saving action in the world. Great philosophers, the doctrines of the great religions, and even the man on the street have all wrestled with this difficult question. Some even try to justify God's action through some kind of argument.

Many answers have been offered and not all of them are acceptable. None of them are exhaustive. There are some who have resorted to blind fate or fortune since ancient times. There are others who have jeopardised man's free will with their emphasis on predestination. In our own age, there are some who think they need to deny God to affirm man and his freedom.

These are all extreme and one-sided positions which, at least, help us realise what truths are at stake when we try to understand divine providence. How can God's all-powerful action fit in with our freedom? And how can our freedom fit in which his unfailing plans? What will out future be like? How can we ever begin to understand and recognise his infinite wisdom and truth in the face of the world's evils? What about the moral evil of sin? What about the suffering of the innocent?

Our Reasons for Hope

This history of ours – with the rise and fall of nations, with its terrible catastrophes and its sublime acts of greatness and of holiness – what does it all mean? Can it be that a final cataclysm will bury forever all kinds of life? Or else we wonder if there is really a providential and positive being whom we call God. This God who surrounds us with his intelligence, his tenderness, his wisdom. This God who leads us firmly yet gently. This God who guides our world, our life, and even our rebellious will if it yields to him. This God who leads us towards the rest of the 'seventh day', the rest of a creation that is nearing its fulfilment.

Here is the answer. The Word stands poised between hope and despair. Yes, the Word of God gives us great reasons for hope. It is ever new, so splendid is the Word of God. It baffles the human mind with its incredible message.

The Word of God

The Word of God does not take on this much greatness and fascination until we are confronted with man's deepest questions about life. Then we recall with deep meaning that God is here. He is Emmanuel, God-with-us (Isa. 7.14). And in Jesus of Nazareth, dead and risen, God's Son and our brother has 'made his dwelling among us' (John 1.14).

In fact, all of the church's trials through time lead her to constantly and passionately renew her desire for God's abiding presence. In this pursuit, she is always guided by the example of Christ and by the power of the Spirit.

This is why the church must speak out and give the world God's grace and an abiding sense of God's providence. She must share about this incredible love so man can be freed from the overwhelming weight of his doubt. Yes, man must entrust himself completely to this mystery of love which is so great, so immeasurable, and so decisive.

We see, then, that the Christian vocabulary of faith is really very simple. It is the same today as yesterday. God provides. God knows. God wills. We live in his presence. His will is accomplished. Yes, God writes straight on our crooked lines. To sum up, he is our divine providence.

God's Divine Providence at Work

The church announces God's providence not because it is her own idea but because God has decided to reveal himself. It is God who reveals himself and saves his people, unfolding a plan of salvation that he has prepared from all eternity. In this light, holy Scripture is the greatest record of divine providence, since it shows God creating nature in the beginning and then intervening in a wonderful way through redemption. This is the providence of God which makes us new creatures in a world renewed by God's love in Christ.

The Bible particularly speaks about divine providence in chapters about creation and in those which refer specifically to the work of salvation in Genesis and in the prophets, especially Isaiah. There are also the deep meditations of Paul about God's unsearchable designs at work in history, especially in Ephesians and Colossians. Then in the wisdom literature, the authors aim at rediscovering God's designs and ways, while the Apostle John in Revelation completely devotes himself to rediscovering the meaning of God's saving purposes in the world.

It appears that the Christian notion of providence is not merely another chapter of religious philosophy. No, God answers the great questions of Job and of every man like him with the scriptural vision of God's faithfulness and providence to man. Here is a clear theology of God's saving help and intervention as his people respond in faith.

The Truth That Does Not Die

Along the way, we also meet tradition's tireless reflection of faith. Here the church is man's constant companion. She is always ready when man asks in new ways about the providence of God. The First and Second Vatican Councils, each in its own way, are precious voices of the Holy Spirit which we must not neglect. The church calls us to reflect anew upon the vital truth set forth in these councils and other important documents of tradition.

Every serious question must receive a substantial answer. That is why we are dealing with various aspects of divine providence in the great works of creation and redemption.

Let us reflect, then, for a moment about the truth that does not die. This is the transcendent wisdom of God that loves man and calls him to participate in God's saving design. Man is invited to receive God's loving care and to co-operate with his saving grace.

Communion in Love

Divine providence and human freedom are not opposed to each other. Quite the opposite is true. No, they reveal a communion of love as God respects and works with our free will. For example, as we consider our future destiny, we find in divine revelation – specifically in Christ – a providential light which shows us the way of salvation and the will of the Father. God accomplishes this even though he keeps the mystery intact. From such a perspective, divine providence does not deny the presence of evil and suffering in man's life. Far from it! It becomes the bulwark of our hope in time of suffering and even offers us a glimpse of how we can draw good out of evil.

Let us remember, finally, the great light which Vatican II has shown on God's providence when it refers to the progress of the world which will be ours as the kingdom of God grows, revealing the constancy and the wisdom of our loving God. 'Let him who is wise understand these things; let him who is prudent know them. Straight are the paths of the LORD, in them the just walk, but sinners stumble in them' (Hos. 14.10).

A Confirmation of the Work of Creation

God called all of creation into existence out of nothing. But God's creative action has not been exhausted. For everything that has been created would cease to exist if it were not preserved by the Creator. In a sense, God – having created the cosmos once – continues to create by sustaining everything he has created.

We can say that divine providence – understood in the most general sense – is expressed above all in God's preservation of creation. He sustains in existence everything that he has created out of nothing. Providence is like a constant affirmation of the work of creation in all its richness and variety. It reveals to us the uninterrupted presence of God the Creator at work in all of his creation. His is a presence that continually creates and reaches down into the deepest root of all that exists. He operates as the first cause of all being and action.

In Favour of Being and Against Nothingness

In God's presence, we see the eternal will of God constantly expressed as both the Creator and sustainer of all things. His is an utterly sovereign will that governs according to the very nature of the goodness which is proper to him. He continues to take a stand – just as he did in the first act of creation – in sustaining being and opposing nothingness, in favouring life and opposing death, in favouring light in opposition to the darkness (John 1.4–5). In a word, the Creator stands for the truth. He stands for the good and the beauty of all that exists. In the mystery of his providence, God extends in an uninterrupted and irreversible way the judgment he makes in the book of Genesis: 'God saw how good it was . . . he found it very good' (Gen. 1.25, 31).

All Things Work Together for the Good

Speaking about divine providence means to recognise that in God's creative design evil originally had no place. Yet once evil is permitted by God and committed by man, it ultimately becomes subordinate to the good: 'All things work together for the good,' as the Apostle Paul says (Rom. 8.28). This is an issue we will study more a little later.

Well, we have spoken about God the Creator standing for the truth. The truth of divine providence is present in the whole of revelation as well as creation. The truth of God stands as the first and fundamental point of reference in all that God, 'in fragmentary and varied ways', wants to say to men 'through the prophets; [and] in this, the final age, . . . through his Son' (Heb. 1.1). It is important for us to read and reflect on this truth in the Bible where it is presented to us directly. It is also helpful to study indirect references to the truth of God's revelation in holy Scripture.

He Governs All Things Well

Divine providence is found in the very beginning as a fundamental truth of faith. It operates through the Magisterium of the church, its teaching authority, even though only the First Vatican Council has made a dogmatic pronouncement on it. The Council says of God's divine providence in creation: 'All things that God has created he preserves and directs with his providence, which extends from end to end and governs all things well (Wis. 8.1). "All lies bare and exposed to [his] eyes" (Heb. 4.13), even that which will take place through the free initiative of creatures' (DS, 3003).

The text of Vatican I was addressed to the particular needs of Catholics living in the nineteenth century. First, the Council wanted to confirm the established teaching

of the church on providence, and thus its unchangeable
doctrine linked to the whole biblical message. We see this
in the Old and New Testament passages that have been
cited in the Council's text. By confirming this doctrine,
the Council opposed the errors of materialism and of
deism in the nineteenth century. Materialism denies the
existence of God. Deism, even though admitting his existence and the creation of the world, holds that God is not
active in the world he has created. It could be said, then,
that deism directly attacks the truth of divine providence.

You It Is Who Hold Fast My Lot

The separation of the work of creation and divine providence by deism and the total denial of God in materialism
open the door to the falsehood of materialistic determinism. Here man and his life become completely subordinate
to an impersonal process. In the face of this attack, the
truth of the existence of God and his divine providence
guarantee man his freedom and his place in the cosmos.

We see this confirmed in the Old Testament where God
is regarded as a strong and indestructible support: 'I love
you, O LORD, my strength, O LORD, my rock, my fortress, my deliverer. My God, my rock of refuge, my
shield, the horn of my salvation, my stronghold!' (Ps.
18.2–3). God is the solid foundation on which man can
stand: 'You it is who hold fast my lot' (Ps. 16.5), the
psalmist says with confidence.

Divine providence is a sovereign affirmation by God of
all creation and particularly of man who is the crown of
creation. It assures the sovereignty of man himself in this
world. This does not mean that the laws of nature are
annulled because of man's sovereignty. But it does mean
we must altogether reject that materialistic determinism
which reduces the whole of human existence to the realm
of necessity. Such a view practically annihilates man's

freedom of choice. We rejoice that God in his providence is the ultimate support for man's freedom.

God as Creator and Father

Faith in divine providence remains closely linked to the very meaning of man's life. Man can face life when he has the certainty of not being at the mercy of blind fate. Instead, he can depend on God the Creator and Father of all. Thus, faith in God's providence liberates us from the error of fatalism. This faith is summed up in the first words of the creed: 'I believe in God, the Father Almighty.'

Such faith in God is stressed in the teaching of the church, particularly the First and Second Vatican Councils. For instance, the Second Vatican Council teaches that God is the one who 'has a fatherly concern for all' (GS, 24), and particularly 'for the human race' (DV, 3). An expression of this concern is also 'the divine law, eternal, objective, and universal, through which God – in his design of wisdom and love – orders, directs, and rules the whole world and the ways of human society' (DH, 3).

'Man . . . does not exist . . . if it is not by the fact that, created by God in love, he is always preserved by God also in love. He does not live fully, according to the truth, if he does not freely recognise that love and if he does not entrust himself to his Creator' (GetS, 19).

God Guards and Rules

To the question of how God is present today in the world, the Christian faith responds with a luminous and sure answer: 'Everything that he has created, God guards and rules with his providence.' With these concise words the First Vatican Council has formulated the revealed doctrine on divine providence. We find this revelation richly expressed in the Old and New Testament.

Two elements are present in the concept of divine providence: the element of care or concern ('he guards') and the element of authority ('he rules'). These two elements reinforce each other. God the Creator has supreme authority over all of creation. In fact, all things that have been created – by the very fact of their creation – belong to God the Creator and depend on him. In a certain way, every being belongs more to God than to itself. First of all it is 'God's' and then it is 'its own'. And it is God's in such a total way that he guards it with a deep care and concern. Thus, God's care and rule over us surpass all earthly analogies of the relationship between authorities and their subjects.

The Lord Is My Shepherd

The Creator's authority ('he rules') is expressed as a fatherly concern ('he guards'). This truth contains in a certain way the very heart of the truth about divine providence. Holy Scripture uses the image of a shepherd to express this truth of God's fatherly concern: 'The Lord is my shepherd; I shall not want' (Ps. 23.1). What an incredible image! The ancient symbols of faith and Christian tradition expressed the truth of providence with the Latin term *omni-tenens* (all-holding), corresponding to the Greek *panto-krator* (all-ruling). Yet these ideas pale before the richness and beauty of the biblical image of the shepherd. And it now conveys such a vibrant meaning through the revealed truth of divine providence. The shepherd is, in fact, an 'authority full of concern', carrying out an eternal plan of wisdom and of love in ruling the created world and particularly 'the ways of human society' (II Vatican Council, DH, 3). It is a careful and vigilant authority, full of both power and kindness. According to the text of the book of Wisdom that the First Vatican Council cites, it 'reaches from end to end mightily and governs all things well' (Wis. 8.1). That is, it embraces, sustains, guards, and – in a certain way – nourishes. Such is our God who cares for us as a shepherd cares for his sheep.

You Open Your Hand

Who is the God who cares for us? The book of Job describes him as the Lord of all creation: 'Behold, God is sublime in his power. What teacher is there like him? . . . He holds in check the waterdrops that filter in rain through his mists, till the skies run with them and the showers rain down on mankind . . . For by these he nourishes the nations, and gives them food in abundance' (Job 36.22, 27–8, 31).

'With hail, also, the clouds are laden, as they scatter their flashes of light. He it is who changes their rounds, according to his plans, in their task upon the surface of the earth' (Job 37.11–12).

The book of Sirach echoes Job and says of the God of creation: 'His rebuke marks out the path for the lightning, and speeds the arrows of his judgment to their goal' (Sir. 43.13).

The psalmist also extols the 'power of [his] terrible deeds', his 'abundant goodness', 'the splendor of [the] glorious majesty' of God, who is 'compassionate towards all his works'. The psalmist proclaims: 'The eyes of all look hopefully to you, and you give them their food in due season; you open your hand and satisfy the desire of every living thing' (Ps. 145.5, 6, 7, 15–16).

Further, the psalmist says of God's loving care for all he has created: 'You raise grass for the cattle, and vegetation for men's use, producing bread from the earth, and wine to gladden men's hearts, so that their faces gleam with oil, and bread fortifies the hearts of men' (Ps. 104.14–15).

Creative Wisdom

In many passages, holy Scripture praises divine providence as the supreme authority of the world, which is full of concern for all creatures, especially for man. God, as the loving master over all he has made, works through everything he has made. This is God's creative wisdom that sovereignly foresees everything and works through it. It far surpasses human wisdom or prudence. In fact, God, who transcends all things created, makes it possible for the world to display his wonderful order at work on many different levels. It is precisely this providence or wisdom of the Creator that makes it possible for the world to function as the 'cosmos' rather than 'chaos'. 'You have disposed all things by measure and number and weight' (Wis. 11.20). Scripture marvels about the creative wisdom of God.

God Respects His Creation

Even though the Bible's form of expression refers the government of things directly to God, we can still perceive clearly enough the difference between the action of God the Creator as the first cause and the activity of creatures as second causes. Right here we find a question which very much concerns modern man: How much autonomy or independence is creation meant to have? What is man's role in inventing, creating, and building in the world?

According to the Catholic faith, the Creator's wisdom makes it possible for God's providence to be present in the world, while the created world possesses a certain autonomy in its own right. The Second Vatican Council speaks about this mystery. On the one hand, God sustains all things and makes it possible for them to be what they are: 'It is from their very condition as creatures that things receive their consistency, their truth, their goodness, their laws, and their order' (GetS, 36). On the other hand, because of the way God rules the world, creation – particularly man – can have real autonomy, which is 'in accordance with the Creator's will' (GetS, 36).

God's providence is expressed precisely in that 'autonomy of things created', in which God's power and tenderness are both exhibited. We see that the Creator's providence will always remain for man on earth a mysterious wisdom that embraces everything (or 'reaches from end to end'). It is realised in everything with its creative power and its clear order. Yet it leaves intact the creatures' role in the formation and development of the world. Such is the wisdom of our God.

Man Is Called to Rule and Guard God's Creation

Man has a special role to play in the development of the world. This has been his role from the very beginning. It reflects who he is as a son created in God's image and likeness. According to Genesis, man was created to 'have dominion' over creation and to 'subdue' the earth (Gen. 1.28).

By participating in the Creator's dominion over the world as a rational and free subject but yet a creature, man becomes in a certain way a 'providence' himself, according to the beautiful expression of St Thomas (S Th., I, 22, 2 and 4). He is called to guard and rule over God's creation with a shepherding love and concern. However, for that very reason, man bears a special responsibility to God and to creation.

Stop Worrying

Our understanding of divine providence in the Old Testament is confirmed and enriched in the New. Among all of Jesus' sayings on this topic, those reported by the Evangelists Matthew and Luke are particularly striking: 'Stop worrying, then, over questions like, "What are we to eat, or what are we to drink, or what are we to wear?" The unbelievers are always running after these things. Your heavenly Father knows all that you need. Seek first his kingship over you, his way of holiness, and all these things will be given you besides' (Matt. 6.31–3; also Luke 12.29–31).

'Are not two sparrows sold for next to nothing? Yet not a single sparrow falls to the ground without your Father's consent. As for you, every hair of your head has been counted; so do not be afraid of anything. You are worth more than an entire flock of sparrows' (Matt. 10.29–31; also Luke 21.18).

'Look at the birds in the sky. They do not sow or reap, they gather nothing into barns; yet your heavenly Father feeds them. Are not you more important than they? . . . As for clothes, why be concerned? Learn a lesson from the way the wild flowers grow. They do not work, they do not spin. Yet I assure you, not even Solomon in all his splendour was arrayed like one of these. If God can clothe in such splendour the grass of the field, which blooms today and is thrown on the fire tomorrow, will he not provide much more for you, O weak in faith!' (Matt. 6.26–30; Luke 12.24–8). With such a strong exhortation, the Lord Jesus not only confirms the Old Testament teaching on divine providence. No, he shows why we should never doubt that providence. Jesus tells us never to worry because we can rest in the Father's love for us.

The Mystery of the Father

No one would question the magnificence of the stanzas in the psalms that exalt God as a refuge, a protection, and a fortress for man. For example, in Psalm 91 we read: 'You who dwell in the shelter of the Most High, who abide in the shadow of the Almighty, say to the Lord: "My refuge and my fortress, my God, in whom I trust" . . . Because you have the LORD for your refuge; you have made the Most High your stronghold . . . Because he clings to me, I will deliver him; I will set him on high because he acknowledges my name. He shall call upon me, and I will answer him; I will be with him in distress' (Ps. 91.1–2, 9, 14–15).

These expressions are very beautiful and touching. But Christ's words to us have even greater meaning. In fact, they are uttered by the Son who penetrates the mystery of God's providence with more understanding than ever before. His words bear perfect witness to the mystery of the Father – the mystery of providence and of fatherly concern that embraces all of creation, even the grass of the field and the sparrows. How much more will this providence embrace man! And this is what Christ highlights first.

Man Takes Priority over Things

If God the Father shows such concern for creatures which are far inferior to man, think how much more he desires to care for the sons and the daughters of men! In this Gospel passage on God's providence, we find the hierarchy of values which is clear at the very onset of creation: man has priority over all other things. He has primacy because he is made in God's image. He sees it in the attention and care offered to him by his heavenly Father. He finds it in the very heart of God where a special place has been reserved for him.

Jesus further insists that man, who has such a privileged place in the heart of his Creator, has the duty to co-operate with the gift he has received from God's providence. He cannot be content with only the values of this world. No, he must seek first God's 'kingdom and his righteousness', because 'all these things' (that is, earthly benefits) 'shall be yours as well' (Matt. 6.33 RSV).

Christ's words lead us to contemplate this incredible

example of God's tender love and care: his providence. At its very heart, this providence respects man's make-up as a free, rational creature.

Man's Freedom

On our way towards a deeper understanding of the mystery of God's providence, we often encounter this question: If God is present and operating in all things, how is it possible for man to be free? And above all, what significance and what role does freedom play in our lives? And what bitter fruit of sin comes from misuse of freedom? How can all of this be understood in the light of divine providence?

Let us remember the solemn teaching of Vatican I: 'All things that God has created he preserves and directs with his providence, which extends from end to end and governs all things well (Wis. 8.1). "All lies bare and exposed to [his] eyes" (Heb. 4.13), even that which will take place through the free initiative of creatures' (DS, 3003).

The mystery of divine providence is at work in all of creation in a deep way. As an expression of God's eternal wisdom, the plan of providence comes before the work of creation itself. As an expression of God's eternal power, it presides over that work and carries it out. In a certain way, it can even be said that providence is realised in its work. It is a transcendent providence, but at the same time it is present in all things. This applies to the church teaching we have just re-read, above all with reference to man with his intellect and his free will.

Man Fulfils Himself Through the Giving of Himself

Providence embraces in a particular way those creatures which have been made in God's image and likeness. They enjoy 'the autonomy of created beings', in the full sense intended by the Second Vatican Council (GetS, 36). Among those creatures, we must include those that are purely spiritual in nature. But we shall refer to them later. These make up the invisible world.

In the visible world, the object of divine providence in a special way is man, 'who' – in the words of Vatican II – 'is on earth the only creature which God has loved in itself' (GetS, 24). For that reason, he 'cannot fulfil himself fully except through a sincere giving of himself' (GetS, 24).

The Wisdom Which Loves

Yes, the visible world is crowned by the creation of man! This discloses to us a completely new understanding about the mystery of divine providence. This is stressed by the dogmatic teaching of the First Vatican Council when it underscores that in the eyes of God's wisdom and knowledge all lies 'exposed' and 'bare' – even those acts that a rational creature carries out by virtue of his freedom: the result of a conscious choice and a free decision by man. God's providence preserves its superior, creative, and ordering purpose which carefully and lovingly leads man towards his goals, while also respecting his freedom. Such is the might and the love of God's providence.

The Kingdom of God in the Created World

At this point in our encounter with God's eternal plan of creation, we are faced with an unsearchable and awesome mystery. The mystery is the intimate relationship between divine actions and human decisions. We know that this freedom of decision is innate to a rational creature. We also know by experience that the reality of human freedom is genuine, even when it is wounded and weakened by sin.

With its relationship to divine action, we should consider human freedom in the light of what St Thomas Aquinas has to say about divine providence. He describes it as the expression of divine wisdom that orders and directs all things to their goal. He calls it 'the rational ordering of things towards their goal' (S Th., I, 22, 1). All that is created by God receives that orientation and becomes an object of divine providence (ibid., I, 22, 2).

In man – created in God's image – all visible creation approaches God and finds its way to final fulfilment. This notion is expressed by others, including St Irenaeus (*Adv. Hae.* 4, 38; 1105–9). It is echoed by the teaching of Vatican II about the development of the world by the work of man (GetS, 7). In sum, the true development or progress that man is called to carry out in the world must not only have a technical character but an ethical one. This is essential to bring about the kingdom of God in the created world (GetS, 35, 43, 57, 62).

The Law of Life

Created in God's image and likeness, man is the only visible creature which the Creator has 'wanted in itself' (GetS, 24). This God who governs the world with his transcendent wisdom and power gives man goals to achieve in this life. But man is an end in himself as well, unlike all other creatures. Man needs to reach fulfilment as a person created in God's image and likeness. Enriched with a special gift which is also a task, man is intimately involved in the mystery of divine providence. For instance, we read in Sirach: 'The Lord from the earth crafted man . . . he endows man . . . with power over all things else on earth . . . He forms men's tongues and eyes and ears, and imparts to them an understanding heart. With wisdom and knowledge he fills them; good and evil he shows them. He looks with favour upon their hearts, and shows them his glorious works . . . He has set before

them knowledge, a law of life as their inheritance . . .'
(Sir. 17.1, 3, 5–7, 9).

My Soul Also You Knew Full Well

Endowed with a mind and an immortal soul, man starts
his journey in the world. He begins to write his own
history. God in his providence accompanies him all along
the way. We now read in the book of Sirach: 'Their ways
are ever known to him, they cannot be hidden from his
eyes . . . All their actions are clear as the sun to him, his
eyes are ever upon their ways' (Sir. 17.13, 15).

The psalmist strikes the same chord as Ben Sirach: 'If I
take the wings of the dawn, if I settle at the farthest limits
of the sea, even there your hand shall guide me, and your
right hand hold me fast. . . . My soul also you knew
full well; nor was my frame unknown to you . . .' (Ps.
139.9–10, 14–15).

The Life of Man Under God's Watchful Eye

God's providence is always present in the life of man and
in the history of the world. God is there: in man's thinking, in his freedom, in his heart, in his conscience.

In man and with man, the action of God's saving presence acquires an historical dimension. Providence does
this by following the rhythm of man's life and by adapting
itself to the ways of human nature. Yet the mysterious
providence of God always remains intact and unchanging.

Yes, providence is an eternal presence in the history of
man – both of individuals and of communities. The history of nations and of the whole human race develops
under God's watchful eye and through his all-powerful
action. If all created things are guarded and ruled by providence, God's authority – which is full of fatherly concern
– supports it. He shows full respect for the freedom of

men as free, rational beings created in the image and likeness of God.

Man Can Make His Own Free Choice

Respect for created freedom is so essential that God, in his providence, even allows for the sin of man and of angels. The rational creature – exalted yet limited and imperfect – can abuse his freedom and disobey God the Creator. This possibility torments the human mind. The book of Sirach reflects on this reality in depth:

'When God, in the beginning, created man, he made him subject to his own free choice. If you choose you can keep the commandments; it is loyalty to do his will. There are set before you fire and water; to whichever you choose, stretch forth your hand. Before man are life and death, whichever he chooses shall be given him. Immense is the wisdom of the LORD; he is mighty in power, and all-seeing. The eyes of God see all he has made; he understands man's every deed. No man does he command to sin, to none does he give strength for lies' (Sir. 15.14–20).

True Freedom Leads to Love

'Who can explain sin?' is the question asked by the psalmist (Ps. 19.13, according to the Latin text). God's providence sheds its light on the tragic rebellion of man, so that we can learn to avoid sin.

Man was created as a free and rational being in a world where sin was not only possible but was shown to be a real fact from the beginning. Sin is radical opposition to God. It is something that God decidedly and absolutely does not want. Yet he has permitted it in creating free beings like man. He has permitted sin, which is the result of an abuse of created freedom.

From this unalterable fact, which is known from revelation and experienced in our fallen world, we know that it must be more important for freedom to exist in the created world, even with the risk of a misuse of that freedom, than that we be deprived of it to exclude the possibility of sin. This is the perspective of God's providential wisdom which sees the end and the purpose of all things.

However, even though on the one hand God has allowed sin, on the other hand our loving Father has foreseen from eternity the way of redemption and of salvation through love. Freedom, in fact, is oriented towards love. There can be no love without true freedom. And, in the struggle between good and evil, between sin and redemption, love will have the last word.

To Man First of All

The question of man's destiny is a concern of every heart. It is a great and difficult question: 'What will become of me tomorrow?' we ask. There is a risk that we will get the wrong answer and be led into fatalism, despair, or a proud and blind sense of false security: 'You fool! This very night your life shall be required of you' is God's admonition (Luke 12.20).

Yet it is here that we find the inexhaustible mercy and grace of divine providence. To the contrary, he is speaking about divine providence in the Sermon on the Mount and ends with this ringing exhortation: 'Seek first [God's] kingship over you, his way of holiness, and all these things will be given you besides' (Matt. 6.33; also Luke 2.31).

We have reflected on the deep relationship that exists between God's providence and man's freedom. It is precisely to man – created in God's image – that Jesus addresses his words on God's kingship and on the need to seek it before all things.

This bond between providence and the mystery of God's kingdom – which must be accomplished in the created world – orients our thinking towards man's destiny in Christ: his predestination in Christ. The predestination of man and of the world in Christ gives the doctrine of divine providence a decidedly salvific and final ring to it. Jesus himself indicates this in his conversation to Nicodemus: 'Yes, God so loved the world that he gave his only Son, that whoever believes in him may not die but may have eternal life' (John 3.16).

That All May Praise His Glorious Favour

Jesus' words 'God so loved the world that he gave his only Son, that whoever believes in him may not die but may have eternal life' (John 3.16) constitute the heart of the doctrine of predestination. We find this doctrine in the teaching of the apostles and especially in the letters of St Paul.

We read in the letter to the Ephesians, for example: 'The God and Father of our Lord Jesus Christ chose us in him before the world began, to be holy and blameless in his sight, to be full of love; he likewise predestined us through Christ Jesus to be his adopted sons – such was his will and pleasure – that all might praise the glorious favour he has bestowed on us in his beloved' (Eph. 1.3–6).

These glorious statements about our destiny in Christ explain in a genuine and authoritative way the essence of what we call 'predestination'. In fact, it is important to clarify the meaning of this term so it can be free from erroneous or improper meanings, which have crept into common usage. These include using predestination as a synonym for 'blind fate' or the capricious 'wrath' of some jealous deity. In divine revelation, the word 'predestination' means the eternal choice of God. It is always fatherly, intelligent, and positive. It is a choice made in love.

The Choice in Love

God's choice in love and its decisive result always pertain to the intimate life of the Blessed Trinity. This dynamic life in love involves the Father together with the Son in the Holy Spirit. Man shares in this divine life as he is called to the creative and redemptive plan of God. Man was predestined for this divine election before the very creation of the world (Eph. 1.4).

Man, even before being created, was 'chosen' by God. This choice took place in the eternal Son ('in him', Eph. 1.4). That is, it took place in the Word through whom the world was created. Thus, man is elected in the Son to participate in his very sonship through divine adoption by the Father. This is the very essence of the mystery of predestination. It is the manifestation of the Father's eternal love for us. As Scripture says, 'He likewise predestined us through Christ Jesus to be his adopted sons' (Eph. 1.5). Predestination, then, sums up the eternal call of man to participate in the very nature of God. It is a vocation to holiness through the grace of adoption as sons: we are 'to be holy and blameless in his sight' (Eph. 1.4).

Predestination

Predestination precedes the foundation of the world. By applying to divine life the analogies of human language, we can say that God wants 'first' to communicate himself in his divinity to man, because man is called to be his image and likeness in the created world. 'First' he chooses him in the eternal Son to participate in that sonship through grace. 'In turn', God desires to draw all of creation to himself in Christ.

In this way, the mystery of predestination is integral to the whole plan of divine providence. The revelation of this grand design discloses before our very eyes the perspective of God's kingdom. It leads us to the very heart of this kingdom, where we discover the ultimate purpose of creation. God's mind is revealed to us.

The Lot of the Saints in Light

We read in the letter to the Colossians: '. . . giving thanks to the Father for having made you worthy to share the lot of the saints in light. He rescued us from the power of darkness and brought us into the kingdom of his beloved Son. Through him we have redemption, the forgiveness of our sins' (Col. 1.12–14). The kingdom of God is the kingdom of the 'beloved Son' in a special way, because it is by his work that 'redemption' and the 'forgiveness of sins' are accomplished. The Apostle Paul's words allude to man's sin. Predestination, then, is not only effective because of man's relation to the creation of the world and his place in the world. No, fundamentally man's predestination has to do with the redemption by the Son, Jesus Christ.

Redemption becomes the concrete expression of God's saving providence. We see the careful government that God the Father exercises, especially with respect to those creatures he endows with freedom.

Man in the World

In the letter to the Colossians we find that the truth of predestination in Christ is closely united to the truth of creation in Christ. Paul writes: 'He is the image of the invisible God, the first-born of all creatures. In him everything in heaven and on earth was created . . .' (Col. 1.15–16). We grasp a marvellous truth here. The world bears in itself from the very beginning of creation, the call and even the pledge of predestination in Christ, because it is created in Christ and is offered to God as the first gift of providence. This is the Word of God through whom the world was created, and this is the Christ who extends salvation to all men and finally to the world. 'It pleased God to make absolute fullness reside in him' (Col. 1.19).

The fulfilment of the last things on the earth, especially the transformation of man, is brought about precisely by the work of this fullness which is in Christ. Christ brings us the fullness of God. In him is accomplished, in a certain sense, that final chapter of our history as divine providence guards and rules the things of the world and particularly man in the world.

The Eternal Plan of Salvation

We now understand another fundamental aspect of divine providence: Its emphasis on Christ's saving work of salvation and its final fulfilment at the end of time when Christ comes again. In fact, God 'wants all men to be saved and come to know the truth' (1 Tim. 2.4). We need to modify our naturalistic view of providence as limited to the good government of physical nature or even to natural moral behaviour. Actually, divine providence is expressed through God's eternal plan of salvation summed up in the saving work of Christ. Thanks to Christ's 'fullness', we know that in him and through him comes the victory over our sin, which is essentially opposed to the completion of Christ's work at the end of time, the fulfilment that the world and man find in God. Speaking about the fullness which has made its abode in Christ, the Apostle Paul proclaims: 'It pleased God to make absolute fullness reside in him and, by means of him, to reconcile everything in his person, both on earth and in the heavens, making peace through the blood of his cross' (Col. 1.19–20).

Seek First His Kingship Over You

Against the background of these reflections drawn from the letters of St Paul, we can better understand Christ's exhortation about the providence of the heavenly Father which embraces everything (Matt. 6.23–34 and also Luke 12.22–31) when he says: 'Seek first his kingship over you, his way of holiness, and all these things will be given you besides' (Matt. 6.33; also Luke 12.31).

By saying 'first', Jesus indicates what God desires 'first' of all for each of us. What God first intended in the creation of the world and what he desires at the end of the world itself is to establish 'his kingship . . . and his way of holiness' in our lives. The whole world has been created with a view towards this kingship or kingdom. It is to reach its fulfilment in man and in his history in God's time. This is the 'kingship' and this is the 'righteousness' that is eternally predestined for the world and man in Christ.

Unto Hope Which Draws Its Life

Alongside the Pauline vision of predestination, we find the words of St Peter: 'Praised be the God and Father of our Lord Jesus Christ, he who in his great mercy gave us new birth; a birth unto hope which draws its life from the resurrection of Jesus Christ from the dead; a birth to an imperishable inheritance, incapable of fading or defilement, which is kept in heaven for you who are guarded with God's power through faith; a birth to a salvation which stands ready to be revealed in the last days' (1 Pet. 1.3–5).

Yes, 'praised be . . . God' who reveals to us how his providence is his tireless, loving, and careful intervention for our salvation. It is always at work until the moment when the last things draw near. Then our predestination in Christ will be accomplished completely through 'the resurrection of Jesus Christ', who is 'the alpha and the omega' of our human destiny (Rev. 1.8).

The Reality of Evil and of Suffering

Let us consider again the text of St Peter's first letter: 'Praised be the God and Father of our Lord Jesus Christ, he who in his great mercy gave us new birth; a birth unto hope which draws its life from the resurrection of Jesus Christ from the dead; a birth to an imperishable inheritance, incapable of fading or defilement, which is kept in heaven for you' (1 Pet. 1.3–4).

A little further on, the Apostle Peter makes a point which is both illuminating and comforting: 'There is cause for rejoicing here. You may for a time have to suffer the distress of many trials; but this is so that your faith, which is more precious than the passing splendour of fire-tried gold, may by its genuineness lead to praise . . .' (1 Pet. 1.6–7).

Yes, in this passage we can take comfort! For the predestination of the created world and above all man in Christ is the indispensable foundation for the relationship between God's providence and the reality of evil and suffering. Here we have a sure hope that we will eventually triumph over evil and suffering in all its many forms by the victory of Christ. We are predestined in Christ to be more than conquerors through him who loved us (Rom. 8.37).

The Bible: A Great Book on Suffering

The reality of evil and suffering are for many people their main difficulty in accepting the truth of God's providence for their lives. In some cases this difficulty becomes extreme. God is bluntly blamed for the evil and suffering which are present in the world, even to the point of rejecting the truth about God and denying his existence. This is the position of atheism. In a less radical but still disturbing way, many people critically question God and his motives. Doubt, questioning, or blunt contradictions emerge out of an attempt to reconcile the truth of divine providence with the reality of evil and suffering experienced by men.

We need to turn to Scripture to study this problem. The vision of the reality of evil and of suffering is present in all its fullness in the pages of holy Scripture. The Bible, is, above all, a great book on suffering. For suffering is one of the things that God instructs mankind about 'in . . . varied ways . . . through the prophets' and 'in this, the final age . . . through his Son' (Heb. 1.1). It fits into the context of God's revelation of himself and into the context of the good news of salvation. That is why the only really adequate means for seeking an answer about the question of evil and of suffering in the world is to seek it in the Bible.

There Are All Kinds of Evil

First of all, we must understand what we mean by evil and suffering. It takes on many forms. A distinction is commonly made between evil in the physical sense and evil in the moral sense. Moral evil is distinguished from physical evil mainly by the fact that it includes guilt, since it depends on man's free will. Hence, it is always an evil which is spiritual in nature. It is distinguished from physical evil because the latter does not necessarily and directly include man's will. That does not mean that physical evil cannot be caused by man or be the effect of man's guilt. Physical evil is caused by man in many situations. Sometimes it is cause only by ignorance or carelessness, sometimes by negligence or directly by harmful actions.

But we know that in the world there exist many cases of physical evil which come about independently of man. It is enough to call to mind the examples of disasters or other natural calamities and psychiatric disorders for which man is not guilty.

God Is Good

Facing all of these questions, we feel, like Job, how difficult it is to give an answer. We look for that answer not in ourselves, but humbly and confidently in the Word of God. In the Old Testament we find the resounding and significant declaration: 'Wickedness prevails not over wisdom. Indeed, she reaches from end to end mightily and governs all things well' (Wis. 7.30–8.1). We see that in the presence of many kinds of evil and suffering in the world the Old Testament bears witness to the primacy of wisdom and of God's kindness – to his divine providence.

This attitude is developed in the book of Job, which is completely devoted to the topic of evil and sorrow. This important book on evil is seen sometimes as a tremendous test for the just. But this understanding of the book is secondary to the author's clear but painstaking conclusion that God is good. In Job, we begin to grasp the limits and the fleeting nature of all created things. We recognise that some forms of physical evil may be due to the fallen nature of our world. Also we become aware that material things are in a close relationship to one another. As the old saying goes, 'the death of one is the life of another'. To a certain extent, then, even death serves life. This law also includes man since he is both flesh and spirit, mortal and immortal. Along these lines, St Paul's thoughts disclose even wider horizons: 'Our inner being is renewed each day even though our body is being destroyed at the same time' (2 Cor. 4.16). And he says further: 'The present burden of our trial is light enough, and earns for us an eternal weight of glory beyond all comparison' (2 Cor. 4.17).

Evil Is Subordinate to Good

The assurance of holy Scripture that 'wickedness prevails not over wisdom' (Wis. 7.30) reinforces our conviction that in the providential plan of the Creator, evil is ultimately subordinate to good. In the light of divine providence, we begin to understand the two truths: 'God does not want evil as evil', and 'God permits evil.'

To understand why 'God does not want evil as evil', it is timely to remember the words of the book of Wisdom: 'God did not make death, nor does he rejoice in the destruction of the living. For he fashioned all things that they might have being' (Wis. 1.13–14).

To understand why God permits evil among physical things it is helpful to remember that material beings – among them the human body – are corruptible and undergo death. We need to point out that this affects the very structure of the physical being of these creatures. But this is logical. It would be difficult to think that every individual bodily creature could exist without limits in the present state of our material world. Thus, we can understand that if 'God did not make death' as the book of Wisdom asserts, yet he allows it in view of the overall good of the material cosmos.

The Victorious Cross of Christ

Now we consider moral evil. By this we mean various forms of sin and guilt and their consequences in our physical world. This kind of evil God absolutely does not want. Moral evil is completely opposed to God's will. If in the life of man and his world this evil is present and sometimes quite oppressive, this has only been permitted by God's providence because he wants freedom to exist in the created world.

The existence of created freedom has meant for us the existence of pure spirits, such as the angels. This freedom is indispensable for man to reach the fullness of creation and to respond to God's eternal plan. To bring about complete goodness and fullness in creation, the existence of free beings is for God a much more important and fundamental value than the tragic fact that those beings can abuse their own freedom and turn against their Creator. We see, then, that man's freedom can lead to moral evil.

We undoubtedly receive great understanding from our reason and from God's revelation about this mystery of divine providence which – though not wanting evil – tolerates it with a greater good in mind. However, a full understanding of the mystery of moral evil can only come to us through the victorious cross of Christ.

O Happy Fault

We have faced the questions and cries of men of all times concerning God's providence. We have faced the reality of evil and suffering.

The Word of God fully claims that 'wickedness prevails not over [God's] wisdom' (Wis. 7.30), and that God permits evil in the world for the sake of greater goods, even though he does not want evil. Today we want to listen to Jesus Christ. Through the paschal mystery, he offers a complete response to these tormenting questions of men.

Let us reflect first on how St Paul announces the crucified Christ as 'the Power of God and the wisdom of God' (1 Cor. 1.24) in whom salvation is given to believers. His is certainly a great and an admirable power if it is manifested in the weakness and abasement of death on the cross. And it is an exalted wisdom, unknown to men outside of divine revelation.

In God's eternal plan and his saving providential action, every evil – particularly the moral evil of sin – becomes subordinate to the far greater good of redemption and of salvation through Christ's cross and resurrection.

It can be said that in Christ God 'draws good out of evil'. He draws it in a way out of the very evil of sin, which was the cause of suffering for the blameless Lamb who was offered as a victim for the sins of the world.

The liturgy of the church does not hesitate to speak frankly about our 'happy fault' that has won for us so great a redeemer. This is the 'Exulter', the great hymn we recite at the liturgy of the Easter Vigil.

God Is with Every Man in His Suffering

To this question of how to reconcile the evil and suffering that are in the world with the truth of divine providence, we cannot give a complete answer without referring to Christ. On one hand, Christ confirms through his own life of poverty and humiliation, and most especially through his passion and death, that God is with every man in his suffering. Yes, Christ even takes on himself all the sufferings of man's earthly existence. At the same time, Jesus Christ reveals that this suffering possesses a redemptive and salvific value and power. In it is prepared that 'imperishable inheritance' that St Peter speaks about in his first letter: 'an inheritance . . . which is kept in heaven for us (1 Pet. 1.4).

Thus, the truth about providence acquires its final eschatological meaning through the 'power and wisdom' of the cross of Christ. The complete answer to the question of evil and suffering is offered by divine revelation through predestination in Christ. For this predestination shows us that man's vocation is to have eternal life – to participate in the very life of God himself. And this is exactly the answer that Christ has brought us. He has confirmed it through his cross and resurrection.

A Wisdom Which Is Full of Love

Now we can see how everything – even the evil and suffering that are present in the created world – are under the scrutiny of that unsearchable wisdom about which St Paul exclaims in wonder: 'How deep are the riches and the wisdom and the knowledge of God! How inscrutable his judgments, how unsearchable his ways!' (Rom. 11.33). It is in the context of our salvation that wisdom over wickedness prevails (Wis. 7.30). It is a wisdom full of love since 'God so loved the world that he gave his only Son . . .'(John 3.16).

When Jesus Christ Appears

The apostolic writers take a great interest in this wisdom that is so rich in compassion and love towards the suffering of man. They recognise in this wisdom the help that the troubled need to pass through hard times with God's saving grace. This is how St Peter writes to the first generation of believers: 'There is cause for rejoicing here. You may for a time have to suffer the distress of many trials' (Pet. 1.6), he tells them. Then he adds: 'But this is so that your faith which is more precious than the passing splendor of fire-tried gold, may by its genuineness lead to praise, glory, and honour when Jesus Christ appears' (1 Pet. 1.7).

In this last passage, Peter is referring to the Old Testament, especially to the book of Sirach. In Sirach we read: 'For in fire gold is tested, and worthy men in the crucible of humiliation' (Sir. 2.5). Peter takes up this same issue of testing later in his letter when he writes: 'Rejoice instead, in the measure that you share Christ's sufferings. When his glory is revealed, you will rejoice exultantly' (1 Pet. 4.13). Indeed, Christ crucified and risen from the dead is our hope of glory! This is the wisdom of divine love and providence.

The Birthpangs of Creation

The Apostle James expresses himself in a similar way when he exhorts Christians to face trials with joy and patience: 'My brothers, count it pure joy when you are involved in every sort of trial. Realise that when your faith is tested this makes for endurance. Let endurance come to its perfection so that you may be fully mature and lacking in nothing' (Jas. 1.2–4).

Finally, in his letter to the Romans, St Paul compares human and cosmic sufferings to the 'birthpangs' of all of creation. He underscores that these are the 'groanings' of those who possess the 'first fruits' of the Spirit and who await the fullness of adoption, that is, 'the redemption of our bodies' (Rom. 8.22–3).

God's Way of Teaching Us

Then Paul adds later to this understanding of suffering: 'We know that God makes all things work together for the good of those who have been called according to his decree . . .'(Rom. 8.28). In the same vein, he states: 'Who will separate us from the love of Christ? Trial, or distress, or persecution, or hunger, or nakedness, or danger, or the sword?' (Rom. 8.35).

With this profound understanding of God's goodness and love in Christ, the Apostle Paul concludes: 'For I am certain that neither death nor life . . . nor any other creature, will be able to separate us from the love of God that comes to us in Christ Jesus, our Lord' (Rom. 8.38–9).

Here is God our Father eternally loving us in Christ. This is the Father who in his loving providence also teaches us: 'Endure your trials as the discipline [or education] of God, who deals with you as sons. For what son is there whom his father does not discipline [educate]? . . . God does so for our true profit, that we may share his holiness' (Heb. 12.7, 10).

The Real Sense of Suffering

Suffering seen through the eyes of faith – even though it can still appear as darkness to us – allows us to see the mystery of God's providence. This mystery is summed up in the revelation of Christ, particularly in his cross and resurrection. No doubt man – as he raises his age-old questions about evil and suffering in a world created by God – may not find immediate answers. This will be especially true if he does not possess a living faith in Jesus Christ.

But gradually with the help of faith nourished by prayer, we can discover the real sense of the sufferings that everyone experiences in life. It is a discovery which depends on the word of divine revelation and on 'the word of the cross' (1 Cor. 1.18 RSV) of Christ, which is 'the power of God and the wisdom of God' (1 Cor. 1.24).

The Enigma of Pain and Death

As the Second Vatican Council teaches us: 'Through Christ and in Christ, we are enlightened about the enigma of pain and of death, which outside his gospel overwhelms us' (GetS, 22). If we discover through faith this power and this 'wisdom', we are then treading the salvific ways of divine providence. The meaning of the psalmist's words are then fully realised for us: 'The Lord is my shepherd . . . Even though I walk in the dark valley I fear no evil; for you are at my side' (Ps. 23.1,4). Yes, in divine providence, we see that God is walking at man's side.

The Truth of the Kingdom of God

The truth about God's providence, which is so closely linked to the mystery of creation, must be understood in the context of the whole revelation, the whole creed which we profess as Christians. In this way, we see an organic link between providence and revelation. Into the truth of providence there comes the revelation of the predestination of man and of the world in Christ. There also comes the revelation of the whole economy of salvation and its accomplishment throughout history.

The truth about divine providence is also very closely tied to the truth of the kingdom of God. That is why the words uttered by Christ in his teaching about providence have such a fundamental importance for our lives: 'Seek first [God's] kingdom and his righteousness, and all these things shall be yours as well' (Matt. 6.33 RSV; Luke 12.13). Yes, the truth about divine providence is revealed in the rule of God over the whole created world. It becomes fully understandable to men through the truth about the kingdom of God. Through that kingdom God eternally establishes – even in our created world – the predestination in Christ, who is 'the first-born of all creatures' (Col. 1.15).

God's Relationship to the World

The truth of divine providence is revealed in the opening lines of our creed – which are so deep and so full of truth – 'I believe in God, the Father Almighty, Creator of heaven and earth.' That majestic truth is addressed by the teaching authority of the Second Vatican Council in an excellent way. In many conciliar documents, in fact, we find good references to this great truth of faith, but it is particularly expressed well in the constitution *Gaudium et Spes* of the Second Vatican Council.

As is well known, *Gaudium et Spes* undertakes the topic of *the Church in the Modern World*. However, from the very first paragraphs, it is clear the Council Fathers cannot deal with this topic without going back to the revealed truth of God's relationship to the world and ultimately to the truth of God's saving providence.

Christ: the Centre and Source of All Things

We read: 'The world . . . which the Council is thinking about is that world . . . of men . . . , the world which

Christians believe to have been created and to be preserved in existence by the love of the Creator. It is a world which is certainly subject to the slavery of sin, but which through Christ's death and resurrection has been liberated with the defeat of the evil one and is destined, according to the divine purpose, to be transformed and to reach its fulfilment' (GetS, 2).

This description embraces the whole doctrine on providence, understood either as God's eternal plan in creation, or as the accomplishment of this plan in history, or understood as the salvific and eschatological fulfilment of the universe. This is especially true of the human world according to its 'predestination in Christ', who is the centre and source of all things.

In this way, Vatican II refines with different terms the dogmatic teaching of Vatican I: 'All things that God has created he preserves and directs with his providence, which extends from end to end "and governs all things well" (Wis. 8.1). "All lies bare and exposed to [his] eyes" (Heb. 4.13), even that which will take place through the free initiative of creatures' (Const. *De Fide*, DS 3003).

From the onset, *Gaudium et Spes* focuses on an issue which is both relevant to our topic and dear to modern man: How the growth of God's kingdom and the development of the world come together.

There Where God Awaits Him

In the visible world, the main mover of historical and cultural development is man. He is created in God's image and likeness and preserved by him in existence. He is guided by God with fatherly love in the task of exercising dominion over the other creatures. As we recall, man is in a certain way a 'providence for the world'.

The Second Vatican Council expresses this aptly. 'Individual and collective human activity – that enormous effort with which men throughout the centuries seek to improve their own conditions of life – considered in itself corresponds to God's design. Man, in fact, created in God's image and likeness, has received the command to subdue the earth with all that it contains. He is to rule the world in justice and in holiness, and also to bring himself and the entire universe back to God, recognising God the Creator of all things. In this way, in the subordination of all realities to man, God's name is glorified in all the earth' (GetS, 34).

The same conciliar document also states: 'Man is not mistaken when he regards himself as superior to bodily things and when he considers himself to be something more than a mere particle of nature or an anonymous part of humanity. In fact, because of his inner life man transcends the universe. He turns to that deep inner life when he enters into his heart, there where God awaits him – the God who searches the heart – there where under God's glance, he decides his own destiny' (GetS, 14).

In the Service of the Brethren

Man is called to develop the world, to work towards the development of better economic and cultural systems. This task is part of man's vocation, for he is called to have dominion over the earth. That is why modern scientific and technological thought and human culture and wisdom of all ages should be shaped by man to fit God's design for his creation.

The Second Vatican Council recognises the value and function of work and culture in our times. In fact, the constitution *Gaudium et Spes* describes our new cultural and social situation with its possibilities for rapid change and progress. These possibilities amaze many and raise the hopes of others (GetS, 53–54). The Council does not hesitate to recognise the admirable achievements of man. It sets these achievements in the context of God's design and command to men. It relates them to the gospel of brotherhood preached by Jesus Christ: 'Man, in fact, as he cultivates the earth with the work of his hands or with the aid of technology for it to bear fruit and to become a worthy abode for the universal family of men – and when he consciously participates in the life of social groups – is carrying out the design of God manifested at the beginning of time. He is called to subdue the earth, perfect creation, and to perfect himself. Thus, he puts into practice Christ's great commandment to devote oneself to the service of the brethren' (GetS, 57; also GetS, 63).

A Fundamental Imbalance Rooted in Man's Heart

However, the Council does not close its eyes to the enormous problems man encounters in developing the earth, both within himself and in his life with others. It would be a delusion to ignore them, as it would be an error to present them in an improper or inadequate way by not referring to God's providence and will. The Council says: 'In our times the human race, moved by admiration for their own discoveries and their own power, often raises the level of expectancy about the current state of development in the world, on man's role and task in the universe, on the meaning of their own individual and collective efforts, and even on the ultimate end of things and of men' (GetS, 3).

Then the Council goes on to explain: 'As is the case in every crisis where there is change, this transformation carries with it considerable difficulties. Thus, while man achieves so much power, he does not always succeed in putting it to his own service. He strives to reach the innermost part of his soul, but he often appears more uncertain about himself. He readily discovers with more clarity the laws of social life, but then he continues to hesitate on how to channel them' (GetS, 4). The Council expressly speaks about 'contradictions and imbalances' brought about by 'rapid and disorderly' change in the socioeconomic conditions in customs, in culture, in man's thinking and conscience, in the family, in social relationships, in the relations between groups, communities, and nations. This results in 'mistrust and enmities, conflicts and bitterness, of which man himself is the cause and the victim at the same time' (GetS, 8–10). Finally, the Council arrives at the root of the problem when it states: 'The imbalances from which the modern world suffers are linked to a more fundamental imbalance rooted in man's heart' (GetS, 10).

The Great Temptation of Modern Man

In view of the situation of man in today's world, it seems totally unjustified to subscribe to the view that his dominion over the earth should be absolute, or that it should be carried out without the help of God's providence. It is a vain and dangerous illusion to build your own life and to make of the world a kingdom based solely on your own happiness, relying only on your own strength. This is the great temptation into which modern man has fallen. Men have forgotten that the laws of nature condition even our industrial and post-industrial civilisation (GetS, 26–27).

The Deception of Self-Sufficiency

It is easy to yield to the alluring deception of self-sufficiency in our gradual dominion over the forces of nature. We can do this to the point of forgetting about God and even usurping his rightful place. In our day, such presumption reaches into the realm of science where there are at times various forms of biological, genetic, and psychological manipulation. Beware. If it is not submitted to the moral law and to the kingdom of God – it can result in the tyrannical dominion of man over man with tragic consequences. The Council recognises the greatness of modern man but also his limits in ordering the legitimate autonomy of all created things (GetS, 36). The Council Fathers remind man of the truth of divine providence that comes to aid him as he builds the world and seeks to serve others. In this relationship to God the Father, the Creator and Provider, man can continually rediscover the source of his salvation. Let him come to the Father and not rely blindly on his own strength and initiative.

Man is the Steward of Nature

We shall refer frequently to the reflections that Vatican II offers on the condition of modern man. He has a unique place in God's creation. On one hand, he is sent forth by God to subdue creation. On the other hand, he is submitted to God the Father and Creator as a creature himself.

Today more so than in any other age, man is aware of the great scope of his task as a steward of nature. He must subdue it and use it wisely and responsibly.

Yet there is a serious obstacle to the development of the world. It is sin and its destructive fruit of alienation. The Vatican II constitution *Gaudium et Spes* bears witness to this tragedy: 'Constituted by God in a state of holiness, man was tempted by the evil one and abused his freedom from the very beginning of history. He rose up against God and tried to obtain his goal without God' (GetS, 13).

The inevitable consequence of this abuse of freedom was that 'human progress – which is otherwise a great benefit for man – now carries with it a great temptation to sin. In fact, once the order of values is upset and good is mixed with evil, individuals and groups will only think about their own interests and not about those of others. That is how the world ceases to be the realm of genuine brotherhood, while the increase of human power threatens to destroy the human race itself' (GetS, 37).

The Spirit of God

Modern man is certainly aware of his role. But 'if . . . the independence of earthly realities is taken to mean that created things do not depend on God, and that man can use them without reference to the Creator, then the false-hood of such an opinion cannot escape anyone who believes in God. In fact, the creature ceases to exist with-out the Creator . . . Indeed, the complete absence of God would deprive the creature itself of all light' (GetS, 36).

We recall a text which allows us to grasp the other aspect of the development of the world by man. The Council says: 'The Spirit of God who – as an admirable providence – directs the course of time and renews the face of the earth is present in this development' (GetS, 26). The Spirit uses us to build the new creation by helping us overcome sin and other evil in our lives. Then we can renew the face of the earth and fulfil our destiny. Overcoming evil by the Spirit of God means to want the moral progress of man and not just his material and physi-cal progress. Then man's dignity can be safeguarded. He can give an answer to the most essential demands of a truly human world. In this way, the kingdom of God gradually develops in human history, finding its own spiritual 'matter' and showing man signs of God's presence.

Progress and the Kingdom of God

The Second Vatican Council has stressed very clearly the ethical significance of man's development and progress in this world. The Council has shown how the ethical ideal of a more human world is consistent with the teaching of the gospel. While they clearly distinguish the development of the world from salvation history, the Council Fathers explore the relationship that exists between the two: 'Although it is necessary to clearly distinguish earthly progress from the development of the kingdom of Christ, nevertheless, if that progress can contribute to the better ordering of human society, it is of great importance for the kingdom of God. In fact, goods such as man's dignity, brotherhood, and freedom, and all the good fruits of nature and of our work – after we have spread them on the earth in the Spirit of the Lord and according to his commands, we shall find them once again. But then they shall be purified from every stain, enlightened, and transfigured. At that time Christ will give back to the Father "the eternal and universal kingdom: a kingdom of truth and of life, a kingdom of holiness and of grace, a kingdom of justice, of love and of peace." The kingdom is already present here on the earth in mystery. But with the coming of the Lord, it will reach perfection' (GetS, 39).

The Church in the World

The Council attests to the convictions of believers when it proclaims that the church recognises all the good things that can be found in today's social order: above all, the desire for unity, the development of 'a healthy socialisation' among peoples, and an emphasis on 'civil and economic solidarity'. In fact, 'the promotion of unity corresponds to the intimate mission of the church, which "in Christ is meant to be a sacrament and a sign of intimate union with God and of the unity of the whole human race" . . . The energy which the church contributes to modern human society is that of faith and love which are actually lived out, and not that of an outward dominion through merely human means' (GetS, 42).

For these reasons, a deep link and even a certain common identity are forged between the development and progress of man in society on the one hand, and salvation history on the other. The plan of salvation has its roots in the real aspirations and in the deepest concerns of men. The call to redemption is constantly proclaimed to man in the world. For the church always encounters the world when she addresses man's aspirations and concerns. Yes, salvation history takes place in the riverbed of the world's history, considering that history as its own in a certain sense. The opposite is also true. The great achievements of man and the genuine victories of history are also the substratum of God's reign on earth. Such is the unity and purpose of God's plan who is over all and in all.

The True Good of Mankind

We read in the Vatican II document *Gaudium et Spes*: 'Human activity, just as it is derived from man, is also oriented to man . . . Development, if it is well understood, is more valuable than the external riches that one can amass. Man is more valuable by what he is than by what he has. Similarly, all that men do to obtain greater justice, more brotherhood, and more human order has more value than progress in a technological field . . .

'This is the norm of human activity: that, according to the design of God's will, such activity has to correspond to the true good of mankind and it has to allow men – both as individuals and as members of society – to cultivate their total vocation and to carry it out' (GetS, 35; also GetS, 59).

This document on the church in the modern world goes on to say: 'The social order and its development must constantly yield to the good of the person, since the order of things must be subordinate to the order of persons and not the other way around. The social order requires constant improvement: it must be founded in truth, built on justice and enlivened by love. The Spirit of God, who, with wondrous providence, directs the course of time and renews the face of the earth, assists in this development' (GetS, 26).

The Action of God's Spirit

We need the guidance and the action of God's Spirit in the development of society. This can only happen when we constantly appeal to the voice of conscience and are faithful in our response to it.

The teaching of the Second Vatican Council tells us: 'In faithfulness to conscience, Christians are joined to other men in the search for truth and for the right solution to so many moral problems which arise both in the life of individuals and from social relationships. Therefore, the more a correct conscience prevails, the more do persons and groups turn aside from blind choice and try to be guided by the objective standards of moral conduct' (GetS, 16).

With realism, the Council calls our attention to the most troublesome obstacle blocking the real progress of man – the moral evil of sin. Because of sin, 'man is divided in himself. As a result, the whole life of men, both individual and social, shows itself to be a struggle, and a dramatic one, between good and evil, between light and darkness. Man finds that he is unable by himself to overcome the assaults of evil successfully, so that everyone feels as though he were chained' (GetS, 13).

The Kingdom of God Is in Man

'The whole of man's history has been the story of dour combat with the powers of evil, stretching – so our Lord tells us (Matt. 24.13) – from the very dawn of history until the last day. Finding himself in the midst of the battlefield man has to struggle to do what is right. It is at great cost to himself, aided by God's grace, that he succeeds in achieving his own inner integrity' (GetS, 37).

In conclusion we can say that even if the growth of God's kingdom is not identified with the world's development and progress, it is true nonetheless that the kingdom of God is in the world and, above all, in man who lives and acts in the world. The Christian knows that through his own efforts and the help of God's grace, he is bringing about the kingdom. The work of every Christian leads towards the fulfilment of all things in Christ, according to the plan of divine providence.

The Call of Vatican II

It is good for us to reflect together on the significance of the extraordinary synod which was held in 1985. It reminded us of how the church is meant to follow the spirit of Vatican II. What is this spirit? Paul VI touches upon it in his first encyclical *Ecclesiam Suam*. On the one hand 'this is the time in which the church must deepen the awareness of herself, must meditate on the mystery which is hers, must explore . . . the doctrine . . . concerning her own origins, her own nature, her own mission, her own final destiny.' On the other hand, Paul VI continues, 'The church must enter into dialogue with the world in which she lives. The church becomes a word; the church becomes a message. These are the two directions that are laid out for the church: The church must simultaneously fulfill her mission within and without. She must understand and deepen her own sense of identity, while she also makes the message of Christ relevant and life-giving to those around her.'

Well, the Second Vatican Council fulfilled these expectations. With an admirable unity of heart, of mind, and of will, the church felt intimately united to her apostolic origins. She also understood the way that she should follow to be faithful to Christ in the world of our times. To sum up, she felt immersed in the love of Christ that she reaches out to share with others: 'As the Father has loved me, so I have loved you, live on in my love . . . The command I give you is this, that you love one another' (John 15.9,17).

The Extraordinary Synod

Why was the synod called? Twenty years after the close of the Council, it seemed helpful, or frankly necessary, to take a look at the direction of the church. This is especially true because we have witnessed certain trends or interpretations of Vatican II which could lead us away from the road mapped out for us by the Council.

And this has proved the basic guideline for the synod, which has been welcomed with much media attention and closely followed with great interest by the public. As I highlighted at the end of the synod, the spirit of collegiality among the bishops was shown in a particularly strong way during the proceedings.

On that special occasion, we saw the church, represented by her bishops, gathered together to reaffirm the great work of Vatican II. Twenty years after its close, they gathered to examine the fruits of this great work, to see how the church had carried out the initiatives and guidelines of Vatican II during the last two decades. We saw the need to pause for reflection so we could objectively assess the state of the church in the light of God's word and with the help of the Lord's grace. We gathered with a renewed vigilance in the Holy Spirit so we could identify 'the signs of the times' and design a pastoral plan of action along the lines of the conciliar documents. We wanted to see what really valid things had been accomplished and what further steps were needed to carry out this great work of the church.

Gratefulness to the Paraclete

The Holy Spirit has blessed and protected the work of the synod. Just as twenty years ago we showed gratitude to the Holy Spirit for the gift of the Council, so we should thank the Spirit for the clear call to the church that has gone forth through the synod.

We must thank the Holy Spirit for these meetings with the presidents of the bishops' conferences from all over the world, the Cardinal Prefects of the Roman Curia, the Superiors General of various orders, members of the religious life and the laity – all men and women of our time gathered together under the wise leadership of the Secretary General and his collaborators.

We must also lift up grateful hearts to the Spirit because the sessions of the synod at all levels were effective, confirming that synods are a good way for the church to examine her work. Thus, the whole church has been united in Christ as 'one heart and one mind' (Acts 4.32). She has been called once again to apply the teaching of the Council to her life and to commit herself anew to its fulfilment in love. Yes, this is the mission entrusted by Christ to Peter and to the apostles: 'Live on in my love' (John 15.9).

The Call of the Synod

The *Relatio Finalis* – which is the concluding document of the extraordinary synod – witnesses eloquently to the bishops' collegial concern and to the entire church's common effort to grow in greater appreciation of the Second Vatican Council. Here we take a fresh look at the problems of the post-conciliar church with studied objectivity and a keen pastoral eye. We closely examine our situation after twenty years with all the important changes and improvements that have come into the life of the church. We see both problems and successes in this examination.

Considered in depth, the *Relatio Finalis* gives us appropriate suggestions for change and throws light on crucial problems in the life of the modern church. There is decided emphasis on the universal call to holiness. We see that this holiness must spring from the church's very life and call. Above all, it must be rooted in her response to the Word of God and the universal call to evangelise by sharing the good news. All Christians are called to go forward in this important call to holiness guided by the teaching authority of the bishops and the ongoing work of the church's theologians.

Second, the liturgy must lead us into a genuine experience of sacredness and reverence in God's presence. The reality of the church in its liturgy should be expressed as a communion with Christ and his mystical body.

Third, we see the need to move ahead in important areas addressed by the Council. We see the need for dialogue and growing unity between the churches of east and west. We need to appreciate the important contributions of the bishops' conferences. We must continue to make the church relevant to the needs and problems of modern man. We must foster understanding with non-Christian religions and with non-believers. We must always promote the cause of the poor and the oppressed and uphold the true human dignity of man by following the social teaching of the church. This is our heritage as the church, the heritage of the Second Vatican Council.

The Spirit Has Spoken to the Church

Another important issue that has been very close to the heart of those attending the synod is our need to form and train future priests. The church of the third millennium will be entrusted into their hands and their pastoral care. Their lives and their ministry must be a living translation of the Council's teachings. They will bear an enormous responsibility for implementing this teaching in the lives of God's people.

The call to ecumenism has also been very well received. In fact, the synod fathers have strongly emphasised the continued enrichment that Vatican II has brought to the church through the ecumenical movement. We witness a sure and steady progress toward unity, which is now bearing some promising fruit. That ecumenical commitment was underscored by the prayer service where I participated recently with ten observers from different communions and churches that are in theological dialogue with the Roman Catholic Church.

All these issues have moved us deeply at the synod and called forth a response. Once again the Spirit has spoken to the churches with 'the roar of rushing waters' (Rev. 1.15; 2.7, 11, 17, 29; 3.6, 13, 22). Let us listen to him. The document of *Relatio Finalis* is now in the hands of the church. It is an important collection of reflections and goals for the future that all are to draw from. These are not only words. No, this is a serious endeavour that calls for prayer, listening, and application. These are guidelines for the church's pastoral action in these closing years of the second millennium. Let us listen to the Spirit.

Some Specific Tasks

Let us now turn to some specific tasks which have been designated as priorities at the end of the assembly of the extraordinary synod. They are:

- the publication of the Code of Canon Law for the churches of the Eastern Rite;
- the preparation of a catechism that can be used by all Roman Catholics worldwide.
- a significant study of the nature of the bishops' conferences, which are organised nationally.

The Council of the General Secretariat of the Synod has been called to collaborate in developing a plan for implementing these recommendations of the synod. Concerning the Codé of Eastern Canon Law, a respective commission is working to make sure that the venerable churches of the east will receive a code very soon. This new code will recognise not only their traditions but, above all, their role and mission in the future of the universal church.

Let us pray for the strength and direction of the Holy Spirit to complete all these tasks.

The Catechism

The preparation of the catechism for Catholics worldwide reflects the synod's desire to put an end to certain teachings and interpretations of faith and morals that are not in accord with the Magisterium – the teaching authority of the church. The synod fathers see a clear need for doctrinal clarity and certainty so these errors can be refuted.

To this end, the synod has proposed a compendium of all Catholic doctrine that relates to faith and morals. Our aim is that this can serve as a point of reference for all catechisms prepared for all parts of the world. This is not the first time that the pastors of the church have requested greater clarity and understanding in the instruction of the faith. It had already been mentioned in a special way in the ordinary synod of 1977. In the apostolic exhortation *Catechesi Tradendae*, I also addressed the bishops' conferences and called on them to undertake 'with not only patience but with firm resolution, the enormous task . . . of making available catechisms which are well done and faithful to the essential content of revelation'.

We want our new generation to have a solid faith grounded in the truth of Christ. Let us all pray for this important work of compiling a catechism that can guide all of us worldwide into a clear knowledge of the truth. O come, Holy Spirit, enlighten our minds.

The National Bishops' Conferences

The National Bishops' Conferences have become a concrete, living reality in all parts of the world. The synod sees a need to deepen our theological understanding of these conferences and, above all, of their doctrinal basis. These conferences have made many valuable contributions to the work of the church in different countries. This is good. But their growth and their increasing influence also raise doctrinal and pastoral problems for the church. We ask, 'How should they develop? What is their role in the life of the church?'

The recommendation that we deepen our understanding of the doctrinal basis of these National Bishops' Conferences is supported by the Council's own decree on the bishops and their important role in the life of the church. In the Code of Canon Law, there is also reference to these episcopal conferences. The code states that the bishops 'jointly exercise some functions in order to better promote the good that the church offers to men'. This is especially true when this authority is exercised through forms of apostolate which are appropriate to the specific circumstances of a certain time and place (can. 447).

Let us pray that the Holy Spirit will give us wisdom about the important work of these conferences, so all the nations of the earth can be effectively pastored and built up in the faith.

It Is the Holy Spirit Who Guides the Church

Let us all adore and thank the Holy Spirit who guides the church of our time in the difficult but joyful way of renewal set forth by the Second Vatican Council. It is under the Spirit's guidance that the extraordinary synod of bishops has reached its conclusion with a renewed awareness that without the help of the Holy Spirit nothing can be done. Everything that is holy and decisive in carrying out the mandate of Christ must be accomplished in the Holy Spirit. Without your Spirit, O Lord, nothing can be done.

The Holy Spirit guided the work of the Second Vatican

Council and has guided the work of successive synods through the fire of his love and the breeze of his refreshment and renewal. You are rest for our labours, Holy Spirit. You have filled the hearts of all the pastors of God and the people of God. Holy Spirit, fill the hearts of your faithful.

Thus, the Spirit has led us to knowledge of the truth. As Jesus says of the work of the Holy Spirit, 'He will guide you to all truth' (John 16.13). This is the Spirit whom Christ promised to the apostles in the upper room before his passion and resurrection. He continues to manifest his presence in all ages of the church, particularly in critical times such as ours. All of us, under the inspiration of the Spirit, cry out, 'Lord and giver of life, Holy Spirit, come.'

The Mission of the Church

It is the fundamental mission of the church to proclaim to the world the good news of redemption. As she offers to others the good news of redemption, the church strives to understand their cultures. She seeks to know their minds and hearts, their values and customs, their problems and difficulties, their hopes and their dreams.

Once the church has got to know and understand these various aspects of the culture of a people, she can then start the dialogue of salvation. She is in a position to offer – with respect but clearly and with conviction – the good news of redemption to all those who freely desire to listen and to respond. This is the evangelical challenge of the church for all ages.

As Pope Paul VI once said of non-Christian religions: 'They carry in themselves the echo of millennia of seeking after God. . . . They possess an impressive heritage of deeply religious texts. They have taught generations of people to pray. They contain innumerable seeds planted by the Word and can constitute a genuine "evangelical preparation" ' (EN, 53).

In her esteem for the value of these religions, the church sees in them at times the action of the Holy Spirit, who is like the wind that 'blows where it wills' (John 3.8). Yet the church always remains strong in her conviction that she must accomplish her own task of offering the world the fullness of revealed truth, the truth of redemption in Jesus Christ. Let us pray that all men would come to the saving knowledge of Jesus Christ. He is the Saviour and the Redeemer of the world.

God Alone is the Love That Does Not Pass Away

'For this reason I bow my knees before the Father . . . that according to the riches of his glory he may grant you to be strengthened with might through his Spirit in the inner man' (Eph. 3.14, 16 RSV). Such is the prayer of the Apostle Paul in his letter to the Ephesians.

These words of the apostle I want to include in our prayer as we join together with Mary the Mother of Christ. And who could be closer to the heart of the Son if not the mother? Therefore, together with her, 'We bow our knees before the Father.' And together with her, we pray that our devotion to the heart of the Redeemer may accomplish for us all – through the Holy Spirit – the strengthening of the inner man. Yes – through the Holy Spirit. This is his work.

The Love of Christ Surpasses All Knowledge

The meaning of that 'strengthening with might in the inner man' – which is the working of the Holy Spirit acting in our hearts – is explained in the letter to the

Ephesians. We read: 'May Christ dwell in your hearts through faith, and may charity be the root and foundation of your life. Thus you will be able to grasp fully . . . and experience [Christ's] love which surpasses all knowledge, so that you may attain to the fullness of God himself' (Eph. 3.17–19).

This can only be accomplished by the power of the Holy Spirit at work in our human spirit. Only the Holy Spirit can open up for us this fullness of the 'inner man' which is found in the heart of the Christ. Only he can make it possible for our hearts to gradually draw strength from this fullness. Our hearts – our 'inner man' – must not be solely concerned with the things that pass away. No, it must have its 'root and foundation' in that love which does not pass away.

May the humble handmaid of the Lord preside over our prayer, so that our human hearts can have their 'root and foundation' in God, for he alone is the love that does not pass away. And this love is revealed in the human heart of Mary's Son.

A Vocation in Christ

In the hidden depths of the human heart, the grace of a vocation takes on the form of a dialogue. It is a dialogue between Christ and the individual in which a personal invitation is extended. Christ calls the person by name and says, 'Come, follow me.' This call – this mysterious inner voice of Christ – can be heard most clearly in the silence of prayer. Accepting it is an act of faith.

A vocation is either a sign of love or an invitation to love. In the Gospel account of Jesus' conversation with the rich young man, Mark says that 'Jesus looked at him with love' as he challenged him to sell all and follow the Lord (Mark 10.21). The Lord's call always requires a choice, a decision that calls for the exercise of our freedom.

The decision to say 'yes' to Christ's call carries with it

many important consequences. We need to renounce other priorities. We need to be willing to leave loved ones behind. We need to start with zeal and deep trust in God by drawing ever closer to Christ.

This response in love to our vocation is aptly expressed by the psalmist when he states: 'I say to the LORD, "My Lord are you. Apart from you I have no good." O LORD, my allotted portion and my cup, you it is who hold fast my lot. You will show me the path to life, fullness of joy in your presence, the delights at your right hand forever' (Ps. 16.2, 5, 11).

This grace requires our response. We must make a conscious effort to comprehend a mystery which is beyond us and yet has been revealed to us by God. God calls to us. Will we answer him?

Entering into the Mystery of God

Every vocation is a call to enter more deeply into the mystery of God. Theological and philosophical studies offer the opportunity for a deeper knowledge of the person of Christ. But this deeper knowledge does not depend only on our intellectual efforts. It is above all a gift of the Father who, through the Holy Spirit, allows us to know the Son. A person must be 'conformed to Christ' and not merely educated in the faith.

All our conscious collaboration with the grace of a vocation must follow the wisdom of Christ set forth in the parable of the true vine. Christ says, 'I am the true vine and my Father is the vinegrower' (John 15.1). He says to us, 'I am the vine, you are the branches. He who lives in me and I in him, will produce abundantly, for apart from me you can do nothing' (John 15.5).

The period of religious or seminary formation has the goal of deepening our union with Christ. Christ issues the same call to each one of us in our vocation.

The Branch and the Vine

Under the influence of the Holy Spirit, the spiritual link between the branch and the vine must be strengthened. The individual who is called and Christ the Lord must be more intimately united. And this necessarily means discipline and sacrifice – particularly the discipline of study and prayer. It is the sacrifice which liberates our hearts so we embrace the word of God with zeal. It is the sacrifice that calls us to give ourselves in service to our neighbours. For St John tells us: 'The fruitful [branches] he trims clean to increase their yield' (John 15.2). Therefore, do not doubt God's love when you face difficulties or sufferings, because the Lord 'trims' those he loves to increase their yield.

To be one with Christ, we must also completely accept his word. This word is communicated to us through Scripture and the tradition of the church. The church herself preserves and presents this word of God in all of its purity, integrity, and power. Through the action of the Holy Spirit and through the charism of the Magisterium, she hands on the gospel to all generations. Yes, a loving obedience to the authentic teaching authority of the church ensures our possession of the word of God. And without this word, there can be no union with Christ that will actually give life. Faithfulness to the Magisterium is an indispensable condition for a correct interpretation of 'the signs of the times'. It keeps us connected to the vine which gives us life.

Towards God Through Faith

Jesus Christ repeats to us: 'I am the way, and the truth, and the life' (John 14.6). These words refer to our pilgrimage through faith. We walk towards God through faith. We follow the way which is Christ.

He is the Son of God, and he is of the same divine

substance as the Father. God of God and Light of Light –
he has become Man, to be for us the way that leads to
the Father. In the course of his earthly life, he spoke
constantly about the Father. To the Father, he directed
the thoughts and the hearts of those who listened to him.
In a certain sense, he shared with them the Fatherhood of
God. He accomplished this in a very special way by teaching his disciples to pray the Our Father.

At the end of his mission on earth, the very day before
his passion and death, he said to the apostles: 'In my
Father's house there are many dwelling places; otherwise,
how could I have told you that I was going to prepare a
place for you?' (John 14.2). If the gospel is a revelation
that human life is a pilgrimage towards the Father's house,
it is also a call to faith. Yes, we walk like pilgrims. We
are called to a pilgrim faith.

We Only Pass Through the World

Christ says: 'I am the way, and the truth, and the life.'
Yes, human life on earth is a pilgrimage. All of us are
aware that we are in the world for just a brief time. Man's
life begins and ends quickly. It starts at the moment of
birth and is snuffed out at the moment of death. And in
this pilgrimage of life, the call to Christ helps us to live
in such a way that we will reach our true destination.

Man is constantly faced with the transitory nature of
a life which he knows to be extremely important as a
preparation for eternal life. Man's pilgrim faith orients him
towards God and directs him in making choices which will
help him in his journey towards eternal life. Thus, every
moment of man's earthly pilgrimage is important – it is
important in its challenges and in its choices.

Human Culture

One thing that touches man very closely in his pilgrimage is the reality of human culture. The Second Vatican Council has insisted on the fact that 'there are many relations between the message of salvation and human culture. In fact, God continually revealed himself to his people, until he fully manifested himself in the incarnate Son, who speaks according to the type of culture proper to the different historical periods' (GetS, 58). The Council also teaches: 'Christians, on their way towards the heavenly city, must seek and taste the things of above. However, this does not diminish but increases the importance of their duty to collaborate with all men for the construction of a more human world' (57).

The Earth is a Place of Pilgrimage

The church proclaims that man in his pilgrimage through life is so much more worthy of respect, of love, and of care because he is destined to live forever. Thus, every human culture that respects the dignity of man and his ultimate destiny aids him in living a noble and righteous life while he is on his earthly pilgrimage. St Paul himself addresses this point in his exhortation to the Christian community at Philippi: 'Finally, my brothers, your thoughts should be wholly directed to all that is true, all that deserves respect, all that is honest, pure, admirable, decent, virtuous, or worthy of praise' (Phil. 4.8). While he passes from birth to death on this earth, man must be fully aware that he is a pilgrim on his way to God.

And in this very quest for the absolute there is already an experience of the divine. Among all those who in the course of the ages have sought God, we can remember the famous Augustine of Hippo, who having found God, exclaimed: 'Where then have I found you in order to know you, if not in you, far above myself?' (*Confessions of Saint Augustine*, 10, 26).

We Are Pilgrims Seeking God

In both the Old and the New Testaments, man lives in the visible world in the midst of temporal things. Yet he is deeply aware of God's presence which shapes his whole life. This living God is in reality the ultimate bulwark for man in the midst of all the trials and sufferings of earthly existence. He yearns to possess this God in a complete way when he experiences his presence. He strives to see his face. In the words of the psalmist: 'As the hind longs for the running waters, so my soul longs for you, O God. Athirst is my soul for God, the living God. When shall I go and behold the face of God?' (Ps. 42.2–3).

While man strives to know God – to behold his face and to experience his presence – God turns to man in order to reveal his very life to him. The Second Vatican Council speaks at length on the importance of God's intervention in the world. It explains that 'through divine revelation, God wanted to manifest and to communicate himself and the eternal decrees of his will concerning the salvation of men' (DV, 6).

At the same time, this merciful and loving God who communicates himself through revelation continues to be for man an inscrutable mystery. And man – the pilgrim ever seeking the absolute – continues all through his life to seek the face of God. But at the end of the pilgrimage of faith, man reaches 'the Father's house'. And in this heavenly house, he hopes to behold God 'face to face' (1 Cor. 13.12).

Seeing God Face to Face

Seeing God face to face is the deepest desire of the human heart. How eloquent are the words of the Apostle Philip in this respect when he says: 'Lord, . . . show us the Father and that will be enough for us' (John 14.8). Philip's words are eloquent because they bear witness to the deepest thirst and desire of the human spirit. But Jesus' answer is even more eloquent.

Jesus explains to the apostles: 'Whoever has seen me has seen the Father' (John 14.9). Jesus is the full revelation of the Father; he explains to the world what the Father is like – not because he is the Father – but because he is completely one with the Father in the communion of divine life. In Jesus' own words: 'I am in the Father and the Father is in me' (John 14.11).

Thanks be to God! Man does not have to seek God all alone any more. With Christ, man discovers God and discovers him in Christ.

Yes, in Jesus Christ, God's revelation of himself reaches its fullness and its summit. The author of the letter to the Hebrews highlights this point when he says: 'In times past, God spoke in fragmentary and varied ways to our fathers through the prophets; in this, the final age, he has spoken to us through his Son' (Heb. 1.1–2). Thus, Christ is forever the way for us. We have a Saviour and a mediator with God.

Christ Is the Way and the Truth

Christ is the way because he is the truth. He, himself, is the ultimate answer to the question, 'Who is God?' This is the testimony of the Apostle John: 'No one has ever seen God. It is God the only Son, ever at the Father's side, who has revealed him' (John 1.18). By means of his incarnation, Jesus Christ manifests the love, the concern, and the mercy of the eternal God. And he does that as the Son of Mary – as God made man – in a way that mankind can understand.

We reach God through the truth about God himself and through the truth concerning all that exists outside of

God, through creation – which is the macrocosm – and through man – who is the microcosm. We reach God through the truth proclaimed by Christ and through the truth that is Christ. We reach God in Christ, who continues to repeat: 'I am the truth.'

Reaching God through the truth that is Christ is indeed reaching the source of all life. It is the source of eternal life that begins here on earth in the 'darkness of faith'. We endure this darkness until we behold God face to face in the light of glory where he actually is.

God Dwells in the Heart of Man

As he parted with the apostles on the eve of his passion, Jesus said: 'Anyone who loves me will be true to my word, and my Father will love him; we will come to him and make our dwelling place with him' (John 14.23). Just a few moments before being handed over to death, he reveals the heights and depths of an immense love. He reveals to us the mystery of God's indwelling presence. Yes, man is called to become a temple for the Blessed Trinity. What greater degree of communion with God could man ever aspire to?

What greater proof than this could God ever give us of his saving love? The God of all wants to enter into communion with man. All the age-old history of Christian mysticism, even with some of its most sublime expressions, can only speak imperfectly to us about the unutterable presence of God in the heart of man.

Christ is Present in His Church

From Christ's presence in the innermost part of man, we now consider the mystery of the church. The reading of the Acts of the Apostles leads us to reflect on the beginnings of the church. It is a community which is born out of Christ's paschal mystery. This new-born church is guided and quickened by the Holy Spirit. The apostles go forth preaching in the power of the Holy Spirit, for instance.

In the church's very beginnings, we see a close link between the human responsibility of the apostles and the divine inspiration of the Holy Spirit. 'It has seemed good to the Holy Spirit and to us . . .', the church of Jerusalem writes to the gentiles (Acts 15.28 RSV). There is a hint of almost a partnership between the Holy Spirit and the apostles.

This is no accident. Just as the Christian's soul is inhabited by the Blessed Trinity, so also the church – which is the Christian community – is inhabited by the Blessed Trinity. In fact, the Christian is a temple of the Blessed Trinity inasmuch as he is a member of the mystical body of Christ, inasmuch as he is a living branch grafted onto the true vine which is Christ.

Even here on the earth, despite the miseries of this life, the church enjoys an intimacy with God which is the foundation of her infallibility.

The Heavenly Jerusalem

Together with this historical understanding of the church as the Christian community, the liturgy shows us her mystical character as Jerusalem, the holy city, 'coming down out of heaven from God' (Rev. 21.10). This heavenly Jerusalem is the church triumphant and glorified in Christ. It is made up of those who now enjoy the prize of eternal life because of the saving redemption of Christ.

Like St John the Evangelist, we must always have the eyes of our hearts set towards this heavenly and glorious Jerusalem, which is the final goal of our life's journey. We must always behold this 'blessed vision of peace', which encourages and comforts us as the object of our hope. The brethren who have reached salvation await us in God's holy city. And in the very throne room of God, they pray and intercede for us so that we, too, may join them one day.

The Guiding Light of the Spirit

The church, born of the cross of Christ and of his resurrection, is constantly guided by the Holy Spirit. 'The Holy Spirit whom the Father will send in my name will instruct you in everything, and remind you of all that I told you' (John 14.26).

The earthly church is constantly led by the Spirit of the risen Christ towards a deepening of that selfsame truth which she has received from the very lips of the divine teacher. In the course of the centuries the church comes to a deeper understanding of the truth because of the guiding light of the Spirit. That way the pilgrim church draws ever closer to the full knowledge of Christ. This saving knowledge is already possessed by the church in heaven, 'the Jerusalem on high' (Gal. 4.26). The Spirit comforts the church here below with the dazzling vision of the church in glory. Thus, the earthly church is encouraged and presses on to join her.

Our Hope of Glory

In her universal mission of salvation, the church is constantly spurred on by the Spirit of the risen Lord. She earnestly desires to lead all men to that heavenly bliss which the saints already enjoy. Within the ranks of the heavenly Jerusalem, the saints do their part by interceding for the pilgrim church on earth. For her part, the church looks with the eyes of faith towards the heavenly Jerusalem and finds there the light and the hope she needs to go forth and share the way of salvation and holiness with the world.

Thus, the church in the world guides man to the everlasting temple located in the eternal Jerusalem, according to the Revelation of St John. 'I saw no temple in the city. The Lord, God the Almighty, is its temple – he and the Lamb' (Rev. 21.22).

The heavenly Jerusalem – by contrast to the church here below – is completely pure and holy. She is completely consecrated to God. There is in her nothing profane which needs to be distinguished from the sacred things of God. In her, there are no temples because there is no need for such a mediating presence. No, everything in heaven manifests splendidly the beatific vision of the Blessed Trinity. In this sense, God's abiding presence in the temple is in everything and everyone in heaven.

God's presence certainly abides in the church here below, too. But it lies hidden in the steadfast faith and expectant hope of the people of God. And, thus, we do not see the glory of Christ as clearly as the church in heaven. But we wait with longing for the Second Coming of Christ and the resurrection of the dead. Then the church will be fully one in heaven with Christ.

Rejoice! This is the church in her full glory. This is the church as the object of contemplation by St John in the book of Revelation.

Be Joyous Witnesses of a Genuine Christian Life

The pastoral strategy which the church has developed in post-conciliar years offers us timely helps for a solid and strong spiritual formation and for a renewed love of men. First, I exhort you to participate in the efforts to evangelise men to Christ and to instruct the faithful in the way of the sacraments. This approach to the Christian life will help you understand and welcome the gifts and graces Christ wants to give you.

By regularly frequenting the sacraments in the right spirit, you will become joyous witnesses of a genuine Christian life. You will find the support you need to follow the Lord of life. He will be able to use you to reveal to the men of this astounding and restless age the true face of God, which is always 'rich in mercy' (Eph. 2.4).

In frequenting the sacraments, work together with your pastors, for union with them is providential for the full flowering of the Holy Spirit in your life. This will enable them to guide you in building the church on earth, which is meant to be a community of love, reflecting the very life of the Blessed Trinity (St Augustine, *De Trinitate*, 49).

Be Builders of the Civilisation of Love

Eagerly co-operate with the Redeemer. He manifests to us the mercy of the Father. The Father in Christ is always inclined towards us to shower on us his blessings. See, he comes with life and strength. He comes offering us forgiveness and a personal relationship with him; he sends us his Son, from whom the mercy of God overflows.

Yes, be conformed to Christ, the perfect image (S. Th., I, q. 35) of the infinite love of the Father. Like Jesus, be close to man. Above all, be near to him when he is sick and when his dignity is demeaned. Be promoters and builders of the civilisation of love. Be tireless in sharing true charity, which elevates and transfigures man. Thus, you will participate fully in the redemption of Christ.

The church says to you, builders of the civilisation of love: 'The experience of the past and of our own times shows that justice alone is not enough . . . for ensuring human life in all its dimensions, if it does not yield to that deeper force which is love' (*Dives in Misericordia*, 12).

The First Sacrament of Salvation

Through the rite of Baptism – which is the first of the sacraments of salvation instituted by Jesus – the human person is incorporated into Christ and united to the family of the living God. St Paul repeats for us what he wrote to the Christians of Rome in his own time: 'Are you not aware that we who were baptized into Christ Jesus were baptized into his death? Through baptism into his death we were buried with him, so that, just as Christ was raised from the dead by the glory of the Father, we too might live a new life. If we have been united with him through likeness to his death, so shall we be through a like resurrection' (Rom. 6.3–5).

The Apostle Paul teaches us that Baptism is a figure and expression of the passion of Christ. In fact, in Baptism we are immersed in Christ's death, cleansed of the filth of sin, introduced to the new life of the resurrection, and made living temples of the Spirit. Through Baptism we are incorporated into the life of the church. This is the community of Christ the Lord, created and nourished by love. This is the community of faith and new life which accompanies us in life and sustains us in our weaknesses. Then we are no longer slaves of the greatest evil of all which is sin. We may begin to live in the fullness of freedom as the children of God.

Confirmation

'May the Holy Spirit confirm you with the richness of his gifts' (Rite of Confirmation).

St Peter's Basilica opens wide its doors to the Christ who is 'the faithful witness' (Rev. 1.5) of the invisible God, to the Christ who is 'the good shepherd' (John 10.11) of our souls.

St Peter's Basilica opens wide its doors to the Holy Spirit who was given to the apostles so they could witness boldly to the crucified and risen Christ.

St Peter's Basilica welcomes with joy all those who come to the Lord's table. St Peter's especially welcomes all young people who have received the holy Sacrament of Confirmation. The Basilica welcomes you who are confirmed with the richness of the gifts of the Holy Spirit, you who have been anointed with the holy chrism. I greet all of you with great affection.

A New Generation

Who are you?

You are a new generation of followers of Christ who have received Baptism. Through that first sacrament you were welcomed into the community of the church. For most of you this sacrament of initiation was received during the first several weeks of your life. Your parents and your godparents took you to Baptism. Thus, you began living in sanctifying grace. God placed his indelible and invisible sign on you. You became children of God whose souls bear the mark of grace.

This grace and this spiritual sign of Baptism you owe to Christ – to his death and resurrection. In fact, through Baptism you have been immersed in the death of Christ so you can rise again with him to new life. As the Apostle Paul teaches us in the letter to the Romans: 'Through baptism into his death we were buried with him, so that, just as Christ was raised from the dead by the glory of the Father, we too might live a new life' (Rom. 6.4).

From the moment of Baptism, you have become partakers in this life which is in Jesus Christ – the life of the Son of God. And you have become yourselves sons and daughters of God by adoption. You have been raised to the dignity of sonship in Christ, the only-begotten Son of the Father. Since the Son shares the fullness of life in unity with the Father and the Holy Spirit, you too have received the Baptism of new life. You have been baptised in the name of the Blessed Trinity: in the name of the Father, and of the Son, and of the Holy Spirit.

Baptism is 'man's new birth from water and from the Spirit' (John 3.5). So you have become immersed in the new life which is in God and which is from God. You are carrying within yourselves the pledge of eternal life.

The Covenant with God

Through the giving of the Sacrament of Confirmation, the church has brought to its fullness the life of grace of which you have become partakers through Baptism. To help make this a living reality for you, you have renewed the promises of faith in that covenant with God which was accomplished for you on the day of Baptism.

At the time of your Baptism, these vows were spoken for you by your parents and godparents. Now you have claimed the words of this covenant as your own. You renounced Satan and made your profession of faith. You have reached a personal and a mature faith in Christ that you can call your own.

More Than Anything Else You Are Called to Be Disciples of Jesus

You have had time to ponder these truths that the church proclaims and professes. These truths make up the foundation of the New Covenant with God in Jesus Christ.

You have reached the goal of Christian education. From the very first years of life in your families and parishes, you have heard the call to be followers and disciples of Jesus Christ. This has been the goal of your prayer. Your prayer with your family and your parish community has brought you ever closer to the mystery of Christ's presence.

This has been the goal of your education as a Christian. You were already children of God thanks to Baptism. Now you have become disciples of Jesus Christ.

I think you and I should thank God for your parents and your pastors. We should thank God for all those who have helped you understand the truth revealed by God in Jesus Christ and proclaimed by the church.

The Laying On of Hands

The sacrament which you have received in Confirmation makes your relationship with the truth of the gospel grow strong. You become mature in Christ. You have already known this truth. Now desire to be strengthened in it. Together with the church, let us turn to the Spirit of truth, so that the faith you profess may remain in your minds and in your hearts. May it be confirmed in all you say and do.

Baptism is a sacrament of water, which is carried out through the washing of the body to forgive sins and to make those in slavery to sin children of God. The chrism or holy oil is the sacrament of those who know Christ and now go forth to witness to him as the apostles did after Pentecost.

That is why part of the rite of Confirmation is the laying on of hands by the bishop. He confers the sacrament by anointing your forehead with holy chrism. The bishop presides at your Confirmation because he has a special vocation in Christ to all of the people in his diocese. He is called to be a shepherd and a pastor to his people as one who carries on the work and ministry that started with the apostles.

The Anointing with Holy Chrism

The bishop, surrounded by the priests of your parish, asked the Holy Spirit to give each of you his gifts: 'Give them . . . a spirit of wisdom and of understanding, a spirit of counsel and of fortitude, a spirit of knowledge and of piety, and fill them with a spirit of reverence before the Lord.'

The anointing of the holy chrism followed that prayer.

The bishop has asked that the Holy Spirit may make you fully conformed to Christ, the Son of God. In fact, the Son of God has become man in order to lead all men to the fullness of the Holy Spirit, the one whom he bestows unceasingly upon the sons of men. This is the Christ, the Messiah, which means the anointed one. He is the first to be anointed with the Holy Spirit and with power. Through the Sacrament of Confirmation, we become in a particular way sharers in this Spirit which Christ has brought to us and of this power which is in him.

The bishop, anointing each confirmand's forehead, prayed: 'Be sealed with the gift of the Holy Spirit.' And each one of you responded: 'Amen.' Then he greeted you by saying, 'Peace be with you!' (John 20.19). These are the very words of Christ after the resurrection when he gave the Holy Spirit to the apostles. Your response was: 'And with your spirit.' Yes, let us rejoice in this gift of the Holy Spirit for our young people. The Holy Spirit is the fountain of God's peace welling up in man to everlasting life. Praise be to God!

The Sponsors

I invite all of you who were present at the Confirmations of our young people to remember this blessed event. It is so important in the life of the Christian community. They so need our support and prayers. I ask this especially of the sponsors who have committed themselves to stand by each one of those confirmands as they move into spiritual maturity in Christ.

All of you sponsors are special trustees of this gift of the Spirit, which was received by these confirmands for the first time in Baptism. Now he is bestowed on these young people anew. You are called to stand with these young people. They are entering into maturity in Christ. New tasks and new responsibilities lie ahead for them. They need your support.

God Is Spirit

On the eve of his death on the cross, Christ said to the apostles: 'The Spirit . . . will bear witness on my behalf. You must bear witness as well' (John 15.26–7).

These words refer also to each one who comes to receive the Sacrament of Confirmation. The sacrament you have received is a sign of a new beginning in Christ. Being aware of the power of the Holy Spirit and aware of the great apostolic heritage which is continued in the church from one generation to another – you cannot exclude yourselves from this gift. No, you cannot stay away from it!

May the Holy Spirit work in your hearts as he worked in the hearts of the apostles when they were sent out to announce the good news. Be aware of the gift of God which you have received! Be firm in your faith and strong in professing it! Live according to its truths! Remember that God wants true worshippers. They are those who worship him in Spirit and truth (John 4.23).

In fact, this is a great mystery. God is Spirit.

Remain in My Love

'I am the vine. . . . He who lives [or, remains] in me and I in him, will produce abundantly' (John 15.5). Christ remains in us through the Eucharist. Jesus' invitation to 'remain in him' reminds us of another truth he mentioned, this time in the context of his great discourse on 'the bread of life'. 'The man who feeds on my flesh and drinks my blood remains in me, and I in him' (John 6.56). So Jesus tells the multitudes.

This parallel passage shows us how the symbol of the vine also has eucharistic significance. We see how our remaining in Jesus, the true vine, is fulfilled by taking him as our very food. The Eucharist is precisely Jesus who remains in our midst in a true and real way. Even though to us he appears under the sacramental signs of the bread and the wine, he is truly present with us. It is true that these signs do not give us the joy of seeing him with our senses, but they do offer us the assurance of his full presence in our midst. We are the beneficiaries of his ability to be multiplied in all places and at all times sacramentally as food for our souls. Let us all draw near to the table of the Lord to receive this precious food.

A Love Which Becomes Food and Drink

The Eucharist is a special point of encounter with Christ's love. Jesus tells his disciples, 'Live on [or, remain] in my love' (John 15.9). This is an amazing love which makes itself personally available to each one of us. This is a love which becomes food and drink that satisfies our hunger and thirst for true spiritual life. Yes, Jesus himself invites us to 'drink of the fruit of the vine' (Mark 14.25).

This 'remaining' in Christ is the first and absolute condition for bearing fruit. Just as Jesus bore fruit through his obedience to the Father's plan of salvation, so his disciples will bear fruit as they willingly accept God's discipline and reject sin in their lives.

My Father Is the Vinegrower

In the light of the parable of the vine and the branches, the Eucharist becomes the main focus of God's salvific work in man. This work is summed up in the words – 'My Father is the vinegrower' (John 15.1). He cultivates the vine by caring for each branch. Since as Creator he is also our Father, he wants all men whom he created in his image to receive this life which comes from him through the Son.

Since creation, the work of the Father has been to care and provide for everything he has made. He cares above all for the persons he has made in his image. In the parable, they are called 'branches', which the Father 'trims', cleanses, and purifies so they can grow and have abundant life. The divine vinegrower shows himself to be a loving Father. He behaves towards us like a Father and wants to be treated as such. All of this recalls to us the superior reality of our spiritual life, the fullness of our salvation.

We see how the Father continuously watches over us and encourages us to desire his attention and nurturing love. With his fatherly interventions in our lives, he reminds us that we do not live in a blind and fatalistic universe. No, we live under the watchful eyes of our Father who is good to us. He is always close to us and ready to help.

He asks that we do our part and collaborate in this work of mercy and of salvation. The divine vinegrower renews us with the regenerating grace of the sacraments of purification and renewal. These are Penance and the Eucharist. Through them, he trims us and accomplishes anew the great paschal mystery of the Son's death and resurrection.

God's Human Face

The liturgy gives an ample answer to the question: 'Who is man?' We find this answer in the book of Sirach: 'The LORD from the earth created man, and in his own image he made him. Limited days of life he gives him and makes him return to earth again. He endows man with a strength of his own, and with power over all things else on earth' (Sir. 17.1–3).

Here we have the answer to the question of man and his destiny: 'In his own image he made him.' Man is, therefore, 'God's human face', according to a brilliant expression of Gregory of Nyssa (PG 44, 446). For an adequate understanding of man, one should never lose sight of this biblical revelation, which, from Genesis to the Apocalypse, brings to full light the true dimension of

man. He is created in God's image. And God, to rescue
and deliver him from sin, has become man.

Man in Communion with Christ

From the time when God manifested himself to Abraham
– which meant the resuming of the dialogue between the
creature and the Creator that had been interrupted with
Adam's sin – true biblical humanism has not ceased to
affirm the eminent and unique dignity of every human
person. Each human person is made in the image of God.
Each human person is rescued by Christ and called to
enter into communion with him.

This is the position that man occupies in the world and
in the scale of values. It is true that literature and the arts
often show his weaknesses, his deficiencies, his sensuality,
his hypocrisy, and his cruelty. But we know that he is
above all a being capable of amazing us with brilliant
thinking, his scientific discoveries, the inspiration of his
poetic lyricism, the splendour of his artistic creations, the
resources of his moral heroism, and, most importantly,
the testimony of his holiness in Christ.

We are Grafted onto the Vine

The Eucharist is the sacrament of life-giving union with
Christ. It is also a sacrament that builds up the community. The vine and the branches are images of this
community which includes all those who are united in
Christ through grace and truth. The image of the vine
and the branches reminds us of the need to live the reality
of the church in a deep communion with Christ and the
brethren. The church is the mystical body of believers;
Christ is its head and all of the faithful are its members.

This is a body whose life comes from the supernatural
sap of grace and whose growth is animated by the light
of the Holy Spirit. Herein lies the 'power' (2 Tim. 3.5) of

our faith; herein lies the connecting tissue which gives meaning and unity to the Christian communities living throughout the entire world.

This truth is illustrated by an image drawn from agriculture called 'grafting'. In Baptism we have been grafted onto Christ (Rom. 11.17). We have become branches sustained by the vine. Therefore, we have been called to live united to Christ and to the brethren. Thus, we are the community of the baptised and redeemed. And we are part of that redeemed community as long as we remain united to Christ and live in communion with our brothers and sisters. Jesus shows us what happens when we separate ourselves from him and our brethren. The illustration from Scripture makes it very clear. If the branch does not remain united to the vine, it withers. It is cut off and is thrown into the fire.

But the Eucharist does not only imply an intimate relationship between Christ and every single believer. It has been instituted also for the union of all the Christian faithful as the Lord's body. It forms in us a deep awareness of our unity, of our brotherhood, of our solidarity, and of our friendship in Christ. It encourages in us a deep sense of spiritual and social cohesion, for we are among those who are nourished by the same bread to form a single body in Christ (1 Cor. 10.17).

Preach the Word

All of us must be convinced that in this time of the life of the church we need to trust God and not give way to discouragement over the many difficulties we face. There is a danger that we can become perplexed and perhaps even despair and turn bitter. The Lord guides his church. Yet even though he uses her to accomplish his purposes, he does not exempt her from the difficulties, adversities, and worries of this life.

In meeting these challenges, we must meet, discuss, and

plan for the future. We must explore ideas and seek out approaches that can strengthen the church and further the sanctification of souls and their continual evangelisation to Christ. In the depths of our difficulties lies the transforming message of Christ. He is the source of our strength. In him we have strength for everything (Phil. 4.13).

To the crowd that asked Jesus, 'What must we do to perform the works of God?' Jesus answered: 'This is the work of God: have faith in the one whom he sent' (John 6.28–9). This is the fundamental command for us which is valid for all time, for all peoples, and for all ages. The memorable words that St Paul wrote to his disciple Timothy are also significant for us: 'Preach the word, . . . stay with this task whether convenient or inconvenient – correcting, reproving, appealing – constantly teaching and never losing patience' (2 Tim. 4.2).

Popular Piety

There is a particular point which I would like to discuss with you: popular piety and its relationship to the liturgical life of the church.

Vatican II's Constitution on the Sacred Liturgy makes reference to the problem, when it speaks about the 'pious exercises of the Christian people', commending and recommending them as long as 'they are conformed to the laws and norms of the church'. It follows that we should not ignore or treat with indifference or contempt displays of piety or devotion that are still alive in the midst of the Christian people. I am thinking of patronal festivities, pilgrimages to shrines, and the various forms of devotion to the saints.

In fact, popular piety or popular religiosity, as Paul VI already remarked in the apostolic exhortation *Evangelii Nuntiandi*, is rich in meaning. 'It manifests a thirst for God that only the simple and the poor can know; it makes people capable of generosity and of sacrifice to the point of heroism, when the manifestation of faith is at stake; it carries with it a keen sense of God's deep attributes, his Fatherhood, his providence, his loving and constant presence; it generates inner attitudes to the same degree – patience, a sense of the cross in daily life, detachment, openness to others, devotion' (n. 48).

Certainly in these religious practices not everything is of equally high value. Since those who practise them are human, their motivations may be mixed with emotion and with a simple desire for security more than with stepping out in faith or showing gratefulness and adoration to God. Besides, they are expressed in signs, gestures, and formulas which may sometimes take on an excessive importance, even to the point of being sensational. However, in their substance they are expressions of the deep inner reality of man. They acknowledge the fact that man, as a creature, is fundamentally dependent on his Creator.

The Richness and the Risk of Popular Piety

We see that popular piety is at once a richness and a risk. Thus, the pastors of the church need to be watchful to check abuses. But they need to carry out their pastoral care with a great measure of patience. As St Augustine noted in his own time when confronted with some forms of devotion to the saints, 'What we teach is one thing, and what we are forced to tolerate is a different thing' (*Contra Faustum*, 20, 21: CSEL 25, 263).

What really counts is to become aware of the deep religious need in man which shows itself in a variety of ways. We must make every effort to constantly purify it and bring it to the level of evangelisation to Christ. This is the approach that the church has followed in every age in dealing with the challenge of indigenous cultures that are non-Christian and the challenge of popular piety and devotions.

This is what the church practised when she had to welcome crowds of new converts after the edict of Constantine. This is what she practised in Christianising the barbarian peoples of Europe. This is what happened once again with the peoples of the new world where it was necessary to announce the gospel. This is what continues to happen today in seeking to adapt the Christian message to the ethos and traditions of various peoples.

We should never forget the norm that Pope Gregory the Great gave to the Apostle of England, St Augustine of Canterbury: 'Pagan temples should not be destroyed, but rather purified and consecrated to God; the same should happen with the religious customs with which the people were habituated to celebrate religious events in life' (Gregory the Great: Jaffe, *Regesta Pontificum*, n. 1848, letter of July 10, 601).

Models of Life

In a nation of ancient Christian traditions such as Italy, popular piety has an undeniable Christian character. Many customs of this nation have their origin in church festivals and are still linked to them. Their origins should be noted. In cases where the customs tend to stray away from those origins, efforts must be made to bring them back.

With personal devotions we should make sure that they never degenerate into a false piety, superstition, or magical practices. Thus, the devotion to saints – which is expressed in patronal feasts, in pilgrimages, in processions, and so many other forms of piety – must not be reduced to a mere quest for protection, for material possessions, or for bodily health. The saints must be held up to the faithful, above all, as models of life and of imitation of Christ. They must be presented as a way that leads to a greater devotion to Christ.

The best way to safeguard against abuses is to bring the word of the gospel into these occasions of popular piety. We need to lead those who live with these forms of popular religiosity from an initial and sometimes hesitant movement towards faith to an act of genuine Christian faith. We must seek to evangelise popular piety so we can remove its defects. By purifying it, evangelisation will consolidate it, making it possible for those things which are ambiguous to take on a clearer meaning in the context of true Christian faith, hope, and love.

Make Disciples of All the Nations

The words of Jesus our Saviour come to my mind once again: 'Go, therefore, and make disciples of all the nations. Baptize them in the name of the Father, and of the Son, and of the Holy Spirit. Teach them to carry out everything I have commanded you. And know that I am with you always, until the end of the world!' (Matt. 28.19–20).

These words – which were the last ones spoken by the Lord before he visibly left the earth to return to his Father – represent in their strength and effectiveness the Magna Carta of Christian dynamism. They also shape the very identity of the church – her nature as a trustee – to which the task has been entrusted not to keep the treasure of truth and divine salvation for herself but to give it away to others. The words of St Matthew's text are the constitution of the church, for she is essentially a missionary institution.

Evangelisation is the mandate to announce to the whole world the salvation of man in Christ Jesus, who died and rose to be the Lord of the living and the dead. And that is why – as the Second Vatican Council says, repeating an idea of St Augustine – 'the apostles, on which the church was founded, according to Christ's example, preached the word of truth and gave rise to churches' (AG, 1).

The Duty of Promoting Human Good

Before they were scattered all over the world, the apostles waited in prayer – together with Mary, mother of the church – for the coming of the Holy Spirit. Jesus had promised to send him as the divine helper to lead them into all truth and to give them the grace to live the call of the gospel. In fact, it is only through the power of the Holy Spirit that the church can enlighten all men. Only through the Spirit, can she be 'the salt of the earth and the light of the world' (Matt. 5.13–14). Only through the Spirit can she renew and save all men, bringing them to Christ.

When the Congregation for the Propagation of the Faith was first officially constituted, the exciting years of great geographical discoveries were in full course. New worlds were opening up to the missionary activity of the church and the need to create a structure to serve that purpose was greater than ever if the propagation of faith was to be encouraged in all places.

Nowadays we are in a different age. The exploration of the earth has been completed. Entire continents are being developed and opened to the message of the gospel with young and promising churches. A rich harvest is in need of labourers who can be the light and the salt of the earth.

Two thousand years after the foundation of the church, the gospel has been proclaimed to the whole world in the geographical sense. But, in the context of her evangelising mission, the church does not forget the duty of promoting human good, of social development, of the defence of the rights of men.

The Duty of Re-evangelisation

Tragically, there are many parts of the world where people either do not know the truth of the gospel, or where they have forgotten it. In the modern age – which boasts of being the information society – there are millions of human beings who are eager to hear the gospel but who know little or nothing about the Saviour of the world, Christ Jesus. And in the old world, raised for centuries in the school of Christian faith, there exist false ideologies and a materialism which are so strong as to make one fear that entire regions of the world may sink into the dark abyss of atheism. Thus, along with the need for evangelisation, we find in other countries a strong need for re-evangelisation.

All of us – priests and laypeople – are called to raise the consciousness of Catholic public opinion about the pressing need for evangelisation and re-evangelisation. We especially need to reach our youth with this message. They are so often distracted by empty expectations. We need to stress with them the urgency of missionary work, the call which personally challenges all those who have been baptised. It is also our task to make Christian communities grow in closer solidarity with the needs and sufferings of their brethren in mission territories.

Spreading the Gospel

The Second Vatican Council, in its decree *Ad Gentes*, has made a wonderful synthesis of both the reason for and the duty of evangelisation. It therefore touches on the missionary activities of the church: 'The reason for the missionary activity comes from God's will, who "wants all men to be saved and to come to know the truth. And the truth is this: God is one. One also is the mediator between God and men, the man Christ Jesus, who gave himself as a ransom for all" (1 Tim. 2.4–6), and "there is no salvation in anyone else" (Acts 4.12). Consequently, it is necessary for all to turn to him, after having known him through the preaching of the church, and to vitally adhere to him and to the church, his body, through Baptism. . . .' 'Even though God, through ways known only to him, may lead those men who without any guilt of their own do not know the gospel to that faith "without which it is impossible to please him" (Heb. 11.6), it is nevertheless the unavoidable task of the church to spread the gospel, so that missionary activity fully preserves – today as always – its validity and relevance' (n. 7).

Announcing the gospel is a permanent task for the church. It is absolutely necessary and can never be substituted for anything else. The salvation of men is at stake. That is why, as Paul VI wrote in the apostolic exhortation *Evangelii Nuntiandi*, 'It is imperative that the apostle consecrate to it all of his time, all of his energies, and, if necessary, that he sacrifice his own life for it' (n. 5).

Bringing Glad Tidings to the Poor

The messianic mission of Jesus of Nazareth has been carried out in India – primarily in Calcutta – in a particularly eloquent way that is a real testimony to God. It is a testimony the whole world has marvelled at. It is a witness that shakes the conscience of the world. I am referring to the testimony of the life and work of a woman who – even though she was not born in India – is known as Mother Teresa of Calcutta.

Some years ago this woman was spurred by the love of Christ to serve the Lord among those who suffer the greatest misery and greatest sorrow. She left a teaching institute to found the Missionaries of Charity. Her well-known service to the poorest among the poor carries out in a concrete way Jesus' messianic mission to 'bring glad tidings to the poor' (Luke 4.18). It has given the world an encouraging lesson of compassion and of genuine love towards those in need. Her example has shown the power of redemption. It has inspired men and women to perform heroic service. And, in fact, that kind of example helps sustain them in that service year after year.

The Pre-eminent Value of Love

This incredible charity and self-sacrifice of Mother Teresa, which is accomplished out of love for Christ, is a challenge to the world. This world is too often characterised by selfishness and pleasure seeking, by greed, by the pursuit of prestige and power. Facing the evils of our modern age, this witness proclaims – not with words but with actions and sacrifice – the pre-eminent value of the love of Christ our Redeemer. This love calls the sinner to conversion and invites him to follow Christ's example: 'to bring glad tidings to the poor' (Luke 4.18).

Who Are the Poor?

But who are the poor in our times? The gospel speaks about the 'blind', the 'prisoners' and the 'captives' (Luke 4.18). And the poor include all those who live without the indispensable necessities of life, both materially and spiritually. Besides, in today's world, there are millions of fugitives who have had to leave their countries. Millions of people, sometimes whole tribes or populations, are exposed to the threat of extinction because of drought or famine. And how could one not acknowledge the poverty and ignorance of those who have never had the opportunity for an education? Or consider the absolute helplessness of innumerable people facing injustice and underdevelopment? And there are also many people who have been deprived of their right to religious freedom and have suffered immensely because they cannot worship God according to the dictates of a right conscience.

Mother Teresa

Our times face various kinds of moral poverty, which threatens the freedom and dignity of the human person.

There is the abject poverty of those who live without understanding the meaning of life. There is the poverty of a conscience that has gone astray or is in error. There is the poverty of separated or broken families. It is all the poverty of sin.

In this modern world, which suffers from so many forms of poverty, the church strives to 'bring glad tidings to the poor' (Luke 4.18). And she does that by drawing on the efforts of people like Mother Teresa and others like her. Their love for Christ and their service to the poorest of the poor is deeply prophetic and deeply evangelical in its call to the whole church.

This work of self-sacrifice and Christian love is really a source of great comfort and blessing. For me and for the whole church, it is an 'encouragement . . . in Christ', a 'solace that love gives', a 'fellowship in spirit' (Phil. 2.1).

The Voice of Christ

After having seen the work borne out of great love for Christ in the heart of this woman – she who is a simple servant of the Lord – I want to make mine the exhortation which the Apostle Paul makes to the Philippians: 'In the name of the encouragement you owe me in Christ, in the name of the solace that love can give, of fellowship in spirit, compassion, and pity, I beg you: make my joy complete by your unanimity, possessing one love, united in spirit and ideals' (Phil. 2.1–2).

Were these words of the apostle to the gentiles addressed only to the church in Philippi? Or only to the church in Calcutta? No! They are addressed to the whole church in every part of the world! To all Christians! In fact they are addressed to the followers of all religions, to all men of good will. Such is the testimony of brotherly love. Such is St Paul's exhortation: 'Make my joy complete by your unanimity, possessing one love, united in spirit and ideals. Never act out of rivalry or conceit' (Phil. 2.2–3).

No! Never act in ways that can feed upon hatred, injustice, or suffering! Never act in favour of the arms race! Never act to encourage the oppression of peoples and of nations! Never act in a way inspired by hypocritical forms of imperialism or inhuman ideologies that crush the human spirit.

Finally, let those who have no voice speak! Let Mother Teresa's poor speak, as well as all the poor of the world! Their voice is the voice of Christ! Amen.

Man's Right

War and violence spring from our ignorance of the fundamental rights of man. Man's fundamental right is to be treated as a unique and irreplaceable person. He is a creature made in God's image and likeness. And through Baptism, he has become God's adoptive son and a partaker in the redemption secured by the incarnate Son of God, our Lord Jesus Christ.

Where a brother is used as a means for satisfying one's own interests, needs, and desires – where the other is abused – violence is committed and discord and war are sown. But where the good of the other is sought – considering that he 'is the only creature that God has loved in itself' (GetS, 24) – where there is true love, there peace is born. The foundation of peace is love.

That is why peace comes ultimately from God, who is the source of all love. The life of God in the Blessed Trinity is a life of love. There is love of the Father towards the Son and of the Son towards the Father. This is a love which is so strong and so personal that it is manifested as a divine person, the Holy Spirit. If the Holy Spirit descends into our hearts, especially when we receive the sacraments, we will be capable of that love and will be able to be genuine peacemakers.

Political Refugees

The nations of the world must work together to offer refugees who want it a new country to settle in. Only large-scale political co-operation will be able to bring a satisfactory resolution to this serious age-old problem. In his encyclical letter *Pacem in Terris*, Pope John XXIII addressed the condition of those exiled for political reasons (PT, 103–108). Among other things, he emphasises: 'These refugees are persons, and all their rights as persons must be recognized. Refugees cannot lose their rights, not even when they become deprived of citizenship in their own countries' (PT, 105).

With these stirring words Pope John XXIII gave the fundamental reasons why we Christians must have a concern for refugees. They have come to us out of situations of suffering and persecution. It is our duty to guarantee their inalienable rights, which are inherent to every human being and are not conditioned by natural factors or by sociopolitical situations.

The Path of Solidarity

I said in my Message for the International Day of Peace: 'The right path towards a world community, in which justice and peace may reign without boundaries among all peoples and in all continents, is the path of solidarity, of dialogue, and of universal brotherhood. This is the only possible path.'

That sense of solidarity must stand above all temptations to close doors. It carries with it the re-establishment of a new solidarity that respects and values the cultural and moral traditions of every people. It makes of those traditions a place of encounter for mutual understanding and for reciprocal and renewed respect. The sort of solidarity for which modern society is in need goes beyond vague and inconclusive expressions and requires the affirmation of the value of life, of every life. Because in every human existence, there is a reflection of the divine being. Therefore, mere tolerance is not enough, much less simply resignation. Acceptance of the status quo is not enough. What is needed is an active commitment to respect and to affirm the dignity and the rights of every person within the bounds of his own cultural identity.

This active commitment seeks the good of the other, forges new links, offers new hope, and works for peace. Only with understanding can we solve conflicts and correct injustice. And only then are we able to offer a true perspective on solidarity in freedom and in hope. Only then can we open the way for harmony among nations, which is an indispensable prerequisite for real peace.

The Good of Man

I am convinced that if our age is going to be remembered some day as a century of civilisation that will happen not so much because of the technological and cultural progress which it has achieved; but rather because of the social development which it has achieved for the good of man. In that social development, finding homes for the millions of refugees in the world today occupies first place.

The stark reminder of the suffering that mankind underwent during World War II should make us acutely aware of this sort of senseless and horrifying tragedy. During that terrible war, millions of people were forced to flee leaving their own homes and their own lands behind. This should lead us to work tirelessly to resolve discords and divisions, ideological struggles and power rivalries. The inhuman logic of selfishness must be abandoned. Then the logic of respect for man can prevail. Thus, we will finally begin to see the construction of a civilisation based on truth and love, based on co-operation with all the nations of the earth.

Jesus Prayed for Unity

On the eve of his passion, at the Last Supper with his disciples, Jesus prayed for unity among all those destined to believe in him. He said, 'I do not pray for them alone' – referring to the apostles – 'I pray also for those who will believe in me through their word, that all may be one as you, Father, are in me, and I in you; I pray that they may be one in us' (John 17.20–21).

We join this prayer of Christ's, the only priest of the New Covenant. Christ, the priest, offers himself in sacrifice. He offers his own body and blood. He offers up his life and his death. And, with this sacrifice – which is holiness *par excellence* – he reconciles the world to himself. The Christ dies on the cross 'to gather into one all the dispersed children of God' (John 11.52).

The words of Jesus' priestly prayer spring from the very heart of this sacrifice. His prayer and his sacrificial death have the same goal – 'that all may be one'.

The Unity That Binds Us Together Through Baptism

What kind of unity is Christ referring to? He is speaking of the unity that comes from Baptism. St Paul speaks about this unity in his letter to the Galatians where he writes: 'All of you who have been baptised into Christ have clothed yourselves with him . . . All are one in Christ Jesus' (Gal. 3.27–8).

Through Baptism we have been immersed not only into water but above all into Christ's redeeming death. And just as Christ's death marked the beginning of his new life revealed through the resurrection, so for us the sacramental immersion in the waters of Baptism marks the beginning of a new life. This is a life through grace, the same life that was revealed in Christ's resurrection. It is Christ's life given to us by the Father in the Holy Spirit.

This saving life is one and unique. It is present in all those who receive Baptism. And that is why all those who are baptised are one in Christ. Baptism both expresses and achieves the fundamental call of all Christians to be one. It is also a call to unity in the one body of the church through the Holy Spirit.

The Communion of the Faithful

That unity which binds Christians into one body is a unity that comes from God. The supreme model of this unity is the Blessed Trinity, the communion of the three divine persons – the Father, the Son, and the Holy Spirit. That is why Jesus prayed at the Last Supper: 'As you, Father, are in me, and I in you, I pray that they may be one in us' (John 17.21).

All those who through the same faith and the same Baptism become sons of God are called to this union. 'Each one of you is a son of God because of your faith in Christ Jesus' (Gal. 3.26), says the Apostle Paul. Therefore, through faith we are sons of God in him who is the only-begotten Son of the Father. We must be united in this supreme source of our unity: the divine unity of the Son with the Father. In turn, the Father and the Son have poured out the Holy Spirit upon the church.

The Spirit dwells in the hearts of all baptised believers encouraging them to pray with confidence and to call God 'Abba, Father'. As the Second Vatican Council has taught, 'The Holy Spirit – who dwells in the believers and fills and rules the whole church – produces that wonderful communion of the faithful, and unites all in Christ so intimately that he is the principle of the church's unity. He operates the variety of graces and ministries (1 Cor. 12.4–11) and enriches the church of Jesus Christ with various gifts "to equip the saints for the work of ministry, for building up the body of Christ" ' (Eph. 4.12 RSV)(UR, 2).

Unity Is a Gift

The unity that comes from faith and Baptism contains a particular reflection of God's glory, that glory which the Father eternally gives to the Son, that glory which he gave to the Son on earth – especially when he was lifted up on the cross. Therefore, the aspiration towards unity is pervaded by the call to share in this glory. That is why Jesus prayed to the Father with these words: 'I have given them the glory you gave me that they may be one, as we are one' (John 17.22).

And what is the glory that the Father gave the Son? The glory of humble service to others. The glory of doing the will of the Father in all things. The glory which culminated in his free acceptance of death on the cross, his sacrifice for the redemption of the whole world. This is the glory of Christ.

This continues to be the way to glory for all the disciples of Christ. The best way to glorify God is to follow the example of Jesus who said: 'Whoever wishes to be my follower must deny his very self, take up his cross each day, and follow in my steps' (Luke 9.23). Whoever gives glory to God in this way shares in God's unity and is one with him, just as the Father and the Son are one.

Unity is a gift of the one God in three divine persons. Where this gift is welcomed in faith there the fruits of the Holy Spirit are found: 'Love, joy, peace, patient endurance, kindness, generosity, faith, mildness, and chastity' (Gal. 5.22). Yes, God helps us to overcome our divisions and rediscover our unity in him. He gives us the light of truth and of grace necessary for a change in our hearts. He liberates us from ignorance, from error, and from sin – from all that causes divisions inside ourselves and in our relationships to others. The Holy Spirit is close to the hearts and minds of those who call upon him. He offers us the fullness of communion with God himself and blesses us with reconciliation with our brothers and sisters.

One in Christ Jesus

Even though unity is something that human beings will never fully achieve in this life, we must nevertheless seek it in Christ and work to achieve it. It is one of the principal characteristics of the church, which is 'one, holy, catholic and apostolic', as we profess in the Creed. But while the church is one, there is disunity among Christians.

The task to re-establish unity among all those who believe in Christ becomes ever more urgent. Past and present divisions are a scandal for non-Christians, a clear contradiction of Christ's will. They are a serious obstacle to the church's efforts in proclaiming the gospel.

The work of ecumenism requires our constant efforts and fervent prayers. It begins with the acknowledgement that the unity of Baptism is deep and meaningful. There is a unity which actually binds all baptised believers to each other and gives them a common sharing in the life of the Holy Trinity – a unity which persists forever despite the fact that there are differences or divisions. St Paul's words remain forever true: 'All of you who have been baptised into Christ have clothed yourselves with him. There does not exist among you Jew or Greek, slave or freeman, male or female. All are one in Christ Jesus' (Gal. 3.27–8).

We must be willing to co-operate with Christ and other believers in working for full unity among the followers of Christ throughout the whole world. We rejoice at seeing the ecumenical progress which has already been achieved. We see the overcoming of old prejudices, of false judgments, and of expressions of contempt. There has been a great development towards mutual understanding and brotherly respect. There has been remarkable progress in dialogue between churches and co-operation among Christians in service to mankind. Increasingly, we see the number of opportunities grow for common Christian prayer that respects the various traditions. Let us go ahead along the path to full unity in Christ. We await full of hope the day when we will really be one as the Father and the Son are one!

Unity – A Condition for the Church's Mission

The unity of Christ's disciples is a condition for carrying out the mission of the church. Even more than this, it is a condition for carrying out the mission of Christ himself in the world. It is a condition for effectively proclaiming and reinforcing our faith in Christ. That is why Jesus prayed: 'I pray also for those who believe in me . . . that they may be one in us, that the world may believe that you sent me . . . that their unity may be complete. So shall the world know that you sent me, and that you loved them as you loved me' (John 17.20–23).

Unity among Christians is essential to the proclamation of the gospel since evangelisation depends on the convincing testimony of the Christian community and not only on the preaching of the Word of God. How can non-believers even begin to believe in the love of God revealed in Christ if they do not see Christians love one another? Love cannot be expressed or penetrate hearts except through the testimony of unity.

The ardent desire for unity and for union must be our starting point. We must pray for the gift of unity. This gift, which the church has received from God, gives her a particular responsibility to the human family. Namely, she has the responsibility to promote dialogue and understanding among all men, to work for unity and peace in our divided world.

Conflicts and tensions are abundant today. Nations are divided between east and west, north and south, friends and enemies. And within the boundaries of every country, one can find groups and factions which oppose each other: rivalries born from prejudice and ideologies, from national stereotypes and ethnic barriers, and from a whole series of other factors, none of which is worthy of our human dignity.

It is in this divided world that today's church is requested to promote harmony and peace.

The Power to Overcome Barriers

The church travels on her way in love and in truth. In that love, she sees every person as a son or a daughter of God, as a brother or sister of equal dignity, no matter what his or her social status, race, or class may be. In that truth which overcomes slavery to falsehood and brings new freedom to minds and hearts, there can be no barriers whatsoever to God's love.

Above all, we as Christians must continue to trust in the power of the cross for overcoming sin and reconciling the world to God. As I emphasised in my Message for the 1986 International Day of Peace, 'Christians, enlightened by faith, know that the definitive reason why the world is a theatre of divisions, tensions, rivalries, barriers, and unfair inequalities – instead of being a place of genuine brotherhood – is sin, which is the moral disorder of man. But Christians know also that the grace of Christ, which can transform this human condition, is constantly offered to the world, because "where sin increased, grace abounded all the more" (Rom. 5.20 RSV).'

Jesus exhorts us to be one, just as he and the Father are one. In our union with Jesus in the communion of the church, we find the power and the inspiration to overcome all barriers and divisions, and build new and tighter bonds of unity: unity in our families and parishes, unity in local churches and between churches of different rites, unity in communion with the Roman Catholic Church and the Bishop of Rome. The world is waiting for this fervent testimony of faith and love. As the Second Vatican Council tells us, 'Let all the faithful remember that the more they strive to lead a life in accordance with the gospel, the better they will promote and live out the unity of Christians' (UR, 7). Let us seek to be one in the unity of Christ Jesus and of his church.

The Cornerstone

In the deepest sense, the unity of the church is a gift of the Father through Christ. He is 'source and core of ecclesiastical communion' (UR, 20). It is Christ who shares with us his own Spirit, and the Spirit 'gives life, unity, and movement to the whole body' (LG, 7).

This intimate unity is wonderfully expressed when the Apostle Paul tells us: 'There is but one body and one Spirit, just as there is but one hope given all of you by your call. There is one Lord, one faith, one baptism; one God and Father of all, who is over all, and works through all, and is in all' (Eph. 4.4–6). These are truly splendid and inspiring words! Actually, these words proclaim the church's task in every age and in every generation. A sacred task of the church is the task of preserving this unity, which is nothing other than full faithfulness to her Lord. And she must struggle to restore that unity where it has been weakened or broken.

The focus of the church's unity is the person of our Lord and Saviour Jesus Christ, the Son of God. He is the 'cornerstone' (Matt. 21.42) of God's building which is the church (1 Cor. 3.9). He – the 'cornerstone' of God's new people, of the entire redeemed mankind – is present in this eucharistic community. He leads us to himself. And he leads us to unite among ourselves in him.

Let us listen to the words of his priestly prayer at the Last Supper. He is addressing the Father: 'O Father most holy, protect them with your name which you have given me, that they may be one, even as we are one' (John 17.11).

Jesus prays to the Father, whose 'name' he has made

known to the disciples. Since he will no longer be 'in the world' with them, he asks the Father to keep them united in the knowledge of the word which has been given to them (John 17.14). The object of his prayer is above all the unity of those he had chosen, the apostles. But he extends it to all his followers in all ages to come. As he addresses the Father, he says: 'I do not pray for them alone. I pray also for those who will believe in me through their word, that all may be one' (John 17.20–21).

Unity Is Built on Truth

Jesus says in his priestly prayer at the Last Supper: 'I consecrate myself for their sakes now, that they may be consecrated in truth' (John 17.19). Unity is built on truth, on the truth of that 'word' that he revealed, on the truth of the very Word of the Father that is Jesus, our Saviour.

The truth of this word is given to the church in Christ and through the apostles who are sent to baptise and to teach in his name: 'As you have sent me into the world, so I have sent them into the world' (John 17.18). Our unity is not only for ourselves but is meant for the whole world, so that the world may believe that the Father has sent his own Son to his eternal glory and for our salvation (John 17.21, 23).

Our unity is the source of our joy and of our peace. On the other hand, division and discord, especially hatred, are completely opposed to unity. They are evils and ultimately they are linked to Satan himself.

A Prayer for Reconciliation

In his priestly prayer, Jesus asked the Father to protect the disciples from the evil one (John 17.15). Thus, the priestly prayer which extols the goodness of unity is also a fervent supplication that all the evil opposing unity may be overcome. It is, therefore, a prayer of reconciliation. This reconciliation occurs on different levels: in man himself; among individuals; among Christians themselves; between Christians and non-Christians; among nations and states; and among developed and less developed areas of the world.

Reconciliation is a deep experience of the human spirit. In its highest form it is the loving Father who opens his arms to welcome the rebellious son. This is the son who fell prey to the temptation to build a world all by himself outside the Father's influence. The emptiness of that choice, the aching loneliness, and the accompanying loss of dignity – all of this inflicts wounds which require a healing. The son must return and experience anew the Father's tender mercy. Yes, reconciliation must run deep in our lives: reconciliation with God, within ourselves, between men, among the various churches and ecclesial communities starting with a deep transformation of the heart.

Reconciliation also has a social dimension. It overcomes barriers of social class and national antagonism. It abolishes forms of unjust discrimination. It considers above all the unique dignity of each human being and works for the respect of human rights wherever they are threatened.

A Community of the Faithful

Modern man is often disoriented and lost in search of genuine fellowship. Many times his social and family life is either too superficial or shattered by brokenness. His work life is many times dehumanising. He longs for an experience of genuine encounter with another human being, for the warmth of true fellowship.

Well! Is this not precisely the vocation of a parish? Are we not called to be a warm, brotherly family together (CT, 67)? Are we not brethren united together in the household of God through our common life (LG, 28)? Your parish is not mainly a structure, a geographical area,

or a building. The parish is first and foremost a community of the faithful. That is the definition given by the
new Code of Canon Law (can. 515, 1). This is the task
of a parish today: to be a community, to rediscover its
identity as a community. You are not a Christian all by
yourself. To be a Christian means to believe and to live
one's faith together with others. For we are all members
of the body of Christ.

But how does the birth of a community take place? A
community is not a reality that can be easily realised.
Community essentially means communion or fellowship.
For fellowship to grow the priest's role is not enough,
even though he plays an essential role as a representative of
the bishop. The commitment of all parishioners is needed.
Each of their contributions is vital. The Second Vatican
Council has underscored the importance of community
and the vital role of the laity (LG, 32–33; AA, 2–3).

Every Eucharist We Celebrate Easter

The question of how a community is born finds a precise
and wonderful answer in Christ: it is not borne mainly
out of our own strength and initiative. It is Christ himself
who raises up Christian community. It is the announcement of the good news that brings the faithful together
(LG, 26; PO, 4). The guiding principle of a parish community is that the Word of God is announced. The people
of God hear it, meditate upon its meaning, and then apply
it to their daily life. They seek to 'apply the perennial
truth [of Christ] to the concrete circumstances of life' (PO,
4). In fact, it is not enough to listen to the Word. It is not
enough to announce it. It must be lived out.

The Christian community is born of the Word, but its
centre and its summit is the celebration of the Eucharist
(CD, 30). Through the Eucharist, it pushes down its roots
into Christ's paschal mystery. Through him the people of
God enter into communion with the Blessed Trinity. Such

is the tremendous depth of the life of a Christian community! Such is the significance of liturgical celebrations – they are rooted in the heart of God's life. In them we encounter Christ who was dead, is risen, and now lives among us.

The Eucharist reveals to us the meaning of our labours, of all our difficulties we encounter on our way through life. The meaning of every sorrow is brought into clear focus. For all of this, united to Christ's sacrifice, becomes an offering to God and a source of life. Nothing can stop the growth of a community that has learned to lead its life as a constant Easter – as a dying and rising again together with Christ (Rom. 6.4–8).

A Foretaste of the Civilisation of Love

The Christian community is born of the Word, and sends down its roots into the paschal mystery of Christ. But there is a third element that builds up the life of the community – the love that has been poured out in our hearts by the Holy Spirit (Rom. 5.5). In fact, what would a community be like without love? What would our community life be like if it did not exercise – what the Council has called the 'law' of the new people of God – the command to love as Christ himself has loved us (LG, 9)? What would it be like without full communion with its bishop and with the Roman Catholic Church?

But that love must become visible. It must characterise every aspect of our life as a community. Spiritual communion must become a communion of rich human relationships. We must have a genuinely Christian way of relating to each other. It is important – as I have remarked on another occasion – for the parish to become more and more a focus of human and Christian gatherings, so that there can be a full community life.

Our communities are called to be a foretaste of the civilisation of love. And this means that – based on the model of the first Christian communities – we need a rich social life characterised by true brotherhood. We need a style of relationships shaped by the spirit of peace and of giving. We need a spirit of co-operation and reconciliation which will heal wounds. We need a rich spiritual life that will unite us with the love of God and the love of our neighbour.

That All May Be One

Today's world is often estranged from God. It wants simply the facts and isn't willing to listen. But Christ calls us to reach out in love: 'This is how all will know you for my disciples: your love for one another' (John 13.35). The parish is a privileged place for giving that witness. We need to repeat in our own times the wonder of the first Christian communities – the wonder of a new life, not only spiritually but socially and historically.

'That all may be one as you, Father, are in me, and I in you; I pray that they may be one in us' (John 17.21). With these words, the Lord Jesus has suggested to us – as Vatican II has said – 'a certain resemblance between the union of the divine persons and the union of God's sons in truth and in love' (GetS, 24). This is the model of every human relationship and life together – the Trinity! From this supreme model flow innumerable implications also for the parish. In fact, the glorious call of a parish community is to strive to become, in a certain way, an icon or an image of the Blessed Trinity, 'blending together all human differences' (AA, 10) in the unity of old and young, men and women, intellectuals and workers, rich and poor.

Characterised by love and the life of the Trinity, parishes will exercise an effective ministry to souls estranged from Christ. They will be led ever closer to new life in Christ.

Our Responsibility for the Future

Every generation earns or squanders for the benefit or the harm of the next. However, no other generation has faced such a great responsibility for the future as ours. Man has never had such enormous possibilities for determining the future in an irreversible way, either for good or for bad. We find ourselves in one of those periods of history which are particularly critical.

Our most important values are at stake. We are at the crossroads between unheard-of advancements for the common good or an irreversible downfall that spells disaster. Man has never had in his hands so much power and, at the same time, so much weakness. And it seems perilous for the one to grow together with the other. It seems almost a paradox. Power is the cause of our weakness. The more we approach the summit of technological progress, the more possibility we see for harm reaching down into the very roots of our life. With technological breakthroughs, risks increase – risks from everywhere: from the earth, from the sea, even from the sky. And the sky has always been the expression of beauty and of our highest aspirations. Let us pray earnestly for our future and for the mercy of God.

We Need to Rediscover the Great Values of Our Civilisation

The unparalleled possibilities for disaster or great advancement invite our generation to rediscover the great values in which our civilisation is rooted.

The dreams of centuries have been made possible by breakthroughs in technology. There is the possibility of halting the advance of the desert and transforming it. There is the possibility of defeating drought and famine. There is the possibility of alleviating the burden of long and exhausting hours of work. There is the possibility of resolving some of the problems of underdevelopment so there can be a more just distribution of the world's resources.

But it is also true that the same technology now threatens man with disaster. We see the ominous possibility of the earth being rendered uninhabitable, the possibility of the sea becoming useless, the frightening possibility of the air becoming dangerous and the sea menacing.

With these enormous possibilities for good or evil, technology must not forget man! Today, more than ever, we see the pressing need for the values of ethics to take priority over those of science and the pressing need for men to become united. All of us need to become involved beyond national boundaries because there are enormous possibilities for good or evil for everyone on our planet. We will all be affected by the outcome.

The great values of Christian civilisation need to guide our future. They must serve vigilantly as guardian against the possibilities for extermination and destruction. The development of new technologies must cause our generation to rediscover the great moral norms of our civilisation. We must ponder anew together the nature of man and the need for dignity and respect for the human person and for all of life.

Our Resource for the Future

It is precisely the great risk to man implicit in technological change that has awakened in our conscience the need for wisdom and the need to recall the moral values of our civilisation. Scientific progress, itself, has imposed the 'moral question' as the new 'social question' of the future. What is the answer?

We must start by pursuing wisdom. Since true wisdom is the mature fruit of the conscience of peoples, the public role that it is destined to play in tomorrow's world becomes clear. For instance, consider the growing field of genetic engineering. Current research indicates there are possibilities for great achievements for man. But there are also possibilities for irreversible harm to our species. Responsible scientists and governments cannot avoid asking themselves the gravest questions of philosophy and theology. Who is man? What is his destiny?

As they search for wisdom, many are beginning to rediscover the answer of Christian truth. They are beginning to see that the only true guarantee for genuine humanity in tomorrow's society is respect for man and life. We are coming back to the root. Man is realising that those values which seemed to be obscure relics of the past are actually our most important asset for the future.

And this wisdom about man and his nature comes from the conscience of the peoples of the earth. If I travel all over the world and meet men of every culture and religion, it is because I have confidence in the seeds of wisdom that the Spirit plants in the conscience of all the peoples. From that source flows the real *resource* for the future of our world, a humane future that will serve man.

Our Youth and Our Future

It is becoming ever more urgent for us to foster a deep and passionate desire for the defence of man and his life, particularly among our youth. We must educate and form our youth to be mature human beings so they can uphold the sanctity of human life in our world. Yes, we must instil in them a deep esteem for true Christian values based on strong personal convictions.

Our duty is to help our youth and not to hinder them in their growth towards full maturity in Christ. They have the right to an education that will form them to lead and guide our world in the future. I appeal to parents, teachers, authors, journalists, scientists, artists, and everyone. Yes, I appeal to everyone who believes in the dignity of man. You are called to make a contribution. The generation of the third millennium must avoid the horrors that have marked with blood this century of ours! Developments for the good of man are still possible for human society. As we head towards the future, there are unheard of possibilities for a better and more humane society inspired by the gospel.

The Builders and Architects of the Future

In our time, the issue of equality between man and woman is being resolved, at least legally, by legislation that recognises the equality of men and women in the workplace. But, as *Pacem in Terris* says, we must guard for women 'the right to working conditions that are consonant with their demands and duties as wives and mothers'. We must build a society in which women have time to rear their own children, who are the builders and architects of the future.

The church is sensitive to this need. As I said at the recent synod of bishops 'the family should be able to live as it deserves, even when the mother cannot be totally devoted to it'. This does not mean that women should be excluded from the world of work or from social and public activities.

'True promotion of women requires that work be structured in such a way that they will not be forced to pay for that promotion by abandoning their own specific call in detriment to the family. For there women have an irreplaceable role as mothers' (LE, 19). This is the teaching of the church. In a society that wants to be just and human, it is essential for the spiritual and material needs of the person to occupy first place in the hierarchy of values. We must protect those needs and uphold the importance of the human person in our families. We must not forget the dignity of motherhood and the important task of child rearing.

The Love that Unites the Spouses

'When the designated time had come, God sent forth his Son born of a woman' (Gal. 4.4). When the Son – the eternal Word – was born of a woman – of the Virgin of Nazareth – a very special union was accomplished: the union of divinity with humanity in the divine person of the Son. We call this the hypostatic union. This union shows a particular love of God for man as revealed through the witness of revelation. This special love bears spousal traits; that is it resembles the love that unites a husband to his wife.

This is unique to the character of God's love for man to which some of the prophets of the Old Testament give witness: namely, Isaiah, Hosea, and Ezekiel. According to them, this love is addressed not just to an individual but to the entire people of Israel. In the New Testament, the letter to the Ephesians makes the same argument: Christ is the Redeemer. But he is also 'the church's husband' and the church is his wife. His love for man has both a redeeming and a spousal character.

Following the teaching contained in the letter to the Ephesians, this spousal love of Christ towards the church is a source and model for that love which unites the spouses in that 'great foreshadowing', that is, marriage (Eph. 5.32).

The Sacrament of Marriage is an image and a participation in the marriage between Christ and the church, which is his bride.

At Cana in Galilee

The wedding feast at Cana in the Gospel of John takes on a particular eloquence against the background of this revealed doctrine. At the beginning of his messianic ministry, Jesus of Nazareth finds himself at Cana in Galilee for a wedding feast. He is not alone. His mother is there, and his disciples are with him.

This shows the importance that Jesus gives this event. Yet at first glance, it may seem surprising. The four Gospels present Jesus as one who is completely devoted to the things of the heavenly Father (Luke 2.49). His mission in his own words is focused on establishing the kingdom of God, which is not a kingdom of this world.

So his participation in a wedding banquet might seem at first to be at odds with his call and with his lifestyle. But actually that is not so. The divine teacher wants to teach us how to orient the things of this world towards the kingdom of God. The wedding at Cana is characteristic of this teaching. Jesus is involved in the affairs of ordinary human life to help us understand that genuine human values can and must serve a destiny which transcends earthly life.

Being Intent on Things Above

Jesus' presence at the wedding of Cana – if we want to understand it fully – is also intended as a gesture to make us 'intent on things above' (Col. 3.2). In this instance, the Lord wants to remind us of the deep, spiritual meaning of conjugal or married love. This love is a sign and a sharing in the very love that exists between Christ and the church. It cannot be at the mercy of the vagaries and unforeseen circumstances of earthly life. No, it can and must be a lasting commitment which is indissoluble and incorruptible. In that way, conjugal love is open to the limitless perspectives of the kingdom of God and of eternal life.

This supreme and transcendent model of married love is illustrated for us in the letter to the Ephesians. In it we discover the basis for choosing marriage so we can be really happy and live in accordance with God's will. The commitment and choice of Christian marriage sustains and deepens our love in the moment of trial, helping it to become pure and ever more fruitful.

We need to evaluate our own affections and feelings in the light of this understanding of married love. That way we can ensure that a genuine love and a truly Christian marriage characterise our life as husband and wife. Then our marriage is truly a sacrament. We begin to glimpse that ideal of love and of fruitfulness which every Christian husband and wife are called to with the help of grace.

The Mystery of Marriage

The mutual consent which a man and a woman give to each other when they enter into Christian marriage is not just an expression of human feeling and love which involves the two of them for the rest of their lives. They say 'yes' to each other in faith, a faith in which they are committed to participate for life. The very mystery of their marriage is a reflection and image of the mystical union and spousal love between Christ and the church.

Therefore, for two Christians, marriage is above all an act of faith.

Their human affection is transformed and made holy by grace. For they have entrusted their love and their life to God, who is now committed to guard it and nurture it with his grace and his blessings. According to the very words of Christ, it is not so much that they are uniting themselves to each other but that the heavenly Father is uniting them to each other. And their main task will be not to break this holy union. A husband and wife will succeed in this as they remember that God himself has become the guarantor of their union. Then when they experience difficulty in their marriage, they will turn to him with full confidence in his provision and love for them.

The Reality of Conjugal Love

Husbands and wives must realise that marriage and family life are not merely a work of man. No, they correspond to the eternal plan of God, which surpasses the changing conditions of our time and remains unchanged throughout the vicissitudes of history. With the institution of an indissoluble union between man and wife, God wants to make man a participant in his highest aims, which are to communicate his love and his creative power to men and all of creation.

That is why marriage and family life offer us a special relationship with God. They are realities which flow from him and are ordered by him. The family starts and has its life here on earth but is destined to be transformed in heaven. Any approach that does not take into account this essential and transcendent nature of marriage and family life runs the risk of not understanding the deep reality of conjugal love.

With Perpetual Faithfulness

Borne out of the creative love of God, marriage finds its fundamental law and its moral value in a genuine reciprocal love. Both husband and wife fully commit themselves to help the other. And out of their common desire to faithfully live out the love of God – who is Creator and Father – they generate new life. This mission received from God requires of them a great commitment and a heightened awareness of their human and Christian responsibilities.

They must seek always to avail themselves of the graces which flow from the Sacrament of Marriage. Such grace is so necessary to meet the challenge of daily difficulties. Christian spouses find the light and the strength for solving their personal problems through this grace. They are able to live out a truly full and universal love – love towards God in the first place, since they must desire his glory and the spreading of his kingdom; love towards their children in the second place, in the light of the Pauline principle that love 'is not self-seeking' (1 Cor. 13.5); and, finally, love towards each other with each of them seeking the good of the other and foreseeing his or her good desires. Here there is no arbitrary or selfish imposing of the will. No, there is only a full and universal love.

This explains how marital spirituality requires a consistent moral effort and lifelong sanctity. It must be nourished by the joys and the sacrifices of everyday life.

Husbands and wives, you must not feel alone in your commitment to these goals, In fact, the Council reminds you that 'the Bridegroom of the church comes to encounter Christian spouses through the Sacrament of Matrimony. He remains with them so that, just as he has loved the church and has given himself up for her, so also the spouses may love each other with perpetual faithfulness' (GetS, 48). Husbands and wives, live in that perpetual faithfulness strengthened by the love of Christ.

The Tragic Break Between the Gospel and Culture

'Genuine conjugal love is assumed into divine love and is ruled and enriched by the redeeming power of Christ and by the salvific work of the church, so that the spouses may be effectively led towards God and helped and strengthened in the sublime mission they have as father and mother' (GetS, 48).

It is necessary to examine the family situation within a wider framework, in the historic and cultural context in which the family lives and functions. As I have already said in the Exhortation *Familiaris Consortio*, we are living 'in a historic moment in which the family is the object of numerous forces which seek to destroy it or to deform it' (n. 3).

The family has been assailed by a series of economic and social changes that have modified the very fabric of its life. The church cannot limit herself to only mentioning these changes. No, she must enter in and help transform and strengthen the family. Christians must become the critical conscience guiding this new mindset. They must be the architects of a new vision of life for the family. This implies evangelical discernment. That is, we must read and interpret the reality of our family life in the light of Christ, 'the Bridegroom who loves and gives himself as the Savior of mankind, uniting it to himself as his own body' (ibid., 13).

Only in the light of the gospel of Christ is it possible to develop the right approach to correcting ways of thinking and patterns of life that undermine God's plan for man and woman. The crux of the matter is that the crisis of the family has originated in the break between the gospel and culture. We must rebuild a truly Christian culture that reflects the values of the gospel.

The Domestic Church

In his work *Pastoral Itinerary*, Cardinal Biffi devotes some interesting pages to the perils and hopes of the family. He emphasises that 'the family is today the great sick one of our society', and is sometimes even held in contempt. That is why healing for the family must involve evangelising our culture. If the wider culture is transformed through its encounter with the good news, the family will return to its roots. The family will be completely renewed and begin to live its own vibrant identity as a communion and community of persons in full respect for all of its members: the husband and wife, the children, and the young and the old.

Thus, far from walling itself off and abdicating its responsibility for society, the renewed Christian family becomes the prime mover in building the society of the future. This is only right since the family is the basic building block of society. Yes, the Christian family must take on service to the wider community, especially on behalf of the poor and those on the margins of society. It must bring the light of the gospel to the world.

The Christian family also has its own place and its own ministry in the church. It is called to share as a family in the saving mission of the church herself. The family achieves this mission by being faithful to its own identity and by developing into a believing and evangelising community itself. It is called to a life of prayer and of service to all men according to the commandment of love. In this way, the family becomes a source of life and of vocations because – as a domestic church – it participates in the threefold mission of Christ's church: the priestly, kingly, and prophetic mission of God's people.

Difficult Family Situations

The church cannot limit herself only to the Christian families that are close to her. No, she must enlarge her horizons to include all families, particularly those that find themselves in difficult situations.

All of us know the serious situations that shape the life of certain families. There are the families of refugees, of the military, of sailors, and of travellers of all kinds. There are the families of prisoners and of fugitives. All these families face long times of separation. There are families with children who are handicapped. There are families with drug addicts or alcoholics. There are families made up of elderly spouses who live in loneliness. You also know the tragedy of families marked by discord and bitter quarrels. There are families where the parents are opposed by their children who are ungrateful and rebellious. There are the painful cases of loss where a spouse dies and their lifelong partner must face life alone. Or there is the tragic

death of a young family member which causes great
mourning and sorrow.

Finally there are those situations which are irregular and
sinful from a Christian point of view. They pose hard
pastoral problems for the church because of the grave
consequences that come from them. The church cannot
be indifferent to those in these difficult situations, for she
must be filled with compassion and concern for the good
of their souls.

Let us pray earnestly for all families, especially those in
difficult situations.

Adopting a Child Is a Service of Love

'Whoever welcomes this little child on my account welcomes me' (Luke 9.48), Jesus tells us. This sheds light on
adoption. The decision to adopt a child is always borne
out of love for children and out of a deep desire to be
parents. Adoption is a unique witness which announces
to the world an openness to share life and love freely with
a child in need of a home and parents.

Though in our day dark clouds gather around the
family, we are comforted that so many testimonies of
generosity are being kindled in Christian families. This
testimony fills our hearts with hope. Christian choices are
often at odds with the mindset of the world around us.
They challenge and comfort those who need to hear the
gospel – those who would rather live closed and selfish
lives. But adoption is a sign by which the Christian family
declares that it does not want to be closed in on itself. It
reaches out to a child in need and assumes a great responsibility joyfully and selflessly.

The decision to adopt a child is never easy – in fact it
carries with it the assumption of complex and serious
obligations. However, it is a decision which enriches the
community.

I would like to emphasise that in our day there has been

a growing number of families that desire to adopt a child. This is certainly a positive development. It is a loving response to a high call. That is why I want to express my support for families undertaking this important work. I also encourage the work of those involved in setting up adoptions. May the Lord bless this wonderful service and bless all the families that have lovingly and freely adopted children.

God Transforms the Hearts of Men

It is God who transforms the hearts of men, as the prophet Ezekiel has eloquently proclaimed: 'I will give you a new heart and place a new spirit within you, taking from your bodies your stony hearts and giving you natural hearts' (Ezek. 36.26). The church never ceases to proclaim the truth that peace in the world has its roots in the hearts of men, in the conscience of every man and of every woman. Peace can only be the fruit of a spiritual change which begins in the heart of every human being and which spreads through all of society to every community. The first of these communities is the family. The family is the first community called to peace and the first community that must seek peace – peace and friendship among individuals and peoples.

That is why our reflection and prayer for today are focused on the family. It is our hope that a great desire for peace and friendship with all men may characterise this essential cell of society.

'I will put my spirit within you' (Ezek. 36.27), the Lord says. When two human beings – a man and a woman – draw near the altar as ministers to each other of the Sacrament of Matrimony, the church invokes the Creator. She asks the Holy Spirit to come down on these two persons who are to become husband and wife and who are about to start a family together. They are going to live under

the same roof and form together a household with a
common life.

Husband and Wife Live in Each Other's Heart

The home is the place where the family lives, the outward
sign of their life. But it is also an intimate mystery they
share in their hearts. Men do not just live in a home; they
create a home. And they create it by living in each other's
heart: the husband in the wife and the wife in the husband;
the children in the parents and the parents in the children.
And the home of our Father in heaven is the true residence
of human hearts. Thus, we see in the home a reflection
of the mystery Christ speaks about in the upper room:
'Anyone who loves me will be true to my word, and my
Father will love him; we will come to him and make our
dwelling place with him' (John 14.23).

The liturgy brings to our mind the incredible image of
community in marriage and family life, which has been
described for all time in the holy Scriptures. We find it in
the letter to the Ephesians where St Paul says about the
union of husband and wife in Christian marriage: 'This is
a great foreshadowing; I mean that it refers to Christ and
the church' (5.32).

The love of husband and wife has its model in Christ's
love for the church and reflects this love to the world.
Jesus gave on the cross the most complete expression of
his love. He sacrificed his own life for the love of his
bride, the church. The Holy Spirit – which every one of
us has received in Baptism and in Confirmation – makes
it possible for husbands and wives to love each other with
the same sacrificial love. That is why St Paul exhorts
husbands with these words: 'Husbands, love your wives,
as Christ loved the church. He gave himself up for her to
make her holy' (Eph. 5.25–6). Christ's love lasts forever
and constantly gives life and bears fruit. In the same way,

Christian spouses are linked to each other in a union which creates and raises up new life.

God Has Not Lost His Trust in Mankind

For every couple that draws near to the altar to become ministers of the Sacrament of Marriage, the church invokes the Holy Spirit so that he may work in them a change of heart – a change which becomes a solid basis for their conjugal covenant.

This change of heart is also a special consecration of marriage (HV, 25). When man and woman commit themselves to each other, they consecrate their souls and their bodies to God in such a way that a full family life may develop from that union: a communion of love and of life expressed in a community of persons.

Husbands and wives receive this communion from God as a gift. It is a gift that they must cherish and deepen over the years. Together, they bring forth life out of this deep communion of love. Their children become a sign and a fruit of that love as a gift of God. With the birth of their child, which calls for sacrificial love, they discover that their own union of love has become deeper to the point of including another. In the words of the Indian sage Rabindranath Tagore, they recognise this truth: 'Every child that is born bears with it the message that God has not lost his trust in mankind.'

The Second Vatican Council teaches that in having children responsible parents must consider 'their own good and the good of their children already born or yet to come, an ability to read the signs of the times and of their own situation on the material and spiritual level, and, finally, an estimation of the good of the family, of society, and of the church' (GetS, 50). The Council goes on to say that 'when it is a matter of harmonizing married love with the responsible transmission of life, it is not enough to take only the good intention and evaluation of motives into account; objective criteria must be used, criteria drawn from the nature of the human person and human action, criteria which respect the total meaning of mutual self-giving and human procreation in the context of true love' (ibid., 51).

Subject Index